THE NEGRO BAPTIST PULPIT

THE NEGRO BAPTIST PULPIT
A Collection of
SERMONS AND PAPERS

By
Colored Baptist Ministers

Edited By
EDWARD M. BRAWLEY

The Black Heritage Library Collection

BOOKS FOR LIBRARIES PRESS
FREEPORT, NEW YORK
1971

First Published 1890
Reprinted 1971

Reprinted from a copy in the
Fisk University Library Negro Collection

The University of Texas
At San Antonio

INTERNATIONAL STANDARD BOOK NUMBER:
0-8369-8783-7

LIBRARY OF CONGRESS CATALOG CARD NUMBER:
74-154072

PRINTED IN THE UNITED STATES OF AMERICA

THE NEGRO BAPTIST PULPIT.

A COLLECTION OF

SERMONS AND PAPERS

ON BAPTIST DOCTRINE AND MISSIONARY
AND EDUCATIONAL WORK.

BY
COLORED BAPTIST MINISTERS.

EDITED BY
E. M. BRAWLEY, D. D.

PHILADELPHIA:
AMERICAN BAPTIST PUBLICATION SOCIETY,
1420 Chestnut Street.

Entered, according to Act of Congress, in the year 1890, by the
AMERICAN BAPTIST PUBLICATION SOCIETY,
In the Office of the Librarian of Congress, at Washington, D. C.

TO
BENJAMIN GRIFFITH, D. D.,
Corresponding Secretary of the American Baptist Publication Society,

AND

HENRY L. MOREHOUSE, D. D.,
Corresponding Secretary of the American Baptist Home Mission Society,

THE REPRESENTATIVES OF THE TWO GREAT AGENCIES THAT
HAVE DONE SO MUCH FOR THE COLORED BAPTISTS,
AND LARGELY MADE THEM WHAT
THEY ARE TO-DAY,

AND TO ALL OTHERS

WHO HAVE IN ANY WAY AIDED IN THE ELEVATION OF THOSE
WHOSE REPRESENTATIVES SPEAK IN THESE PAGES, THIS
BOOK, IN GRATEFUL APPRECIATION OF THESE
SERVICES, IS RESPECTFULLY
DEDICATED BY

THE EDITOR.

CONTENTS.

		PAGE
I.	CONTENDING FOR THE FAITH.	
	By the Editor, ...	11
II.	THE SCRIPTURES.	
	Rufus L. Perry, D. D., ...	28
III.	THE DOCTRINE OF GOD.	
	Walter H. Brooks, D. D., ...	39
IV.	THE FALL OF MAN.	
	Rev. H. N. Bouey, ...	50
V.	THE WAY OF SALVATION.	
	R. B. Vandavell. D. D., ...	56
VI.	THE FREENESS OF SALVATION.	
	Rev. W. G. Parks, ...	60
VII.	REGENERATION.	
	E. K. Love, D. D., ...	64
VIII.	REPENTANCE AND FAITH.	
	Rev. G. W. Raiford, ...	81
IX.	JUSTIFICATION.	
	Rev. Andrew J. Stokes, ...	87
X.	SANCTIFICATION.	
	Rev. C. H. Parrish, A. M., ...	91
XI.	FINAL PERSEVERANCE OF THE SAINTS.	
	Rev. A. W. Puller, A. M., ...	104
XII.	HARMONY OF THE LAW AND THE GOSPEL	
	Rev. J. J. Durham, A. M., ...	113
XIII.	A GOSPEL CHURCH.	
	R. DeBaptiste, D. D., ...	116

CONTENTS.

		PAGE
XIV.	BAPTISM.	
	Rev. M. W. Gilbert, A. M., . . .	129
XV.	THE LORD'S SUPPER.	
	W. J. Simmons, D. D., LL. D., . . .	143
XVI.	THE CHRISTIAN SABBATH.	
	Rev. G. H. Jackson, B. D., ...	157
XVII.	THE RIGHTEOUS AND THE WICKED.	
	Harvey Johnson, D. D., ...	166
XVIII.	THE WORLD TO COME.	
	Rev. S. W. Anderson, A. B., ...	175
XIX.	BAPTISTS AND BIBLE WORK.	
	S. T. Clanton, D. D., ...	188
XX.	BAPTISTS AND PUBLICATION WORK.	
	Rev. R. J. Temple, B. D., ...	200
XXI.	BAPTISTS AND COLPORTAGE.	
	Rev. R. T. Pollard, ...	211
XXII.	BAPTISTS AND SUNDAY-SCHOOL WORK.	
	By the Editor, ...	221
XXIII.	COLORED BAPTISTS AND JOURNALISM.	
	W. H. Steward, ...	233
XXIV.	BAPTISTS AND GENERAL EDUCATION.	
	By the Editor, ...	237
XXV.	BAPTISTS AND HOME MISSIONS.	
	Rev. M. Vann, ...	251
XXVI.	BAPTISTS AND FOREIGN MISSIONS.	
	Rev. P. H. A. Braxton, ...	256
XXVII.	THE WORK FOR BAPTIST WOMEN.	
	Miss Mary V. Cook, A. M., ...	271
XXVIII.	THE DUTY OF COLORED BAPTISTS IN VIEW OF THE PAST, THE PRESENT, AND THE FUTURE.	
	By the Editor, ...	287

PREFACE.

A QUARTER of a century has passed away since the colored Baptists began to live under their new and changed conditions. From a few hundred thousands they have become a million and a quarter in number. As a rule, great loyalty to the denomination characterizes them. If there be any irregularity in doctrine or practice anywhere, it is the result of ignorance rather than of erroneous convictions. The great need, therefore, of our colored churches, is instruction in our denominational principles. They need to understand fully *why* they are Baptists. Many of them understand this in part only. They believe in baptism, and hence are Baptists, just as though baptism were the only tenet of our faith.

The present, and for many years to come the great work of our ministry must be that of development, particularly along the line of Baptist doctrine and work. Much has been done by the living voice to train and lead the people, but the time has come when the pen must also be employed. Our trained leaders must write.

This book, therefore, makes no apology for coming into existence. It is needed. The various parts have all been prepared by men of culture and experience, many of them being the products of Baptist institutions ranking among the foremost in the North. Madison and Bucknell and Morgan Park and Kalamazoo and Denison, and others, are all represented here, while all the writers are loyal men and true.

This book aims to be an exposition, though brief, of the Confession of Faith generally held by Baptist churches. It aims also to present the work of our various denominational societies, particularly as that work relates to the colored Baptists. They are no small part, numerically, of the great American Baptist family, and, as they have been greatly helped during the past twenty-five years by the denomination,—millions having been given for their elevation,—the time has come for them to show that such aid has not been fruitless, and to use their powers to aid themselves.

The work of two societies is made especially prominent, that of the American Baptist Publication Society and the American Baptist Home Mission Society. This is purposely done. No greater work was ever committed to men anywhere than that which is now being done by these two great arms of our denominations; and that work increases yearly in magnitude and importance. Surely, then, because of the greatness and value and necessity of this work, as well as because of the great help which these two societies gave to us in the days of our helplessness, the colored Baptists should gladly and cheerfully do their part toward conquering our land for Christ. *And they will.* Only let them know their duty and they will do it. To show them their duty, and to unfold the great work before us all, a large part of the book is devoted.

As before suggested, the object of the book is also to furnish evidence that what has been done for us is not wasted effort. Nearly all the leading colored Baptist ministers, in the South particularly, were the recipients of a generous benevolence in the days of their student life. They were aided unselfishly, and it was believed that when fully trained they would measure up to the full stature of Christian manhood. This book is, therefore, a modest vindication of the greatheartedness and judgment of those who aided us in that direction, and this book— counted among the first-fruits of our people—prepared for the defense of the doctrines of our common Lord, and in furtherance of his work, is none the less an expression of thanks from beneficiaries to benefactors. Many to whom these words would properly be addressed have already gone to their reward above; but others are left to see the harvest of their own seed-sowing, and to be recipients of our acknowledgments therefor.

While this book is distinctively denominational, and, in a measure, polemical, it is believed to be pervaded by a thoroughly Christian spirit; and although it appears as a volume of sermons, it is not strictly such, but rather a collection of lectures or essays, all of which have been expressly prepared for it.

And, now, with the prayer that God will bless it to the instruction and strengthening of those of our own household of faith, and to the teaching of others the way of the Lord more perfectly, this book is sent forth upon its mission.

E. M. BRAWLEY.

Nashville, Tenn., 1890.

THE NEGRO BAPTIST PULPIT.

I.

CONTENDING FOR THE FAITH.

BY THE EDITOR.

"Ye should earnestly contend for the faith which was once delivered unto the saints."—JUDE 3.

"CONTEND for the faith" has been the inspiring battle-cry of Baptists all along the centuries, and with it they have conquered. It should be ours no less; for Christianity is powerless unless aggressive. It has no days of quietness and repose. It is always on the battle field. Paul's declaration to Timothy rang out clear and strong when he said: "Fight the good fight of faith" (1 Tim. 6: 12); and he exhorted Timothy to do only what he himself had done. For, from his imprisonment at Rome, he wrote among his farewell words: "I have fought a good fight, I have finished my course, I have kept the faith." (2 Tim. 4: 7.)

It seems never to have been God's purpose to grant his churches great prosperity when they failed to go forward; but his greatest blessings have come in darkest times, when the churches have put forth their most earnest efforts, and struck their hardest blows. This seems to be the divine plan. For Christ sent forth his first workers under instructions to antagonize the beliefs and practices of men everywhere, and, having conquered, to make disciples of them. (Matt. 28 : 19, 20.) Paul's ministry exemplifies this divine plan; for no one can follow him in his work over Asia Minor and Greece without seeing that, everywhere and always, he was contending for the faith. His open enemies, within and outside of the churches, kept him busy at this. And Paul's inner life, which in some measure some think has been portrayed for us in the seventh chapter of Romans, shows that his inner experience was identical in character with his outward.

I. We may accept it as a divine law that Christians must always contend for the faith.

1. Loyalty to Christ demands it. Social influence, family ties, wealth and culture, are sometimes powerful in tempting to silence or apology those who stand squarely for a New Testament Christianity. The doctrines which we must preach antagonize human pride and worldly ambition. The richest and the most honored of earth must bow before Christ just as the poorest and most debased, and confess their nothingness, before they can be forgiven. The human heart is deceitful and desperately wicked, and, no matter how much culture a man has, he must be born again. Every believer must publicly profess Christ in baptism, and take upon himself the badge of discipleship. He must deny himself, mortifying his selfishness, which is the root principle of sin, and help to bring this world to Jesus. To say these things to men is often to rouse in them the spirit of opposition. But with those who would obey the New Testament there can be no question as to duty. These and all the other doctrines of grace must be faithfully presented to men. To Christ alone are we re-

sponsible. We must be loyal to him. Those of us especially who are called of God to preach must be true, and aid to stand by the truth all who profess to be the Lord's disciples. And no man can be loyal to Jesus who, for any cause, is afraid to contend for the faith. Loyalty to Christ and contending for the faith stand side by side in the Christian life.

2. Our Baptist predecessors contended for the faith, and thus handed it down to us. The scene before the Sanhedrin in Jerusalem, when Peter and John were commanded to preach no more about Jesus, was re-enacted many times in their experiences. When commanded to preach no more as they had done, and to stop crying out against error and sin, and burying converts in the likeness of Christ, they, in the spirit of the apostles, would say: "Whether it be right in the sight of God to hearken unto you more than unto God, judge ye. For we cannot but speak the things which we have seen and heard." (Acts 4 : 19, 20.) They willingly gave up everything in defense of the doctrines which to-day are our precious heritage. They sang, in substance :

> "And must I part with all I have,
> My dearest Lord, for thee?
> It is but right, since thou hast done
> Much more than this for me.
>
> "Yes, let it go ; one look from thee
> Will more than make amends
> For all the losses I sustain
> Of honor, riches, friends."

An open Bible, with the right of private interpretation, immersion alone as baptism, freedom to worship God according to the dictates of conscience, separation of church and state, baptism of believers only, the spirituality of Christ's kingdom, and the equality of believers, are some of the things for which Baptists have had to contend. Deprived of property, and often of civil liberty, and beaten with many stripes, they yet dared to stand against the civil power, and culture and wealth. They counted all things but loss for the excellency of the gospel of Christ. For this they suffered, and for this some of them died; but they suffered and died because they would contend for the faith. It is but little more than one hundred years since the last of such terrible contentions; but the glorious results of their steadfastness of purpose are to-day blessing our entire land and world. The right of every citizen of our country to worship God as he pleases is one result largely, if not wholly due to Baptists. That article in the National Constitution which guarantees absolute religious liberty to all was secured as an amendment by Baptist influence. Another result secured to us is the bringing of other Christians to the true baptism. In some sections of our country Pedobaptists are baptizing their members, when baptism is requested. The increasing disuse of infant sprinkling is still another result secured by Baptists in contending for the faith. John Bunyan did not suffer for nothing in Bedford jail, nor did Roger Williams, nor did Obadiah Holmes. They all suffered, and thus handed down to us New Testament faith and order. And we must contend for these to-day, that we may hand them down to others.

3. Antagonists will often force us to contend for the faith. The method of attacking Christianity has greatly changed in the last century. Men do not come to us so much now after the manner of Paine and Voltaire. Their

attacks are more specious. With an acknowledgment that some things in Christianity are true, they deny the truth of other things, especially such as are vital. They bring science, falsely so called, to their aid. They would make God unknowable; they would reason away the efficacy of prayer; they would annihilate the doctrine of a vicarious atonement; or they would make the soul material, and thus destroy the doctrine of a future life. When men thus attack the truth we must not be fearful, but must go forth and contend for the faith. Even the gates of hell shall not prevail against us if we go forth in Christ's service, to contend for him. We must meet a false science with that which is true. Against the deductions of a false philosophy we must oppose the word of God. Not one single outpost of gospel truth must be surrendered. And even when sinners come against us after the manner of fashionable society, and would allure our members to the theatre, to the card table, and to the modern dance, we must contend for a simple but pure religion. The dividing line between the church and the world must be sharply drawn.

4. False brethren will cause us to contend. The devil has no more effective agents than false disciples. Being in the churches, they can do more for him than they could do if they were without. Such false brethren will object when the whole truth is preached without apology or excuse. They are very solicitous about the feelings of their friends who are sinners, or who are members of other denominations. Such brethren will cause contentions, disrupt the pastoral relation, and utterly destroy the peace and usefulness of the churches. In such cases our duty is plain. The Apostle Paul bids us (2 Thess. 3: 6) with-

draw from every one that walketh disorderly. Sometimes this will cause considerable personal loss; but we cannot be true, and fail in our warfare.

5. Christians of other names, who fail to obey Christ in some important respects will cause us to contend for the faith. The general excellence of our Pedobaptist brethren often causes us to overlook their errors. Because they have much to commend them their faults are concealed, not positively, perhaps, but negatively. Our intercourse with them being pleasant, we do not care to mention their shortcomings. This is not right. They fail in an important respect when they fail to obey Christ by being baptized. By substituting sprinkling—a thing of human invention—for gospel baptism, they destroy what really is the most perfect symbol of vital gospel truth. Regeneration, justification, the resurrection of Christ, and our own resurrection, all symbolized by the act of baptism, lose an eloquent enforcement as it is cast aside. The "mould of doctrine" is broken. By sprinkling infants, Pedobaptists deny to believers a most precious privilege—that of making a public profession of Christ in his own appointed way. By ascribing to any other agency a regenerating power, as so many of them do, in what they call baptism, they dishonor by so much the work of the Holy Spirit. It is not true charity to these brethren to be silent as to their false doctrines. We should teach them the way of the Lord more perfectly; and this will cause us to contend for the faith.

6. The victories we have achieved should inspire us to contend for the faith. To stand up for the truth when the battle is waging is the strongest evidence of faith; and a strong and abiding conviction of right will hold us up

even in the face of adversity. But the shout of victory brings rejoicing and a strengthening of faith. In the past we have contended, and we have won. This should be the inspiration for future conquests. As a matter of history, infant sprinkling is less practiced than formerly. Baptist influence has caused this. Immersion is becoming more generally accepted as the true form of baptism. No respectable Pedobaptist scholar will now assert that infant sprinkling is found in the Bible, or that anything but immersion is baptism. By contending for the faith we have forced Pedobaptists to admit that the only claim they have for infant sprinkling, so far as the Bible is concerned, is a purely inferential one; and to defend their sprinkling of adults solely on the ground of expediency. The progress that Baptist principles have made in the past one hundred years is great; and if we are only faithful, we shall probably bring our Pedobaptist brethren still nearer to the truth. We owe it to Christ and to them that this be done; and our victories in the past and in the present are an inspiration for us to be thus faithful.

II. But we must not only contend; we should contend *earnestly.*

Christ wants no half-hearted service. Whatever we do for him must be done with all our might. We must be in earnest. Earnestness in a right cause will carry conviction. But we should be careful as to the manner in which we contend. We should never employ denunciation, or direct the force of our argument against any man; for it is not the man, but his doctrines which we oppose. We should carefully disconnect the man from the errors which he holds; and, while for his errors we have nothing but utter destruction, for him personally we have only peace and good will. The man we want to save. Going forth in the spirit of our Lord, we may use the hardest kind of argument if only our words are soft, and fragrant with kindness and love. And with this spirit we shall conquer.

III. And, now, what is the faith for which we must contend earnestly?

It is New Testament truth—the truth and the whole truth. Excluding the commonly accepted evangelical doctrines, some of its elements are:

1. The integrity and sufficiency of God's word. Biblical criticism has been of service; but some of it is entirely too radical and utterly destructive. When criticism is applied to the Bible in such a way as to destroy its very life, then it is time to call a halt. God's book in its entirety, with the doctrine of plenary inspiration, must be contended for, and we must likewise maintain the sufficiency of the Scriptures for all men and for all ages. The Bible is a completed and sufficient book. It is the oracle of God. There may be, and doubtless is, progress in understanding what it teaches. Many things may be plainer to us than to those of preceding years, but the book itself remains intact. It is a sufficient rule of doctrine and practice. It needs no help from tradition, or the enactments of synods and councils. All we have to do is to rely solely upon it, conforming our beliefs and lives to its teachings, doing what the Lord commands, and rejecting everything that man, by a false interpretation, would put into it. The Bible has made Christian civilization what it is, and the same Bible will go on in its glorious work through all time for the healing of the nations. We must stand by the Bible and defend it.

2. Another element for which we must contend is a converted church membership. Baptists have always contended that no one has a right to church membership unless he has been born again, and there is no probability that we shall ever change our requirement in this particular. But, while we will not knowingly receive any one except on profession of faith in Jesus Christ, it is to be feared that some methods we employ in revival meetings result in bringing into the churches many who know not Christ in the forgiveness of sins. Perhaps there never was a time when the churches were free from false disciples, and perhaps they never will be free from them; but we ought to be careful to keep the number as few as possible. Unconverted people get into our churches mainly in two ways. In a revival, when the preaching is more sound than sense; when reliance is placed, not so much upon the simple doctrines of repentance and faith, but rather upon singing and other physical demonstrations; when the members, with doubtless good intentions, gather around those who are seeking Christ, and sing and pray over them until they "get religion"; when, in brief, physical feeling is substituted for judgment and positive conviction; then it is very likely that a large number of those who profess to be converted will be mistaken. They are baptized, but they do not remain in the churches very long. They have nothing to remain for. They go in with the rush of an excitement, and they come out when the excitement has ended. Too much care cannot be taken in preaching to sinners. They should be made to understand that praying cannot save them; nor can singing. *Belief in Christ alone saves.* Hence the doctrines of repentance and faith, the atonement, and free salvation should be

preached in a very plain and simple manner. The work of the Holy Spirit in convicting and regenerating should be explained, and the instrumentality of the word of God in regeneration distinctly shown. All these should be made plain to men's understanding, and then the question of deciding for Christ should be pressed home to their hearts.

Another danger that confronts us is the change that has taken place in the manner of accepting Christ. The older preachers used to make much of what they called the *law work*, and possibly too little of the work of grace. They would have the sinner feel the weight of a broken law, and suffer mental and spiritual anguish because of the weight of sin. They were in no special hurry to have a man converted, but preferred that he should have the experience of Bunyan's Pilgrim from the time he left the City of Destruction, until, at the sight of the cross, the burden of sin fell from his shoulders. More modern preachers reject this method of presenting truth. They go to the other extreme, and underrate the work of the law. And so the gospel is often presented in such a way as to belittle the change needed in conversion. Men are told "to accept Christ," "to believe," "to profess Jesus," in such a way as to leave the impression that the act is purely voluntary and mechanical. Hence many do profess Christ and claim to love Jesus, whose hearts have not been touched.

The proper ground is the middle one. Men must realize their sins. No man can have godly sorrow for sin unless he realizes that he is a sinner without excuse before God. His heart must be ploughed up with deep furrows. Hence if he does not thus realize his sin, and has not godly sorrow, and does not resolve to quit sin, there is no repentance. The law *and* grace,—the thing that Christ saves us from and that by which we are saved,—should be presented together; and when men thus realize their own desperately helpless condition, and have truly repented, then may they be taught that—

> "Nothing either great or small,
> Remains for me to do;
> Jesus died and paid it all,—
> Yes, all the debt I owe."

It is by such an experience, and such alone, that persons should be received as candidates for baptism, and thus for membership in the church. Only in our denomination is this method of entering the church rigidly adhered to, and so it is our mission to proclaim to all men everywhere the doctrine of a pure gospel church, composed only of baptized believers.

3. Still another element of truth for which to contend is, that immersion alone is baptism. A few centuries ago, those proclaiming this truth were called Ana-baptists—a name meaning those who baptized again. But they did not regard sprinkling as baptism any more than we do. It was no baptism at all. So what they demanded was not a second baptism, but "one baptism," and only one. By contending for scriptural baptism, Baptists have at last brought the scholarship of the world to acknowledge the correctness of their position. If any Pedobaptist is rash enough now to deny that immersion is the baptism of the New Testament, the most effective thing to show him is the almost unanimous confession of Pedobaptist scholars. With a unanimity that is gratifying they admit

that the apostolic baptism was immersion, although they seek to defend sprinkling by other than New Testament support.

Baptism is an external rite, but it is full of essential gospel truth. It symbolizes truths upon which the salvation of every believer depends. It sets forth the resurrection of Christ, without which no man could be saved. (1 Cor. 15: 14.) Christ must rise from the grave for our justification. Upon the resurrection of Christ hung the validity of Christianity. That was the pivotal point. That fact must be proven, and it was. Witnesses of the fact were abundant, and the apostles never failed, in preaching, to proclaim it.

Christ's foreknowledge enabled him to grasp the fact of his resurrection, and so he gave to his churches a beautiful yet wonderfully expressive ordinance, which through all coming time would teach men by symbol, that as he died for our sins, even so he arose for the completion of our redemption.

But it must be remembered that we never baptize a man to save him. We ascribe to baptism no saving power. Christ alone saves us by his gracious work upon the heart, and when we baptize a believer, it is on the ground that he is already saved.

4. Another point to be contended for is, the baptism of believers only. We are commanded to make disciples out of all nations, and *then* to baptize them. (Matt. 28 : 19.) We have no authority to administer the ordinance to any but those who make profession of saving faith in the Lord Jesus Christ. To unconscious babes and grown-up sinners alike we refuse the ordinance. This doctrine is vital. Its destruction would mean the disintegration of every

church founded on the New Testament plan. None but Baptists stand and contend for this doctrine, which means so much to the kingdom of our Lord. If, then, we fail to proclaim it, the world will never know it. We have been set for the defense of this truth, and valiantly we should contend for it.

5. Still another element in the faith to be contended for is the Lord's Supper for orderly baptized believers. For believers, for baptized believers, for orderly baptized believers—for them only. Perhaps at no point have Baptists been less understood than at this of restricted communion. Now the Lord's Supper is not a feast, in which Christians are to show their love to one another. It is a memorial, by which they show Christ's death. (1 Cor. 11 : 26.) It is not a personal possession. It belongs to the local church. We can invite none but orderly baptized believers to partake of it, because it is not intended for others. He who partakes must be a believer. He must have personal union with Christ. He must have put on Christ by baptism, and his Christian life must be blameless. We cannot invite others than those who, upon credible evidence of saving faith in Jesus Christ, have been baptized according to his command, and are walking orderly in his church, organized after the New Testament plan. We must contend for the purity and integrity of the Lord's Supper as a church ordinance, and invite none but those who are obedient to the Lord's commands.

IV. How best may we contend?

1. By a vigorous presentation of scriptural truth in its entirety. The circle of doctrines ordinarily preached must be enlarged, and they must be preached with vigor. We may not preach from the New Testament alone, but

from the Old as well. Not only favorite doctrines should be presented, but others possibly less to our taste. It is well for us to remember that all Scripture given by inspiration of God is profitable, and no part of it should be omitted. It is only as we preach all the doctrines of the gospel that we can make symmetrically developed Christians. Doctrine and life are inseparable, and the Lord intended his people to attain unto the stature of men in himself. (Eph. 4 : 13.) The young Christian needs to know of his privileges; and hence he should understand the doctrines of justification, adoption, sanctification, and final perseverance. He needs likewise to know of his duty, and so the doctrines of self-denial and personal sacrifice should be taught him. The great claims of home and foreign missions, colportage, Bible work, ministerial and general education, and the care of the poor, should be pressed hard upon his heart. We have too many undeveloped churches now. Let us reduce the number of them as rapidly as possible. And when our people fully understand the teachings of God's word, then will they be able and willing to contend for the faith.

2. We may contend by a more thorough and aggressive missionary work. Mission work is the truest exponent of Christianity's charter. The command to make disciples was meant to be of universal application. (Matt. 28: 19, 20.) It is not to the credit of God's people that the world should have remained unevangelized for nearly two thousand years after Christ died. We have never properly taught the people to give according to the necessities of Christ's work, nor have we yet undertaken that mission work which we must undertake before the Lord's kingdom will fully come. This is a matter of which all

are conscious. So far as practical results are concerned, it would be far better for us to baptize fewer people, and train those we already have. Really it would be an advantage to the Lord's cause if we would for a while stop preaching to sinners, and devote ourselves, body, mind, and heart, to the development of the great masses now upon our hands who are doing nothing to extend the Lord's kingdom. A great deal can be done without much outlay of money. Nearly every Christian can do something in his neighborhood. Every one of our cities is legitimate mission ground. At our very doors we can do mission work; and we ought to do it. But home and foreign missions should be more vigorously prosecuted. In these ways we can effectively contend for the faith.

3. By building up our institutions of learning we can contend for the faith.

(1) We should make them equal to the best in the land. We should give our money, and plenty of it, to provide teachers, buildings, and apparatus, so that our schools may not be surpassed by any. We need to give our young people a thorough training. Our surroundings demand a complete education, both mental and industrial.

(2) We should send all our students to our own schools. We not only need to educate, but also to educate from a Baptist standpoint. It is worse than folly to place our young people under influences which will destroy their denominational life. We hold truth to be sacred, and we dare not allow it to be displaced by error. Our churches need strong men and women to support the work projected by our ministry, and we can have strong men and women only as they are trained in our own schools. There is no

good reason for sending even one student to any but a Baptist institution.

(3) And we should use our schools directly in the interest of our denomination. Our schools were built with money given by Baptists for the education of Baptists. We did not go to the national government or to State legislatures, and pretend to be undenominational, in order to get public funds. No; we have always sailed under our true colors, and Baptists willingly and knowingly gave. Now, since our schools were planted as missionary agencies, they should always be used as such. It is neither good sense nor sound policy to conduct them on any other basis. We should use our institutions to promote the truth in Christ as we understand it. When we shall become more aggressive in this direction, then will we have still greater success.

4. Again, we may contend by promoting the efficiency of our Sunday-schools, in which the young should be indoctrinated. The Roman Catholics set us a good example in this direction. As soon as a child is able to understand, he is taught their doctrine. Even so should we act. Every Baptist child should be taught Baptist doctrine. Into the Sunday-school he should be placed just as early as he can understand, and there be kept. The catechism should be taught, as well as the Bible. Every church should have a good home school, and one or more missions, if possible. Hold the young! Such a course will enable us to contend for the faith in a very practical manner.

5. By a wide use of the printed page, we may likewise contend for the faith. We must, more than formerly, employ the printing press. Put the Bible everywhere.

It is the strongest possible Baptist book. Only let men know what the Lord commands. Let them read for themselves. When men search the Scriptures for themselves, they will rely less on tradition. Many things which we preach are not known by many people to be in the New Testament; while they vainly imagine that many things they believe and practice are in the Bible. Let us undeceive the people. God's word is a great means of enlightenment.

6. And, lastly, we should use freely such tracts and books as set forth our doctrines. Scatter these leaves far and wide. Many a time a man will refuse to hear us because he is blinded by prejudice; but the printed page will speak to him in his calm moments and carry conviction to his heart. Great have been the victories of the printed page, and greater still will be our future victories, if we rightly and freely employ these means of contending which God has placed in our hands.

Thus, for these various ends, and in these several ways, we should contend for the faith; and, in all this, our only motive should be the honor and manifested glory of our Lord, that his word may have free course throughout the earth, and that his kingdom may everywhere be established.

II.

THE SCRIPTURES.

RUFUS L. PERRY, D. D.,
Editor of The National Monitor, Brooklyn, N. Y.

"Search the Scriptures; for in them ye think ye have eternal life: and they are they which testify of me."—JOHN 5 : 39.

THE speaker in the text is Jesus. The reporter is "the disciple whom Jesus loved." The subject matter is Christ and eternal life. We are told that God, who at sundry times and in divers manners had spoken in time past unto the fathers by the prophets, now spake unto men by his Son, whom he had appointed heir of all things. (Heb. 1 : 1, 2.) If these things be so, then the Scriptures wherein they are recorded must be inspired of God; and if they be inspired, it is our undeniable duty to search them diligently and prayerfully, that we may learn just what they contain.

They promise to teach us what we ought to know about God and about the way to inherit eternal life. They promise to tell us what to do, and when and how to do it. They purport also to tell us what not to do.

But are they true? May the God of heaven send the answer to the heart. Reason, it is true, demands proof of all it accepts as truth. In this demand there is nothing wrong, but rather what is legitimate and praiseworthy. That reason owes to itself. Nor do we discredit God, nor at all dishonor him, to examine honestly and thoroughly the grounds on which we are required to accept the Scriptures as his inspired word. Indeed, the Scriptures themselves tell us to "believe not every spirit, but try the spirits whether they are of God" (1 John 4: 1); to "prove all things; hold fast that which is good." (1 Thess. 5: 21.)

I. Let us briefly examine the grounds of our belief in the inspiration of the Scriptures.

1. The word inspiration, predicated of "all Scripture" (2 Tim. 3: 16), means the inbreathing of a divine and controlling influence. It means that the human agents through whom the Bible came, while writing, wrote "as they were moved by the Holy Ghost" (2 Pet. 1: 21); and hence that which they wrote forms the "holy Scriptures." (Rom. 1: 2.)

2. This belief in the inspiration of the Scriptures is based on the common conviction of the existence of a Creator, who is disposed to reveal himself to his intelligent creatures, and able to do so. The belief that God is, is always accompanied by the belief that he has somehow revealed himself. "The heavens declare the glory of God, and the firmament sheweth his handywork. Day unto day uttereth speech, and night unto night sheweth knowledge." (Ps. 19: 1, 2.) Now, if we admit that the Deity can speak to us by the voice of nature, we must admit also that he can communicate with us through a special revelation.

3. Again, our belief in a divine revelation is founded on its necessity. Human reason could not of itself discover God, as he has revealed himself; for it is finite, and God is infinite. The soul finds itself existing; but whence it came, what it is, and whither it goeth, it does not know. It may formulate philosophical theories as profound as thought can make; it may gather up all its resources and

start out on the highway of agnostic evolution; it may move here and there with all the learned "isms" with which the ages have been so rife, but it will return unsuccessful; for no man *by* searching can find out God. (Job 11 : 7.)

Yet, between God and man there is a necessary relation of sovereign and subject. The laws of the sovereign must be capable of being clearly understood, to justify punishment for their transgression. The sovereign is absolute. He holds all the legislative, judicial, and executive powers of his moral kingdom in his own hands. Then his laws commanding right and forbidding wrong must be intelligible. And so we believe the great " I AM THAT I AM " has spoken to man in language he can understand.

4. The divine inspiration of the Bible is further evinced by the character and situation in time and place of the different writers. They were all godly men. Some were learned, and of high station; others unlearned and lowly. God called them and endowed them with power, and graciously spoke through them to his rebellious people and to the world. The Bible contains sixty-six books. From the first by Moses to the last by John there is a space of more than fifteen hundred years; and yet there is harmony among all the writers. The different writers could form no collusions; and if they could, their good characters would have forbidden so great a fraud.

5. Our belief in the inspiration of the Scriptures is still further based on the claims which they make. They constantly claim divine authority by prefacing a message or command by "Thus saith the Lord." The Old Testament is shot through and through with the expression, "The word of the Lord came"; and Jesus put his seal upon it,

embracing it all by the saying, "As the Scripture hath said." Peter says that the holy men of God "spake as they were moved by the Holy Ghost" (2 Pet. 1 : 21), and Luke, that "The Holy Ghost, by the mouth of David, spake." (Acts 1: 16.) In the New Testament, Jesus stands, who "spake as never man spake," and his promise of "another Comforter" was fulfilled no less to his disciples in their written, than in their spoken word. As the "all Scripture given by inspiration of God" spoken of by Paul (2 Tim. 3 : 16), by their own claims we may justly connect the Old and New Testaments, which form our Bible. What the Scriptures teach, both as to matter and manner, is compatible with their claim to divine inspiration. It is worthy of God. The Bible is "the Scripture of truth" (Dan. 10 : 21), and "the word of truth" (Eph. 1: 13). It teaches holiness. It condemns every evil disposition of the heart; and then, in a spirit of love divine, points out the way of recovery from sin.

6. The antiquity and preservation of the Bible may be taken as evidence of its divine authorship. The writings of Moses are hundreds of years older than those of Homer and Hesiod, of Herodotus and Thucydides—the oldest profane poets and historians. More than thirty-three hundred years have elapsed since Moses wrote. Great cities and empires have fallen; nations and their tongues have died; but the Bible still lives. Wicked men, like Antiochus Epiphanes of Syria, and Diocletian of Rome, have tried to destroy it, by bringing against it all the powers of darkness; but by an overruling providence it has been wonderfully protected from all the attacks its enemies have made against it.

7. Finally, to all these reasons for believing in the di-

vine inspiration of the Bible, add the opinions of pious and learned men of the early ages of the church. Then use the test given by our Lord: "If any man will do his will, he shall know of the doctrine, whether it be of God." (John 7: 17.) If men would do this, all doubt must disappear, and they would joyfully sing:

> "Holy Bible, book divine,
> Precious treasure, thou art mine.
> Mine, to tell me whence I came,
> Mine, to teach me what I am."

II. Since the Bible is the word of God, it becomes our imperative duty to study it.

"Search the Scriptures; for in them ye think ye have eternal life." Whether the word "search" be rendered in the imperative mood, or in the indicative, as will better translate the original word, the duty of searching the Scriptures remains the same. A belief in their divine authority carries with it an undeniable obligation to search them. It is there that God tells us how to view our relations and regulate our conduct toward him and toward each other. This knowledge can be found nowhere else. Then we should read the Bible and heed its teachings, as if God himself were present and speaking to us.

An absent father hears of the misery that has overtaken his children. He loves them; and, knowing just what will lift them out of trouble into the enjoyment of prosperity and happiness, he writes them a letter, telling them what to do. Now, what manner of children are they, if they put the paternal letter on the shelf, and neglect to read it? Man was created in the image of God, and enjoyed the favor and communion of his Creator. But he sinned and fell. Thus alienated from God, he became carnally minded, walking after the flesh and not after the Spirit. (Rom. 8 : 7.) How to recover—to escape from sin and its penalty—he knew not. Ever since the fall of Adam, the soul of man has keenly felt a consciousness of its imperfection, and of its inability to purge itself of sin. When Paul and Silas prayed, and the foundations of the prison were shaken, the trembling jailer cried out: "Sirs, what must I do to be saved?" (Acts 16 : 30.) But this was no new question. It was the echo of a question that had haunted the ages. But no satisfactory answer could be rendered until it was found in the gospel of Jesus Christ. The religions of Egypt and Eastern Asia, of Greece and of Rome, could not give ease to the soul. They could but awaken it to a keener sense of its guilt, and teach it how to seek, but not how or where to find. At its best, the history of the pagan world was a history of moral corruption. Paul tells us, in the first chapter of his Epistle to the Romans (1 : 22–32), just the state of mankind without the Bible ; and what he there says is attested by history. By no process of evolution could there be discovered a remedy for sin, or aught that would give to the fallen "a conscience void of offense toward God and toward man" (Acts 24 : 16), accompanied by a hope of eternal life. "Without me," says Jesus, "ye can do nothing" (John 15: 5), and experience confirms his words.

The invention of printing, the Reformation inaugurated by Martin' Luther, and the formation of Bible Publication Societies, put an end to the age of darkness, and gave to Christian civilization a new impetus. They put the Scriptures within reach of the poorest households. Their benign influence soon showed itself in the character of all who gave them a prayerful study; for they proved to be "quick and powerful, and sharper than any two-edged sword." (Heb. 4 : 12.) They are the conduits of the waters of life that flow from the fountain opened for sin and uncleanness. They reveal God's panacea for all moral and spiritual diseases.

They should, then, be searched, for the benefits to be derived from them. The Bible was given to us as an agency of the Holy Spirit, by which to make us "wise unto salvation" (2 Tim. 3 : 15), and is "the power of God unto salvation to every one that believeth." (Rom. 1: 16; John 17: 17; Ephes. 6: 17; 1 Pet. 1: 23.) It searches the heart, and there discovers, characterizes, condemns what is in disorder, and then prescribes a remedy, whether it be among the high or low. It is "the engrafted word, which is able to save your souls." (James 1 : 21.) "Blessed is he that readeth" it. (Rev. 1 : 3.) This is found to be true in the case of the Ethiopian eunuch, who was reading when Philip joined him in his chariot. He believed, was baptized by Philip, and then went on his way to Ethiopia, rejoicing. (Acts 8 : 27-39.) The Jews of Berea were more noble than those in Thessalonica, "in that they received the word with all readiness of mind, and searched the Scriptures daily." (Acts 17: 10, 11.) The Scriptures "are written that ye might believe that Jesus is the Christ, the Son of God, and that believing, ye might have life through his name." (John 20 : 31.) The Scriptures come to us as a guide. They tell us what to do to be saved, and the Spirit of God making effective the word, puts it into our hearts to will and to do. "Say not in thine heart, Who shall ascend into heaven? That is, to bring Christ down from above; or, Who shall descend into the deep?

That is, to bring up Christ again from the dead. . . . The word is nigh thee, even in thy mouth, and in thy heart: that is, the word of faith which we preach: that if thou shalt confess with thy mouth the Lord Jesus, and believe in thy heart that God hath raised him from the dead, thou shalt be saved." (Rom. 10: 6-9.) "He that believeth and is baptized, shall be saved." (Mark 16 : 16.)

Now, a renewed life is the sequence of a renewed heart. A sinful heart is manifested by a sinful life. "A good tree cannot bring forth evil fruit, neither can a corrupt tree bring forth good fruit." Ye shall know them by their fruit. (Matt. 7 : 18, 20.) The Scriptures lead to perfection. "Thy word," says the Psalmist, "have I hid in my heart, that I might not sin against thee." (Ps. 119 : 11); and our blessed Lord, in his intercessory prayer, affirms the same sanctifying power of the Scriptures. "Sanctify them through thy truth," he said; "thy word is truth." (John 17 : 17.) Again he says: "If ye continue in my word, then are ye my disciples indeed; and ye shall know the truth, and the truth shall make you free." (John 8 : 31, 32.) You shall be freed from the bondage of sin, stripped of ignorance and superstition, and clothed with "the glorious liberty of the children of God." (Rom. 8: 21.) We who read the Scriptures can testify to their cleansing and elevating power; and it is evinced by the history of missions, both foreign and domestic. The Jews were superior to contemporaneous nations, in that they had the oracles of God. Europe rose out of darkness into light through the influence of the inspired Scriptures. All Asia is being led to God by the same quickening truth, as it is preached or read in the native tongues. And by the same power divine,

Ethiopia is now stretching out her hands unto God, as prophesied in the sixty-eighth Psalm (ver. 31).

The Bible is a transcript of the will of God, and is pre-eminently a book of justice. It defines justice, shows how far men have departed from it, and then tells them how to return to it. It is a moral clock that keeps exact time, timing every man alike. In this respect it is superior to any other book that ever appeared in the world. Indeed, it is just this superior quality of the Scriptures that takes hold of the hearts of men, and impresses them with the fact of their divine inspiration. Wherever the Bible is read, there are light and liberty. Vice gives way to virtue, oppression to freedom, and there is at least a partial recognition of the fatherhood of God and brotherhood of man, whatever his parentage may be. There is faith, there is hope, there is charity; and in these three the soul finds sure and steadfast anchorage.

III. As a rule of faith and practice, the Scriptures are to be regarded as of supreme authority.

"They are they which testify of me," Jesus said. In type and service and prediction they bore witness to him, and this fact makes them authentic. They are God's word, absolute and sovereign in their authority. They testify of the Son of God, to whom "all power is given in heaven and on earth" (Matt. 28: 18), and who is "Head over all things to the church." (Eph. 1: 22.) God now speaks to us by his Son (Heb. 1: 2), and tells us to "hear him." (Matt. 17: 5.) Then let us hear him: "Till heaven and earth pass, one jot or one tittle shall in no wise pass from the law, till all be fulfilled. Whosoever, therefore, shall break one of the least of these commandments, and shall teach men so, he shall be called the least in the kingdom of heaven: but whosoever shall do and teach them, the same shall be called great in the kingdom of heaven." (Matt. 5: 18, 19.) No "Thus saith the Lord," no positive command found in the Holy Scriptures, can be set aside by earthly potentates, or ecclesiastical councils. No bishop, no priest, no pope, may annul or alter a single word. "For I testify unto every man that heareth the words of the prophecy of this book, if any man shall add unto these things, God shall add unto him the plagues that are written in this book: and if any man shall take away from the words of the book of this prophecy, God shall take away his part out of the book of life, and out of the holy city, and from the things which are written in this book." (Rev. 22: 18, 19.) These words are spoken of the Revelation. But it is legitimate to infer that the whole Bible is no less sacred than this, which is a part.

The Scriptures are God's covenants (Heb. 9: 15), confirmed by the death of his Son. They set forth God's will; and "no man disannulleth, or addeth thereto." (Gal. 3: 15.) God's heirs must not attempt the dangerous act of altering God's will and testament. It contains the law and the gospel, and must neither be added to nor diminished (Deut. 4: 2), for it is perfect. (Ps. 19: 7.) It contains "all the counsel of God" (Acts 20: 27) concerning man's duty and man's salvation. The Scriptures are God's decrees, God's *verdict*, from which there can be no appeal. What are called distinctive tenets of Baptist churches do but attest the strict obedience of these churches to the commandments of God. They are founded on the word of God. In all things they say: "To the law and to the testimony: if they speak not according to this word, it is because there is no light in them." (Isa. 8 : 20.) With these churches nothing is binding law but the Holy Scriptures; which, in conclusion, I commend as the only safe guide. Search the Scriptures. They testify of Jesus as " the Lamb of God, that taketh away the sin of the world." (John 1 : 29.) They lead to peace with God, to the knowledge and joy of true holiness, and to the attainment of everlasting life. They are the only infallible rule of life in faith and practice; being "profitable for doctrine, for reproof, for correction, for instruction in righteousness : that the man of God may be perfect, thoroughly furnished unto all good works." (2 Tim. 3 : 16, 17.) May the Holy Spirit aid us in searching and learning from them! Amen.

III.

THE DOCTRINE OF GOD: HIS EXISTENCE AND ATTRIBUTES.

WALTER H. BROOKS, D. D.,
Pastor of the Nineteenth Street Baptist Church, Washington, D. C.

"He that cometh to God must believe that he is, and that he is a rewarder of them that diligently seek him."—HEBREWS 11 : 6.

A BELIEF in the existence of God, and an adequate idea of his nature and character as set forth in his works and his Word, form essential elements in the conditions on which one's personal salvation is secured.

Eliminate the idea of God from the religions of earth, and man, robbed of his noblest aspirations, sees nothing in the universe higher than himself, and nowhere the power that redeems from sin, misery, and death. Man's spiritual nature demands God as an object of worship; and that nature fallen, reaches out for him as one mighty to save.

Let us, therefore, examine the source of our knowledge of God, and the reasons which strengthen and confirm us in the possession of it.

I. The testimony of intuition.

The belief in the existence of God is, as we have indicated, innate. We have not come into possession of it by any process of reasoning, nor by tradition. It is an intuition of the mind. The savage and the civilized alike have it. It is self-evident, necessary and practically universal. Men are so constituted that they cannot help believing that there is a God; and those persons who, having impaired their moral vision by false philosophy, pose as agnostics and atheists, do not disprove the position here taken. For they are certainly not more numerous, and not a whit wiser than the unfortunate blind, who may deny the existence of the sun, because they do not, and, under the circumstances, cannot behold him. They are, as all men know, an abnormal element in human society. Nevertheless, inasmuch as they are forever discussing the being of God, we are justified in drawing the conclusion that the idea of his existence enters into the thought of all men, and that it is impossible for any one to free himself entirely from it. The idea of Deity, at the worst, is not extinct in the atheist. It is simply dormant, and may, at any moment, be aroused by the divine power.

As religious beings a longing for God is born in us, and a belief that he somewhere exists accompanies that longing and prompts us to inquire after him. Against this feeling and conviction the atheist, we concede, may so successfully fight, that ultimately he finds little trouble in declaring that he has no knowledge of God, and knows nothing of his will and his works. Nevertheless, the belief in the existence of God is innate in him as in others, and sooner or later the scales of spiritual blindness must fall from his eyes.

II. The testimony of reason.

While it is true that the idea of God is innate, we must look in other directions for anything like an adequate conception of his nature and attributes. Observation and reason are to be relied upon, therefore, to supplement, strengthen, and confirm the idea of God, which is intuitive within us. In discussing this phase of the subject, the lamented Charles Hodge, D. D., of Princeton Theological Seminary, says: "Although all men have feelings and convictions which necessitate the assumption that there is a God, it is nevertheless perfectly legitimate to show that there are other facts which necessarily lead to the same conclusion. Besides, it is to be remembered that theistical arguments are designed to prove not only that there is a necessity for the assumption of an Extra-mundane and Eternal Being, but mainly to show what that being is; that he is a personal being, self-conscious, intelligent, moral. All this may be inclosed in the intuition, but it needs to be brought out and established."

What, then, are those other facts, which bring out and establish the truth concerning God's existence?

1. The theory of the creation of the universe by a self-existent, self-conscious, eternal, benevolent, and all-wise Spirit, who, while upholding all things by the power of his might, is independent of, and superior to, matter and all other existences, human and angelic, is the only one which at all satisfies the human mind in its search for the one *First Cause* of all things.

We presume that no one will deny that the material universe, in its present form, had a beginning. It matters not where nor when; for the mind of man is willing to travel backward through countless cycles of time, and all conceivable conditions of geologic and astronomical changes; but when, at last, the ultimate and original material, the embryo of the universe, is reached, it pauses to inquire, as it did at the start, for the great First Cause. It demands something more and higher than mindless matter, force, and law. These are not, and, in the nature of things, cannot be, self-existent and original. Hence, the mind finds repose alone in the belief that there is a God, and that he is the architect and builder of the universe.

2. Another factor in this series of proofs is the evidence of design, which nature everywhere furnishes.

(*a*) The marks of design, wisdom, and benevolence, which so many single objects in nature present, are an evidence of the existence of the Intelligence whom we call God, and a revelation of a number of his attributes.

You may select for study man or beast, fish or fowl, insect or reptile; or, if you fancy, turn to the vegetable world; and you will scarcely be able to point out a single living thing which does not bear marks of design. But these marks of design are due, as all men know, to the cause that gave rise to them; and we have only to study the ear, the hand, the eye, and like wonders of creation, in order to appreciate the fact that the wisdom and intelligence which pertain to the great First Cause in these cases are nothing less than the expression of the intelligence, will, and benevolence of Deity.

If these marks are not an incontestible proof of a designing mind which is independent of, and superior to the material objects which bear them, then the countless specimens of mechanism which abound in the great centres of civilization prove nothing relative to the existence, intelligence, and purpose of their inventors; and it may be claimed that the locomotive, the Victory printing press, and other wonders of the nineteenth century, originated themselves as the result of force, necessity, or of some inherent influence which has from time immemorial remained latent in matter. But no sane man would listen for a moment to such an explanation of the origin of the great Suspension Bridge, which makes one the cities of New

York and Brooklyn, or of the Washington Monument, which adorns our National Capital. Nothing would satisfy him but the assumption of an intelligent mind as the source of the thought and sentiment which thus find expression. Much more, then, may we insist that there is an intelligence back of the objects of nature to which we have here alluded, *which implies Mind* of the very highest type. But mind pertains to person, and the person here is God.

(*b*) The marks of design, which are evident in the adaptation of objects which are perfectly independent of each other, and exist as parts or properties of separate and widely unlike creatures of nature, are a proof of the existence of the same Intelligence whom we call God, and his boundless wisdom and goodness.

Are not the fins, eyes, and breathing apparatus of the fish made for water, and water adapted to the life of the fish? Are not the wings of the bird made for the air, and the air adapted to the habits and pursuits of the bird? Are not the digestive organs of every creature made for food? And the food which land, water, and open sky afford, are they not adapted to the sustenance of life, the promotion of growth, and the preservation of health? Is not the eye made for light, and is not light adapted to the eye? Is not the ear made for hearing, and sound adapted to the construction and capacity of the ear?

But why cite instances when, on every hand, we are confronted with the most marvelous adaptations. Nature is full of them. If we walk amid beds of flowers, or roam the forests, they are there; if we bore into the solid earth, the rocks declare them; if we dive into the depths, the waters reveal them; and if we ascend on high, lo, they are there. We cannot get away from them. They abound, that men everywhere may know that the universe is under the control of a Being of wisdom and goodness beyond our comprehension; and that being is God.

In the physical world, we find God by searching for a first cause, and by studying the marks of design manifest in the objects of our observations themselves, and in their wonderful adaptations. May we not be equally successful with the study of the mind? Let us see. Notice, then—

III. The moral faculty in man.

The moral faculty in man is a proof of the existence of a personal Being, and of his holiness of character. All men possess a power of mind by which they determine questions of morality, not in the light of their own experience, nor by a process of reasoning, but immediately and intuitively. It is this power of the mind, embodied in the conscience, which condemns vice and crime in all their forms, and fills the transgressor with a keen sense of his guilt and shame; and it is this same moral function which commends virtue, justice, truth, and everything that is good, and rewards those who are obedient to its dictates with the consciousness of their own integrity and moral worth. To what, then, are we to attribute the origin of this function of the soul?

There is a little instrument in many public buildings which is so constructed that if a night watchman is in the habit of sleeping at his post, or from some other cause fails to record the hours or half-hours of the night, as he is instructed to do, as a proof of his being awake and going his rounds, it will faithfully record his shortcomings, and present to him and to his superiors the facts in the case.

It would not be thought for a moment that this instrument,—constructed in the interest of truth, honesty, justice, and the public well-being; which shows such marks of design and wisdom; which is so unerring and faithful in the presentation of its testimony against the undutiful servant;—originated in anything less than a designing mind, which, at the time of its construction, was bent on the promotion of the moral and legal interests of the individual and the community, and the determent and punishment of at least one species of injustice and wrong.

Now the conscience of man is a power which determines the nature, and records the merits and demerits of all his performances, and even of his thoughts and emotions. It is infinitely more comprehensive and far-reaching in its influence than any invention of man. What, then, must we conclude? That it originated with a mind infinitely more exalted and wise than the mind of man—a holy Being, who is both the author of man's spirit and the builder of his mortal frame.

The atheist, if he will, may attribute the origin of this faculty to something less than God, or he may deny its existence altogether, and refer its decisions to other functions of the mind; but the truth will still remain that there is a God, and to him men are personally accountable as the Moral Governor of the Universe; for the evidence of conscience is conclusive.

But let us turn from the study of matter and mind, to the history of man as a moral being.

IV. The moral history and experience of man are a proof that there is a God, and that he loves righteousness.

Events and series of events which ultimately bring to pass results of a benign or afflictive character—results which imply the existence of a will far superior to the will of man—are constantly occurring. These are witnesses of God's existence, and present him as the world's Moral Ruler. An extract or two may confirm our position at this point.

Emerson says: "A little consideration of what takes place about us every day would show us that a higher law than that of our will regulates events. . . Oh, my brothers, God exists."

Dr. James McCosh, whom the literary world recognizes as a scholar who may speak with authority on matters of science and philosophy, puts it thus: "Inquire into the ground of the belief in the existence of God, entertained by the working man or man of business, and you will probably find it not an ingenious inspection of his own frame, or any material object, but an observation of the care which God takes of him, and of the judgments with which from time to time he visits the world." In the same connection he makes the following quotation from Niebuhr: "As the consideration of nature shows an inherent intelligence, which may also be conceived as coherent with nature, so does history, on a hundred occasions, show an intelligence which is distinct from nature, which conducts and determines those things which may seem to us accidental; and it is not true that the study of history weakens the belief in divine providence. History is, of all kinds of knowledge, the one which tends most decidedly to that belief."

We may appeal to every man's personal experience and observation, and to his knowledge of history, in confirmation of the position here taken. Of a truth—

"There's a divinity that shapes our ends,
Rough-hew them how we will."

THE DOCTRINE OF GOD. 47

V. The testimony of the Bible.

From all that has been said on the subject in hand, every one who accepts the views here advanced must conclude that there is a God, a living, personal Spirit, who is infinitely wise, just, and good; a God who loves truth and hates wickedness; a self-existent, self-conscious, eternal being, who, everywhere present, sustains the universe by the power of his might; and, while not destroying the freedom of man as a moral being, regulates all human affairs to the ultimate triumph of his own will. But, after all, there is nothing in matter, or the construction of the mind, which reveals God as "the justifier of sinners," as an object of saving faith, or "the rewarder of them that diligently seek him." In the Bible alone do we find this knowledge; and were it not for its inspired declarations, we should be entirely and forever ignorant of his threefold being, and his infinite mercy.

The proper understanding and right appreciation of his attributes, of the office-work of the respective persons of the Godhead, and of the character and scope of God's mercy, necessitate an intimate knowledge of the whole story of the creation, fall, and redemption of man. But we can give only a brief summary of what we believe concerning the true God, as he is set forth in the Scriptures.

According to the New Hampshire Confession of Faith: "We believe that there is one, and only one living and true God, an infinite, intelligent Spirit, whose name is Jehovah, the Maker and Supreme ruler of heaven and earth; inexpressibly glorious in holiness, and worthy of all possible honor, confidence, and love; that in the unity of the Godhead there are three persons—the Father, the Son, and the Holy Ghost; equal in every divine perfection and executing distinct but harmonious offices in the great work of redemption."

The particular passages in the Bible which support this view are many. A few only are given. John 4: 24, "God is a Spirit"; Ps. 147: 5, "His understanding is infinite"; Ps. 83: 18, "Thou whose name alone is *Jehovah*, art the Most High over all the earth"; Ex. 15: 11, "Who is like thee, glorious in holiness?"; Mark 12: 30, "Thou shalt love the Lord thy God with all thy heart, and with all thy soul, and with all thy mind, and with all thy strength"; Rev. 4: 11, "Thou art worthy, O Lord, to receive glory and honour and power: for thou hast created all things, and for thy pleasure they are and were created"; Matt. 28: 19, "Go ye, therefore, and teach all nations, baptizing them in the name of the Father, and of the Son, and of the Holy Ghost"; Jonn 15: 26, "When the Comforter is come, whom I will send you from the Father, even the Spirit of Truth, which proceedeth from the Father, he shall testify of me"; John 10: 30, "I and my Father are one"; Eph. 2: 18, "For through him [the Son] we both have access by one Spirit unto the Father"; 2 Cor. 13: 14, "The grace of our Lord Jesus Christ, and the love of God, and the communion of the Holy Ghost, be with you all."

Here God is revealed to us under circumstances which render the rejection of the truth concerning his nature and character extremely heinous; for he is, in the language of another Confession, "Most gracious, merciful, long-suffering, abundant in goodness and truth, forgiving iniquity, transgression, and sin; the rewarder of them that diligently seek him; and, withal, most just and terrible in his judgments; hating all sin, and who will by no means clear the guilty." Therefore he who would be eternally saved must heartily accept the idea of God, as it is presented in the Holy Scriptures, and aim to conform his life to his will.

But the Scriptural argument in proof of the existence of God, especially of God as he is presented in the sacred volume, rests entirely upon the trustworthiness of the Bible as a declaration of truth. We cannot discuss this. We must state, however, that the reasons which lead us to accept the statements of the Bible as true, and as altogether satisfactory, are abundant and conclusive. We accept the testimony of our own senses and of our intuitions; and we as readily accept the testimony of worthy men who wrote on the same subject at different times, and in places widely separated from each other, because their statements all harmonize, and their writings bear internal proofs of the influence of the Divind Mind.

But the Bible, aside from what it states concerning God, is itself a proof of his existence. Like the works of nature and the mind of man, it has the seal of Jehovah upon it, and with them testifies of his being. Therefore let those who believe in the reality of nature, and who cheerfully accept the testimony of their senses, their intuitions and their reason, listen to the voice of God as it rings out in the volume of his truth, and, believing in his existence and in the atoning merits of the Lord Jesus Christ, be reconciled unto him through the inward working of the Holy Spirit.

IV.

THE FALL OF MAN.

REV. H. N. BOUEY,
Missionary of the American Baptist Home Mission Society for Missouri.

"Let us make man in our image, after our likeness."—GENESIS 1 : 26.

"And when the woman saw that the tree was good for food, and that it was pleasant to the eyes, and a tree to be desired to make one wise, she took of the fruit thereof, and did eat, and gave also unto her husband with her; and he did eat."—GENESIS 3 : 6.

THE first text is necessary to an intelligent understanding of man's original state. In it we see at once God's great condescension, and man's true greatness in purity and intelligence. It appears that after God had finished his creative work, he looked out upon it and it pleased him; for he saw that it was all very good. And it seems that he needed a crown for it—a being superior to all else he had formed, and next to himself. Under him man was to rule the world of nature according to laws he laid down. Thus he determined to make him in his own image, after his own likeness. Man's uprightness was physical, intellectual, and moral. His fall affected him in each of these features. Right from the hand of the infinitely good and pure and holy God, it was impossible for Adam to be other than a holy, righteous, and pure man. However the fall may perplex us both in its cause and results, one thing is sure, and that is, that Adam was made in the image and likeness of God.

Created in holiness, under the law of his Maker, he

THE FALL OF MAN. 51

enjoyed unhindered communion with him. Adam did not have a sinful nature, and hence no tendencies to sin. He had the ability to sin, which necessarily followed the high and exalted gift of free moral agency. "Lo, this only have I found, that God hath made man upright; but they have sought out many inventions." (Eccl. 7: 29.) The meaning of uprightness admits of no doubt as to man's original rectitude in his godlike nature. He was connected with the divine nature and made in its likeness. And the goal of our restoration in the gospel is the recovery of this, or more than this, by our being made like Christ.

"And the Lord God commanded the man, saying, Of every tree of the garden thou mayest freely eat: But of the tree of the knowledge of good and evil, thou shalt not eat of it; for in the day thou eatest thereof thou shalt surely die." (Gen. 2: 16, 17.) This was the first law that was promulgated upon earth for human government. It was given by a Holy Being to a holy, but subordinate being. And there was nothing in it opposed to Adam's nature; so that there was every reason why he should and could have obeyed it. It was a just law from a holy God to a godlike man, who had not only never committed sin, but who had no sinful proclivities. By voluntary transgression Adam fell from that holy and happy state. This was a mighty fall, in which all Adam's descendants participated to the extent of becoming inheritors of a depraved nature, from which nothing can deliver them save the atoning work of Jesus Christ. Adam's exalted lineage and gift of free agency formed the ground of his responsibility for his action in violating the law given him. There was no excuse for Adam, though he tried to find one; just as there is none for men to-day for not believing on Jesus Christ, who has come for their redemption. His being tempted by Eve formed no valid excuse. He could put upon no one else the responsibility for breaking the law which had been given to him. In the fall resulting from this disobedience, all of Adam's faculties, physical, intellectual, and moral, shared; and all the disabilities arising therefrom were transmitted by him to his posterity.

Before man fell in Adam, he was without any tendencies to sin; but now he is prone to evil "as the sparks fly upward." Nothing but the Holy Spirit produces in him any desires toward God. His communication having been severed by his disobedience, he could obtain nothing from God. "Wherefore as by one man sin entered into the world, and death by sin; and so death passed upon all men, for that all have sinned." (Rom. 5 : 12.) Whatever was Adam's trouble is ours to-day, until we accept Jesus as our Saviour, and become restored to that image which we lost in Adam's fall. In him we lost all, but in Christ we gain all. Here is a meaningful contrast between Adam and Christ, in relation to the tempter to whose power both were subjected. Adam ruined us by yielding, and Jesus opened the way to our healing and redemption by not yielding.

The world cannot have a more striking illustration of God's inevitable condemnation of disobedience than is given by his dealings with Adam. "So he drove out the man: and he placed at the east of the garden of Eden cherubim, and a flaming sword which turned every way, to keep the way of the tree of life." (Gen. 3 : 24.) God's driving Adam out of the garden was an emphatic expression of the fact that he had already excluded himself from that familiar and perfect relationship in which he communed with his Maker.

Two things are clear as to Adam's fall: He was made holy, and he was free and intelligent in his choice. We must keep our eyes upon Adam's ability and power to resist the temptation that assailed him, and his absolute freedom of choice in yielding thereto. Nor could he plead ignorance of the penalty affixed to disobedience. It was too impressive to have been forgotten. "In the day that thou eatest thereof thou shalt surely die."

The penalty pronounced was imposed. Adam died spiritually on that very day in which he ate that forbidden fruit, and some think that he also became subject to physical death. He suffered also in the curse pronounced on creation for his sake. "And unto Adam he said, Because thou hast hearkened unto the voice of thy wife, and hast eaten of the tree of which I commanded thee, saying, Thou shalt not eat of it: cursed is the ground for thy sake; in sorrow shalt thou eat of it all the days of thy life. Thorns also and thistles shall it bring forth to thee." (Gen. 3: 17.) It is to be noticed that no special woe was pronounced upon Adam, as upon the serpent and Eve. God cursed the ground for his sake, it is true; but there was no need for any special curse upon him, for the penalty of the law went into effect immediately. He, for the first time, realized the fearful feeling of condemnation. There was a great change in his disposition, affections, and will. Where he had delighted in God's presence, he now hid among the trees. He needed no special curse. God's broken law was curse enough to affect him so deeply that all of his posterity have suffered because of it, and are suffering until now. Truly it is said that in Adam we all fell. "For . . . by one man's disobedience many were made sinners." (Rom. 5 : 19.) We inherited our sinful nature from our father Adam; for we sin to-day very much as he did. He put his wife (coupled with his own desire for self-gratification) before his God. This we do now, almost daily, by putting some earthly object first in our affections, thus giving it God's place. God is no more pleased with such conduct now than he was in Adam's day. Nor is the penalty any less in our case than in his. Indeed, we are suffering until to-day the spiritual death of separation from the great Source of life, and must continue to suffer until we become heirs of the new life in Christ Jesus. Our sinful natures are too deeply depraved to be changed by anything except the power of God through regeneration. "Because the carnal mind is enmity against God : for it is not subject to the law of God, neither indeed can be." (Rom. 8 : 7.) None of man's devices nor works can reconcile him to God, and remove the stains from his soul. In our fallen state, outside of the Holy Spirit, we cannot offer anything acceptable. There is no saving power in us. Jesus alone is our Saviour. And all are alike. "There is none that understandeth. There is none that seeketh after God. They are all gone out of the way, they are together become unprofitable; there is none that doeth good, no, not one. . . . And the way of peace have they not known: There is no fear of God before their eyes." (Rom. 3 : 11, 12 ; 17, 18.) Here Paul tells us that all men are alike, in that they have all gone out of the way, and thus none are righteous. Neither Jew nor Gentile can boast of a holy birth, nor of an exemption from a positively corrupt nature. Our souls cleave to the dust. Not even the Christian, the regenerated man, can boast of doing good; for whatever of acceptance he may possess comes to him through his relations to the Lord Jesus Christ. We had our conversation in the lusts of the flesh; now we are quickened into life by the Holy Spirit of God. And we know the difference between then and now. Then we were strangers and foreigners; now we are of the household of faith, having been made nigh by the precious blood of Christ. Then we had the spirit of bondage again to fear; now we have the spirit of adoption, whereby we cry, Abba, Father. And so Eden is revenged by Calvary. The disobedience and failure and defeat of the first Adam are redeemed by the obedience and success and victory of the second Adam. In the one we died; in the other we are made alive. Thanks be unto God, who giveth us the victory through our Lord Jesus Christ.

Let us sum up what we have said. God created man pure and holy—in his own image. He gave him a place in which to live, and a single law for him to keep. By his own free, intelligent act he broke that law and became sinful. He fell from the position in which he held communion with God, and was driven from the garden where he lived. And not only did he fall for himself, but also for his posterity. All the race became sinful because of his sin in the garden of Eden. Moreover, it is not a sin from which man can recover himself. And so Christ came. He died for our sins, and lives for our justification. It is only in him that the verdict of Eden can be reversed. *That* because of disobedience meant separation from God, and so death. *This* means union to God again, and so life. Above Jesus Christ, then, hear the words: "He that hath the Son hath life."

V.

THE WAY OF SALVATION.

R. B. VANDAVELL, D. D.,
Pastor of the First Baptist Church, East Nashville, Tenn.

"Not by works of righteousness which we have done, but according to his mercy he saved us, by the washing of regeneration and renewing of the Holy Ghost."—TITUS 3 : 5.

ONE of the great wonders of Christianity is the simple way in which a sinner is saved. The way of salvation reveals alike God's wisdom and love. And yet it is a sad fact that so many do not seem to know how to find Jesus. And it is a sadder fact that so many of our ministers so frequently present Jesus in such a way as to lead to the belief that somehow the sinner has to earn his salvation by a process of mourning and prayers and tears. There is no proper view of the matter of salvation which does not exhibit God as a sovereign, and the way of salvation as through the atonement of Jesus Christ.

I. The gospel is founded on the depravity of human nature.

Man by the fall became disobedient, sinful, and helpless—morally depraved. Hence sin was to him a pleasure; to disobey God more satisfactory than obedience; and he had no moral power to choose a holy life. It is because of this condition of man's nature that salvation is provided and offered.

1. Man cannot save himself by his own works. Sal-

vation is declared to be "not by works of righteousness which we have done." The law under which every man lives is, in a true sense, the law of service. We owe God, as creatures, all the obedience and love of which we are capable. If, therefore, we could perfectly obey God, we would be doing simply what is our duty; and we would never reach a time when we would have anything to our credit more than we owed. But we cannot fulfill the law under which we daily live; and to have any surplus obedience which could be set over against our past life of sin and disobedience is an impossibility. So if we were left to ourselves we must ultimately perish. No, we cannot save ourselves; and our good works, though useful and needful as proof of the change of heart wrought by the Holy Spirit, can never gain for us an entrance into heaven. Moreover, our best acts are marred by defects which make them sinful in the sight of God; and, consequently, they would serve more to condemn than to justify us.

2. In purposing to save man by grace, God's final purpose was his own glory. Whatever else may have been in the divine mind, this was there, because as God's glory is secured, man's salvation is attained.

There are many things which relate to the matter of salvation which men cannot fully understand; but the way in which they are to be saved is made plain. Thank God, a sinner can be saved by simply repenting of his sins and trusting Jesus Christ. He does not have to rely on his own efforts; he does not have to sing or pray his way into the kingdom of God. He has simply to repent and believe the gospel; and in all this God's glory obtains, and should be kept in view.

But although works do not save us, they must be shown in the life of every Christian as the outward evidence of the inward workings of the Spirit. He has been created thereunto. (Eph. 2: 10.) If a man shows no good works in his life, we may reasonably infer that he has never been born again. Indeed, this is the necessary inference; for if the love of God moves upon a man's heart, and Christ dwells there, he cannot avoid showing it in his life. And it is true that good works are the only external evidence of a change of heart. Without such evidence, men may reasonably doubt that the sinner has ever been born again. Hence love to God and love to man should find constant expression in all lines of Christian work. The care of the poor saints, the support of the church, Christian education, missions at home and abroad, Bible work, and all other such activities, should engage the hearts and hands of all who profess to have found Jesus Christ.

II. God's plan of saving men is according to his eternal purposes.

It is a purpose too founded upon justice and mercy. He must vindicate the majesty of his law; and this he does by giving his Son to die for us; but *mercy* shines through it all. When the Holy Spirit convinces us of sin and regenerates us, mercy underlies the whole transaction. By grace we are saved. The purposes of God can never be discovered; they can be known only as revealed. Men are sometimes disturbed because they cannot know just why God does certain things; but a loving, child-like trust should lead us all to believe that God does all things well, and secures, as the result of all his acts, his own greatest glory, and the salvation of all such as will believe.

III. Because the way of salvation is plain, we should seek to make it plain to the understanding of sinners.

There is much that ought to be corrected in the manner of our preaching. We need to preach more emphatically a free salvation. We sometimes present the gospel in such a way that men get the impression that they have to "get religion" by praying, or by singing, or by mourning. And some inquirers will attend protracted meetings for weeks, and then not find Christ. Only let men's understanding be enlightened. Let them be taught that—

> "Nothing, either great or small,
> Remains for them to do,"

but to repent of their sins and trust Jesus, and many more will be saved. Let us, then, study this matter of salvation so that we may be able to present it in the manner laid down in God's word. Let us seek to honor Christ more by being more faithful to his method of saving men. Let us exalt God's plan of salvation, preaching *Jesus only*, and the desert places will blossom as the rose, and the waste places will be built up, and the name of our Lord the Christ magnified.

VI.

THE FREENESS OF SALVATION.

REV. W. G. PARKS,

Pastor of the Mount Zion Baptist Church, Shelbyville, Tenn.

"Whosoever will let him take the water of life freely."—REVELATION 22 : 17.

WE have announced to us at once that:
1. The gospel offers the blessings of salvation free to all. One of the glories of this text is, that it represents man, though vile and sinful, as able at will to accept the proffers made. "Whosoever will" throws open the gate of deliverance to the whole race of Adam, and gives to all the blessed invitation, Come.

"Let him take the water of life freely" does not only assure the lost sinner that his thirst shall be quenched, but also informs him of its abiding nature, for it is the water of "life." The blessed Saviour has not simply made known the provision of this to the lost sinner, but also stands pleading with him for its acceptance. "Ho, every one that thirsteth, come ye to the waters" (Isa. 55 : 1), is the sentiment of every New Testament proclamation. "Come, for all things are now ready." (Luke 14 : 17.) The table is spread, and all are urged to come to it and partake of its bounty. The Lord Jesus himself uttered the words that indicate this gracious provision, and with no respect of persons the announcement is made to the world. "For God so loved the world that he gave his only begotten Son, that whosoever believeth in him should not perish, but have everlasting life." (John 3 : 16.)

This provision of grace is free, because the price of it has been paid by Jesus Christ himself: "Who gave himself a ransom for all to be testified in due time." (1 Tim. 11 : 6.) It is through Christ that all matters between God and man as pertaining to salvation are transacted. Christ gave himself up to death, even the death of the cross, that we might have a right to the tree of life. This ransom was wrought out by his substitution for us, and thus he paid the price of our redemption. Therefore our deliverance does not come by anything that we have done. We do not receive it for any price paid by us; for we had sinned, and were helpless, bankrupt; but Christ assumed all our obligations, and met all the demands of the law, and so proffers the water of life to all mankind without money and without price.

2. It is the immediate duty of all to accept this by means of a sincere, penitent, and obedient faith. "But now [the gospel] is made manifest, and by the Scriptures of the prophets according to the commandment of the everlasting God, made known to all nations for the obedience of faith." (Rom. 16 : 26.) The gospel of Christ was re-revealed or made manifest to the Gentiles and to all nations, to induce them to exercise faith in Jesus Christ and obey his commands. It is disclosed to men in order that they may believe and be saved from their sins. It is an *immediate* duty, because "to-day is the day of salvation," and to delay may fix our eternal destiny. We want to realize the necessity that is laid upon us of believing the gospel: "For therein is the righteousness of God revealed from faith to faith: as it is written the just shall

live by faith." (Rom. 1 : 17.) Therefore the righteousness of God is received by faith, and nothing else can be offered as a substitute. And by this faith we are justified through our Lord Jesus Christ. By this faith God, the Father, accepts us as righteous, and holds us no longer under the condemnation of the law. We can therefore see that the obedience and death of Christ are the ground of a sinner's acceptance with God. He must have an inward change of views and feelings, and must turn away from his sins unto God, having as the fruits of repentance a change of life. He can be saved in no other way.

3. Rejection of the gospel is the only thing that prevents the salvation of those to whom that gospel has been preached. Many unrepentant sinners have read the Scriptures enough to know that they bear witness to our Saviour the Lord Jesus Christ, that he is the Messiah and Redeemer of the world. But they have not the word of God abiding in them, neither have they believed in his Son, whom he has sent. It is, therefore, their own disobedience, and the corruption of their own hearts, that keep them from the blessing of salvation. It is not their will to come; for if it were, they would be saved. "And him that cometh to me I will in nowise cast out." (John 6 : 37.) God assures salvation to all who will come to him renouncing their sins and exercising faith in him. And when they refuse to do this, they themselves bar the way to the free salvation which has been provided. "And ye will not come to me that ye might have life." (John 5 : 40.) For they stumbled at that stumbling stone—Christ Jesus laid in Zion as the foundation stone of all true hope; neither is there salvation in any other. If they will refuse, and continue to reject him, then come to

them in thunder tones the words of our blessed Saviour: "Behold, your house is left unto you desolate." (Matt. 23 : 38.)

4. This rejection involves the sinner in a grievous condemnation. They that fail to hear the gospel's warning voice, repent and accept Christ on terms of faith, must be driven from the presence of God into everlasting exile. "Who shall be punished with everlasting destruction from the presence of the Lord and from the glory of his power." (2 Thess. 1 : 9.) What a miserable state! Christ rejected and heaven lost. And, instead of enjoying the blessings of a free salvation, weeping amid the pangs of an eternal exile.

"Why do you wait, dear sinner?
The harvest is passing away;
Oh, why not accept his salvation?
There are danger and death in delay."

What an awful day, when God shall appoint the finally impenitent and disobedient their portion, and drive them from the glory of his presence. Let poor sinners take warning, and prepare to enter into that rest that remaineth to the people of God. Since salvation is so free, and mercy stands and pleads, will it not be an awful thing to be turned away from his presence filled with an eternal sorrow?

"Almighty God, thy grace impart,
Fix deep conviction on each heart;
Nor let us waste on trifling cares
The life which thy compassion spares."

VII.

REGENERATION.

REV. E. K. LOVE, D. D.,
Pastor of the First African Baptist Church, Savannah, Ga.

"Marvel not that I said unto thee, ye must be born again."—JOHN 3 : 7.

SUCH was the strange language that greeted the ear of the ruler Nicodemus, as he came to the Lord Jesus Christ on that memorable night with his flattering address: "Rabbi, we know that thou art a teacher come from God: for no man can do these miracles that thou doest, except God be with him." (John 3 : 2.) The conversation that followed was a most remarkable one. It was remarkable in circumstance, authorship and significance. It succinctly touched upon the vital points that had to do with the admission of members into Christ's kingdom, and make man at one with God. Jesus knew that Nicodemus had come to interview him about the nature of his mission; and without indulging in a long preface, he proceeded to enlighten the ruler as to the nature and subjects of his kingdom. In his answer, he gave his visitor to understand that neither rank, influence, wealth, learning, nor family descent could gain an entrance into the kingdom he was about to establish ; but that it would demand an entire change of heart and newness of life as a condition of membership. The unexpected answer of the Lord turned the conversation in an unexpected way. When he said, "Verily, verily, I say unto thee, except a man be born again he cannot see the kingdom of God" (John 3:3), Nicodemus did not understand him. This was putting the case to him in a way as new as it was startling. Not that Nicodemus failed to comprehend the language or figure employed, but he could not see how that language or figure could apply to himself and the Jews. They were the seed of Abraham, and the children of the promise. If Jesus had said to this "ruler of the Jews" that the Gentiles "must be born again," he would have found no trouble, either in understanding or accepting the statement. But this "man of the Pharisees" believed that the Jews were by nature the heirs of the kingdom.

The Lord at once struck right at the heart of his mistake by assuring the ruler that the new birth was a necessity for all who would enter his kingdom. And when Nicodemus in a carping or a bewildered mood asked him if a man could be born when he was old, Jesus said: "Except a man be born of water and of the Spirit, he cannot enter into the kingdom of God. That which is born of the flesh is flesh; and that which is born of the Spirit is Spirit." (John 3:5, 6.) The kingdom of heaven is a spiritual kingdom, and a spiritual birth must precede its possession and enjoyment. Nicodemus, more to express his bewilderment than expecting an answer, said: "How can these things be?" "Art thou a Master in Israel and knowest not these things?" Jesus said. And then his succeeding words are in the nature of a reproach. It is as though he had said: If you do not understand this that any Rabbi should know, that a changed heart must precede entrance to Messiah's kingdom, really an earthly matter, how shall ye understand the higher things of which you would have me speak?

Nicodemus was silenced, if not convinced at this time. Afterward he became wholly convinced, and experienced, doubtless, the change of which Jesus spake, although as far as we know he did not openly follow Jesus. He learned, as all men have learned since, wherever the gospel has been preached, that the new birth, spiritual generation, must precede citizenship in the kingdom of our Lord. Before them all appear the weighty and uncompromising words: "Ye must be born again." This is the requirement of all, from which there can be no abatement, and to which there are no exceptions.

I. Consider, then, the necessity of the new birth.

All men are by nature sinners. "Behold I was shapen in iniquity; and in sin did my mother conceive me" (Ps. 51) is a fact that all must admit. If we are conceived in sin and born in sin and have lived in sin, it must follow that a radical change must take place before we can live anew unto righteousness. "How can he be clean that is born of a woman?" (Job 25 : 4) is a question that grows out of the fact that we are all sinners. The total depravity of a man is put beyond the shadow of a reasonable doubt. Those who doubt it must shut their eyes to both reason and revelation. Man was created holy; he sinned of his own free will and accord. It was not God's fault. He could have kept from sinning. He chose to be disobedient, and in the consequences of his disobedience involved all of his posterity. All men since the fall have borne the image of their fallen parents. The effects of the fall and the depravity of human nature are seen in the fact that at the very altar of sacrifice, when the two brothers met, the older murdered the younger. When the world had stood less than two thousand years the awful words fell from the pen of the inspired writer: "The earth also was corrupt before God and the earth was filled with violence." (Gen. 6 : 11.) "And God saw that the wickedness of man was great in the earth, and that every imagination of the thoughts of his heart was only evil continually." (Gen. 6 : 5.) So general and widespread has the curse become that the Apostle John says: "The whole world lieth in wickednes." (1 John 5 : 19.) No man may claim to form an exception to this universal corruption. "There is no man which sinneth not." (2 Chron. 6 : 36.) If man were disposed to charge his corrupt condition wholly to Adam, there would meet him this difficulty : "Have you done everything aright, to the best of your ability? Have you kept the law perfectly, not even violating it in your heart? Have you always loved God with all your heart, mind, might, and strength?" If you cannot answer "Yes" to these questions, then you are personally sinful, and are also included in the solemn statement made by the prophet Isaiah (53 : 6), "All we like sheep have gone astray; we have turned every one to his own way." Man by nature is not disposed to do right. Sin has depraved his disposition, poisoned his affections, spoiled his taste for righteousness, and made his mind diseased. He is a rebel against God, and hates his law, "Because the carnal mind is enmity against God: for it is not subject to the law of God, neither indeed can be." (Rom. 8 : 7) What means the committing of crime everywhere, by people of every nation, but that sin everywhere exists? Why did our Lord command that the gospel be preached everywhere if sin did not obtain everywhere? Why would he taste death for every man if every man had not sinned? Verily, "All have sinned, and come short of the glory of God." (Rom. 3 : 23.) "And so death passed upon all men, for that all have sinned." (Rom. 5 : 12.)

If, then, man would gain what he lost in the fall, he " must be born again." He is not prepared to live a new life, save as that from which life springs is renewed. No one is prepared to work and live for Christ until his will has been subdued, the fallow ground of his heart broken up, a saving knowledge of the word of God placed within him, and the love of God shed abroad in his heart. If we could adjust the condition and nature of a fish to the air, we could make it live out of water. Until we can do this we would attempt it in vain. If we could so adjust the fish to the air, we would call that change a new birth. A person is not prepared to live in the vineyard of the Lord until his nature has been adjusted to its new conditions. That adjustment must be effected by the Holy Spirit, and when it is accomplished we call it regeneration. No one is truly a servant of God until quickened by the Holy Spirit. No human reformation can assure a godly life in Christ Jesus. This life must follow a new birth in the Lord. If we would walk with God, we must be born of God. The love of God must constrain us or we make vows only to break them. "The old man with his deeds" (Col. 3 : 9) must be put off and " the new man which is renewed in knowledge after the image of him that created him" must be put on, or we cannot work the works of Christ Jesus. We are dead in trespasses and in sins, and we must be born again before we can live again. There can be no spiritual life without a spiritual birth, any more than a natural life without a natural birth. A man who is not born again is as truly dead spiritually as a man who dies naturally; and it would be just as serious a mistake to admit such a person into the church and expect good works and godly life of him as to dig from the grave a man who has long lain there, and expect work and activity of him. The Christian Church should let the dead remain in their graves until they hear the voice of the Son of God; then they will arise, and not till then, to walk in the newness of life. Only regenerated persons should compose the church of Christ, for only such are called "saints." "That which is born of the flesh is flesh," and will seek the things of the flesh; will seek to gratify the lust and ambition of the flesh, which things are contrary to the law of God. A new birth is the only remedy. As circumcision was essential to membership in the Jewish theocracy, so the new birth is essential to admission to the privileges of Christ's kingdom.

But all we could say would not make the necessity for the new birth more apparent than the plain, precise statement of Jesus Christ the heavenly Teacher. "Except a man be born again he cannot see the kingdom of God." (Ver. 3.) Here the necessity appears in the statement of our inability to enter the kingdom of God save by means of the new birth. No farther reason should be asked than that Jesus Christ says so. He came from God, and God was with him, and Nicodemus had acknowledged this. As the Lord's declaration was enough for the ruler, so it should be sufficient for us. And we should all seek the new birth, the necessity for which the Lord's words point out. Without it we can have no real peace, and by it alone can we be well-pleasing to God. "Without faith it is impossible to please him." (Heb. 11:6.) And this faith can come alone as fruitage of the new birth and the new life.

II. The character of the new birth required.

The new birth is a change of heart, a change of disposition, a change of affection, a renewing of the mind, and a beginning of a new life. This is properly called a new creation. "Therefore, if any man be in Christ, he is a new creature: old things are passed away; behold, all things are become new." (2 Cor. 5:17.) The words "new creature" mean one "regenerated through Christ." The new birth is the accepting of salvation by Jesus Christ, by whom is formed the disposition to obey his commandment, deny self, and follow him. It is said to be a passing from death unto life. "We know that we have passed from death unto life, because we love the brethren. He that loveth not his brother abideth in death." (1 John 3:14.) "And you hath he quickened, who were dead in trespasses and sins; wherein in time past ye walked according to the course of this world, according to the prince of the power of the air, the spirit that now worketh in the children of disobedience; . . . for we are his workmanship created in Christ Jesus unto good works, which God hath before ordained that we should walk in them. . . . For ye were sometimes darkness, but now are ye light in the Lord: walk as children of light." (Eph. 2: 1, 2, 10; 5:8.) The disposition to conform to these requirements is an evidence of the new birth.

To be born again is to be born of the Spirit. He is the Author of the new birth; and that Nicodemus might the better understand, the Saviour said that except a man be born of water—the gracious influences of the gospel—and the Spirit he cannot enter into the kingdom of God. The violation of the law changed man's condition, and threw him out of harmony with God, and regeneration, wrought by the Spirit through the gospel, must counteract this change and restore man to the favor of God again. The new birth has to do with the spiritual man. This is that for which David prayed "Create in me a clean heart, O God, and renew a right spirit within me" (Ps. 51 : 10); that is, the Psalmist wanted his sins blotted out and a spirit put in him that would incline him to do right. This is that which was promised (in Ezek. 18 : 31) by the Almighty. A new heart also will I give you, and a new spirit will I put within you. Nay, verily nothing but this new birth "can give the guilty conscience peace, or wash away the stain." It cannot be a human reformation. It is beyond human power or conception. It is not confined to race, or sect, or nation. It is not in beautiful religious ceremonies. It is not in observing feasts and fasts. It is not in learning nor eloquence. It is not in natural birth or blood, for "in Christ neither circumcision availeth anything, nor uncircumcision, but a new creature." (Gal. 6 : 15.)

What is this new birth? It is not the making of new faculties. It is not the making of a new heart. It is not the fashioning of a new mind. It is not the creation of a new spirit, nor is it the adding of new organs or senses to the old machine; but it is a renewing of them all, and turning their power to operate in another direction more pleasing, more righteous, more blessed, more lovely, and more divine. "Whosoever believeth that Jesus is the Christ is born of God" (1 John 5 : 1), and will be ready for every good work. Here it is then defined to be faith. "But as many as received him, to them gave he power to become the sons of God, even to them that believe on his name : which were born, not of blood, nor of the will of the flesh, nor of the will of man, but of God." (John 1 : 12, 13.)

Without this regeneration men cannot be truly good. It is true that some men may have lofty ideas of virtue and good morals; they may have a high sense of honor, and may do many charitable deeds, yet, if the heart has not been changed, the foundation is wrong, and there is an under current of evil which God hates, and which will destroy the soul. Nothing can atone for the absence of a regenerated heart. The new birth is Jesus Christ, "the highest expression of God's infinite compassion," formed in the soul as the hope of glory, it is this which creates in the soul the most decided hatred for sin and all that God hates, and begets instead thereof the supremest love for holiness, righteousness, and all that God loves. It is the source of that "joy unspeakable and full of glory," and creates the peace that passeth understanding which the world cannot give nor take away.

"'Tis religion that can give
Sweetest pleasure while we live.
'Tis religion must supply
Solid comfort when we die.
After death, its joys shall be
Lasting as eternity.
Be the living God my friend,
Then my bliss shall never end."

Regeneration is a death to the love of sin, and a birth which begins a new life unto righteousness. It is that which sets the affection on things above, and makes the soul long after righteousness, as the hart panteth for the water brooks. It enlightens the understanding, fills the soul with joy and love, and makes the heart beat in unison with the law of God in which it now delights. If a man who was an inveterate drunkard, a bold blasphemer, and a reckless gambler, should turn and live a quiet, chaste, and sober life, we would say of him, "He is a changed man." Now, if that change was in the heart, that would be regeneration. That would be exactly what Christ meant to teach Nicodemus in the text. If a man who is a member of a political party should change for policy's sake, because the other party had succeeded in an election, and thereby increasing his chance for gain and fame, that would simply be changing position, not condition. That would be like reforming without regeneration. But if he really believed in his heart that he was wrong, and the other party right in principle, and his wrong in principle, his change would be a change of condition, which would cause the change of position. If such a change took place spiritually, it would be regeneration. If a man believes in his heart the record that God has given of his Son, and humbly accepts the terms of reconciliation proposed in the gospel, he is born again. The new birth is not only renouncing the old man and his deeds, but it is the putting on the new man Christ Jesus, and walking in him to the glory of God the Father. Regeneration is that which the Holy Spirit effects in the heart by which we are made children of God and heirs of the kingdom. Sin unfits men for association with God; and the new birth secures to them the divine nature, and so fits them for heaven and its enjoyments. Regeneration is the swallowing up of the human will into the divine will, thus glorifying the soul, and putting obedience into the life. It fits the man for continuing in fellowship with the saints, and for walking by faith in meekness and humbleness to that rest that remaineth for the people of God, where hope shall consummate in fruition and faith be turned into sight.

III. By whom is this new birth effected?

This new birth is effected by the Holy Spirit. In the creation, when everything was chaos, when "the earth was without form and void," then "the Spirit of God moved upon the face of the waters." (Gen. 1 : 2.) As the result of this moving, the waters gathered together in one place, and the dry land appeared. Life roamed the plains and forests and filled the air and seas, while over all was thrown a mantling beauty which God's hand alone could give.

As prior to the creation of matter there was chaos, so likewise is there in the new creation. The soul, before the touch of the Holy Spirit, is chaos—"without form and void." Great darkness, spiritual darkness, envelops it. It is confusion and emptiness—without order and life. It is without holiness, without perfect love, without good thoughts, without the disposition to do right, without peace, without hope, and without God in the world. It is the office of the Holy Spirit to give the soul these needed graces; and until he does, the soul must remain chaotic and dead. There is nothing more fraught with fearful destiny than a graceless, Christless soul. It is the seat of unholy aspirations, selfish ambitions, and lustful passions. Not in all are these developed; but in all their seeds are found.

This condition now can only be changed by the Holy

Ghost. Until he comes and breathes upon the slain, the valley will continue covered with dry bones. Nothing is roused to life without his vivifying touch. He was present at the genesis of the natural world, and he presides over the building of the spiritual. At the commencement of the public ministry of Christ he appeared at the Jordan and lighted upon his shoulders, and immediately led him away into the wilderness, where by personal testing he was fitted for his work. "The Spirit of the Lord God is upon me; because the Lord hath anointed me to preach good tidings unto the meek" (Isa. 61: 1), are words he applied to himself when he emerged therefrom. The Holy Spirit came to the church on the day of Pentecost, and so moved the hearts of the preachers and people that it did not require very great faith to see that a new era had begun for the church. This miraculous visitation of the Holy Spirit in the beginning of the church's career seemed to indicate his place therein, and in the economy of grace. He moved upon both the preachers and the hearers, breathing on the one power, and rousing in the other conviction. He still performs this duty. The disciples were told to wait at Jerusalem "for the promise of the Father" (Acts 1: 4), which was: "Ye shall be baptized with the Holy Ghost not many days hence." (Acts 1: 5.) "It is the Spirit that quickeneth" (John 6: 63), and calls dead sinners from their tombs, and gives the blind their sight. There can be no life without him. Jesus Christ says of him: "When he is come, he will reprove the world of sin, of righteousness, and of judgment." (John 16: 8.) It is the business of the Spirit to teach of Christ. "But when the Comforter is come, whom I will send unto you from the Father, even the Spirit of truth, which proceedeth from the Father, he shall testify of me." (John 15 : 26.) " Howbeit when he, the Spirit of truth, is come, he will guide you into all truth : for he shall not speak of himself; but whatsoever he shall hear, that shall he speak. And he will shew you things to come. He shall glorify me : for he shall receive of mine, and shall shew it unto you." (John 16 : 13, 14.) His office in the salvation of man appears very forcibly in the following passages : " Grieve not the Holy Spirit of God, whereby ye are sealed unto the day of redemption." (Eph. 4 : 30.) " And whosoever speaketh a word against the Son of man, it shall be forgiven him : but whosoever speaketh against the Holy Ghost, it shall not be forgiven him, neither in this world, neither in the world to come." (Matt. 12 : 32.) Here the awful consequence of insulting the Spirit is plainly told by our Saviour. He speaks of Christ and for him. " There are three that bear witness in earth : the Spirit, and the water, and the blood." (1 John 5: 8.) The Holy Spirit has charge of the application of the plan of redemption. No man can come to Christ except by the Spirit. " No man can come to me, except the Father which hath sent me draw him." (John 6 : 44.) This drawing is by the Holy Spirit. " Spirit of grace, to us apply Emanuel's precious blood." It is the Spirit who urges our acceptance of the plan of salvation. He " worketh in us both to will and to do." Our initial turning to God is his work, and any succeeding graces that may spring up are his fruit. If I am asked how the Spirit accomplishes this, my answer is, I do not know. " The wind bloweth where it listeth, and thou hearest the sound thereof, but canst not tell whence it cometh, and whither it goeth ; so is every one that is born of the Spirit." (John 3 : 8.) The Saviour was not pleased to give us a description of the working of the Spirit in regeneration; and if he had, we would not have understood it. It is our duty to believe Christ, and to accept the teachings of the Spirit while he yet strives with us; for God has said: "My Spirit shall not always strive with man." (Gen. 6 : 3.) The Apostle Paul said: "God hath from the beginning chosen you to salvation through sanctification of the Spirit and belief of the truth." (2 Thess. 2 : 13.) Let one more quotation suffice on this point: "Elect according to the foreknowledge of God the Father, through sanctification of the Spirit, unto obedience and sprinkling of the blood of Jesus Christ." (1 Pet. 1 : 2.) We think that it will not be questioned that the Holy Spirit effects the glorious change that takes place in the heart, which is called regeneration.

IV. The effects of the change.

The effect is first personal, having only to do with the individual thus moved upon. It first fills his heart with joy, and peace, and a great satisfaction. All barriers are now broken down, and he is at one with God. But he cannot keep the matter to himself. He has read: "For with the heart man believeth unto righteousness, and with the mouth confession is made unto salvation." (Rom. 10 : 10.) And so he confesses Christ. He tells to all around what a dear Saviour he has found. From this time he affects others. The entire life following this change is meant to bless others. God said of Abraham: "And I will make of thee a great nation, and I will bless thee, and make thy name great; and thou shalt be a blessing." (Gen. 12 : 2.) God blesses men to make them a blessing to others. The disposition to do good to others is one of the first fruits of regeneration. The first thing Christ told the fierce maniac to do after the devils had been cast out was to go home and tell his people what the Lord had done for him. Regeneration is not only the making of a new man, but it assigns him to a new field, and puts him at a new work. He thinks anew, he acts anew, he walks anew, he talks anew. He has new associates, new aspirations, and he loves new objects. His life is to be such as would commend the doctrines he professes. He is to be a living epistle "known and read of all men." There are many who will not read the Bible to learn of Christ from its sacred pages, but they will read those who claim to be born again, and therefore *they* should endeavor to let their lives be as strong letters of recommendation as they can give of Christ, and the glorious gospel of the kingdom. Those who are born again are to be witnesses of Jesus Christ. "But ye shall receive power, after that the Holy Ghost is come upon you; and ye shall be witnesses unto me both in Jerusalem, and in all Judea, and in Samaria, and unto the uttermost parts of the earth." (Acts 1:8.) When a person has received the Holy Ghost, as he does in regeneration, he is made a happy witness of Jesus Christ, of the wonders of his cross, and of the power and sweetness of his grace. He joyfully espouses the cause of Christ, and thus helps the truth to win other victories more signal and more glorious. "That we might be fellow helpers to the truth." (3 John 1:8.) The man who is regenerated is enlightened in his mind, so that he sees beauty in the law of God, and delights to obey his precepts and to persuade others to do the same. He enjoys personal communion with God. He sups with God. He walks with God. His soul is filled with the love of God, and he wants everybody to feel as he feels. Oh, the joy he realizes who knows he is born again! As has been well said: "Tongue cannot express the comfort and peace of a soul in its earliest love."

That was indeed a precious hour when he first believed. He may forget all else, but he can never forget that. That was the hour when he got ready for the dying hour. That was the hour when he received a guide for all subsequent life. He is forever afterward kept by grace. Though he is pursued by sin and Satan still, he forgets the troubles of the way and presses to Zion's hill. There is a secret sweetness that the regenerated soul enjoys that none can understand but those who are born again. Only those who are born again can joy in tribulation, and sing amid the tempest "Praise the Lord." Only the new birth can guarantee eternal life in the new Jerusalem, the city of God which hath no need of the sun, moon, nor stars, to give it light, for the glory of God giveth light to the city. It is a pleasing thought only to those who are born again, that "eye hath not seen, nor ear heard, neither have entered into the heart of man the things which God hath prepared for them that love him." (1 Cor. 2:9.) How true and forceful are the poet's words:

> "Religion is the chief concern
> Of mortals here below;
> May we its great importance learn,
> Its sovereign virtue know.
>
> "Oh, may our hearts by grace renewed,
> Be our Redeemer's throne;
> And be our stubborn wills subdued,
> His government to own.

"Let deep repentance, faith, and love
  Be joined with godly fear,
And all our conversation prove
  Our hearts to be sincere.

"Let lively hopes our souls inspire;
  Let warm affections rise;
And may we wait with strong desire
  To mount above the skies."

Then shall we sit down in the kingdom with Abraham, Isaac, and Jacob, and with Christ our Saviour, and heaven shall ring with praise. Amen.

VIII.

REPENTANCE AND FAITH.

REV. G. W. RAIFORD,
Pastor of the Bethesda Baptist Church, Georgetown S. C.

"Repent ye, and believe the gospel."—MARK 1 : 15.

REPENTANCE and faith when considered in their connection with each other, with man's need of them, in order to pardon of sin and peace with God, and their invariable effect upon the heart and life of those who live in the continual exercise of them, may be considered as second to none among the doctrines of Christianity. If man had continued in his original state of innocence, there would be no need of salvation through our Lord Jesus Christ; but sin has made a terrible wound, which must be healed; and must be laid bare as a preface to its healing. "I wound, and I heal, saith the Lord." Therefore, the painful ordeal through which each believing soul must pass.

Gospel repentance looks toward a change of life both inwardly and outwardly. This is especially true, when taken in connection with faith. When Jesus began to preach in Galilee the gospel of the kingdom of God, and that it was at hand (Mark 1 : 15), the Jews fondly expected the Messiah to appear in external pomp, not alone to free the Jewish nation from the Roman yoke, but to give it power over all its neighbors. They therefore thought that they must prepare for war and victory; but Christ told them they must repent and believe the gospel. They had broken the moral law, and could not be saved under the old covenant, for both Jews and Gentiles had come far short of its obligations. They must therefore have the benefit of a covenant of grace, submit to the remedy proposed by it, viz.: Repentance toward God, and faith toward our Lord Jesus Christ. (Acts 20 : 21.) Peter, on the day of Pentecost, stood up in the midst of the people, and arraigned the Jews for the cruel and malignant murder of Jesus Christ. His stern, accusing words did not fail to produce a good result, for the Jews were both startled and convinced—startled because they had committed so ruthless a crime against the Messiah; convinced that they had need of immediate action. Thus aroused, their cry was "What shall we do?" Peter told them what to do. Then Peter said unto them: "Repent, and be baptized every one of you in the name of Jesus Christ for the remission of sins." (Acts 2 : 38.) Repent! this was the same duty that John the Baptist and Jesus Christ had preached. Be baptized every one of you in the name of Jesus Christ; that is, they must firmly believe in Jesus Christ as a Saviour, and in baptism make a solemn and open profession of him, and come under an obligation or agreement to live a new life. "For godly sorrow worketh repentance to salvation, not to be repented of, but the sorrow of the world worketh death." (2 Cor. 7 : 10.)

In order that there may be a full and genuine repentance there must be:

1. A deep and genuine sense both of sin and God's infinite love and righteousness. This is true on the one

hand, because but for sin there would be no need of repentance; and, on the other hand, but for a knowledge of God, his will, his just and equitable law, there could be no holy concern for his honor, will, or law.

2. Repentance must be attended both with sorrow and shame. Holy shame is as necessary as holy sorrow. The more definite our knowledge of sin, and our sense of God's love and justice, the more genuine will be our sorrow for sin, and the more keen our shame.

3. There must be a hatred of sin. This intense sorrowing for sin quite naturally leads to a hatred of it. Sin must be hated in all of its forms. It strikes at the authority of God, and its blighting influence may be felt in the palace of the noble, as in the most despicable hovel of the most lowly. We must loathe and hate sin. We must loathe ourselves too as sinners in the sight of a holy God. If sin be truly an abomination to us, sin in ourselves will especially be so—the nearer the more loathsome; and if sin lurk at the bottom of love for self, then there can be no repentance without an abhorrence of self. Our self-abhorrence and abandonment of sin will be in proportion to our knowledge of the direful effects of sin, as seen in ourselves, and of the mercy and goodness of God as manifested toward us.

Here is the dividing line between every soul and Jesus Christ. If crossed, it means life; if uncrossed, it means death. Here, to change the figure, is the battleground of every individual; the scene of conflict for the emancipation of the soul, or where its bondage is made more secure. Here we begin to come nearer to God, or to be driven farther from him. How important, then, in view of these facts, that each one should look at repentance and faith in their true light, and estimate them at their true worth!

4. In true repentance there must be a fixed purpose to forsake our sins. Our hatred of sin should be so deep, our contrition so sincere, as to form within us this fixedness of purpose. The very nature of repentance implies this, and the genuineness of our repentance may be determined by its existence. For to form and carry out this purpose carries with it all of the real results of repentance, since the change in our life is due to the faithful performance of this purpose. The carrying out of this purpose alone sets forth the change. In this matter of repentance and faith we want to bear in mind that there is no atoning efficacy in them for sins of the past. There is that in the work of Jesus Christ and in that alone. And it is made effective to us by means of repentance and faith. "For by grace are ye saved through faith, and that not of yourselves, it is the gift of God." (Eph. 2 : 8.) Not only is the being saved by faith the gift of God, but the faith also through which we are saved. The presence of faith in us is the evidence rather than the reason of our being saved. If I should be asked why am I saved, the answer would be, because the Lord chose to save me; but if I should be asked why I know that I am saved, it would be because I believe on the Lord Jesus Christ. The fact that I believe is evidence to me that I am saved.

Spiritual life in man is the immediate result of union with Christ; if to be united with him is to hear him, to come to him to touch him, to have one's life hid with Christ in God. Faith is in no wise the procuring cause of this life; but faith joined with repentance makes that life operative at once. Nor is it faith which a dead soul exercises, but faith which "is the gift of God," bestowed in response to the imploring need of the convicted soul, whereby Jesus Christ is made its own. Faith must unconditionally and unreservedly look to the Lord Jesus Christ; must trust him for his promises. Faith therefore accepts Christ as the promised Messiah, believes in him as the victim that bears away the sins of the world, trustingly accepts his death as satisfactory to Divine justice. Christ alone could do this, and at the same time restore man to the favor of the Father, because in him *alone* were united the qualities requisite to so mighty and mysterious a task. Christ alone was truly human and divine, and his power to save lies in the fact that he possessed both the divine and human nature. Divine and human, Jesus assumed the mighty task. Clad in human form, he came to earth, and by his obedience unto death vindicated the divine law, and made it possible for man to be saved. We walk the earth now with rays of divine light and mercy shining upon our pathway. The terrible clouds of darkness and woe which should justly have gathered and broken with fury upon *our* heads, broke and spent their fury upon Christ's devoted head, when he stood between guilty man and God, against whom man had sinned. For man's sake he alone bore the penalty. In that moment hope sprang up for the world. Through the mist and darkness of human sin and the thunderings of divine wrath light shines forth from the cross of Christ.

> "In the cross of Christ I glory,
> Towering o'er the wrecks of time;
> All the light of sacred story
> Gathers round its head sublime."

Faith evermore looks to that cross; and the soul exclaims meanwhile, as it looks to the past: " I live because he died!" And as it looks to the future: " I live because he lives."

Repent, then, and believe. Let all heed the call; for in the heeding is everlasting life.

IX.

JUSTIFICATION.

REV. ANDREW J. STOKES,
Pastor of the First Colored Baptist Church, Clarksville, Tenn.

"Therefore we conclude that a man is justified by faith without the deeds of the law."—ROMANS 3 : 28.

IN the consideration of this text let us inquire:

I. What Justification is. Justification is one of the great gospel blessings. It does not mean primarily to *make* a man just, but simply to *declare* him so. It is a necessary blessing, if a man is to be restored to the condition superior to that of Adam prior to his fall. It is not easy to show the logical place of justification in the order of redemptive acts; but perhaps we may understand it by the following considerations. Regeneration gives a man a new nature, but it does not essentially alter the old. The man is, of course, spoken of as a new creature, because he really is; and because, also, although the old nature remains active, a new nature has been implanted, which gives the sinner a new standing before God. Pardon is an act of God, whereby the sinner is forgiven. Pardon removes the penalty of sin, but it does not remove its stain. Here justification comes in. The righteousness of Christ is imputed to the sinner, is regarded as really his; and so God, having pardoned the sinner, and seeing him clothed with Christ's righteousness, pronounces him free from the condemnation of the law. (Rom. 8 : 1)

Thus justification is a necessary act, in securing for the sinner a proper status before God. Men cannot be justified by the works of the law. "Therefore we conclude that a man is justified by faith without the deeds of the law." "Now we know that what things soever the law saith, it saith to them who are under the law: that every mouth may be stopped, and all the world may become guilty before God. Therefore by the deeds of the law there shall no flesh be justified in his sight: for by the law is the knowledge of sin." (Rom. 3 : 28, 19, 20.) Like our pardon, it can come only through the grace of our Lord Jesus Christ, and the ground of our justification is the mediatorial work of Christ. It is because of what he was and did that God the Father can justify us. "Being justified freely by his grace through the redemption that is in Christ Jesus." (Rom. 3 : 24.) "In whom we have redemption through his blood, the forgiveness of sins, according to the riches of his grace." (Eph. 1 : 7.) "In whom we have redemption through his blood, even the forgiveness of sins." (Col. 1 : 14.) The effect of justification is to make perfect peace between God and the sinner. "Therefore, being justified by faith, we have peace with God through our Lord Jesus Christ." (Rom. 5 : 1.)

II. This leads to the consideration of the means whereby justification is procured.

It is faith in Jesus Christ as an atoning Saviour. We are justified by faith, not as its procuring cause, but rather as its obtaining means. And see how wonderfully God's mercy appears in this transaction! He has placed the whole matter on simple faith in Christ. Nothing can be easier. Hence, if the sinner is not saved, it is his own

JUSTIFICATION.

fault. Notice that God does not say that we are justified by baptism. Important as the act of baptism is, God has not made it a condition of salvation. If a sinner could not be justified, and hence saved without baptism, many persons who believe would be lost; for often a sinner on his dying bed repents of his sins and dies without receiving baptism. We do not underrate baptism when we say that God never uses it to justify a sinner. It has its own place, and a very important place it is in the Lord's church; but baptism never justifies a man.

Nor has God said that men are justified by church membership. The joining of a church is a thing for every believer to do, and he cannot maintain a healthful Christian life without it; but church membership is not a condition of justification. If it were, many a believing soul would be lost; for, often a man, like the dying thief, repents in his last moments, when joining the church is an impossibility. So far as we can see, God in even his infinite wisdom could devise no simpler way of justification than that which he has provided, through faith alone in Jesus Christ. A man has only to trust Jesus with his whole heart, and the work is done. And what a responsibility does this place on the sinner! If he had to *do* something in order to be saved, he might plead his inability, or lack of opportunity; but he has nothing to do but to repent and believe, and the doing of these things can be accomplished by the aid which God is always ready to give. Thank God! no preacher, no church, no baptism is absolutely essential to the salvation of a man when once he understands the gospel; and because of the wonderful simplicity of the plan of salvation, the sinner's remaining unsaved aggravates his guilt. "And when he is come [that is, the Comforter] he will reprove the world of sin, and of righteousness, and of judgment: of sin *because they believe not on me.*" (John 16 : 8, 9.) Men speculate often as to the way in which sin got into the world; they had better turn their attention to the way by which it may be gotten rid of. They sometimes find fault with God for condemning the human race; they had better give him thanks for providing the means whereby the race may be justified.

May God help us so to present Christ to dying men that every man who hears the truth may repent of his sins, and be justified by faith in the Lord Jesus Christ.

X.

SANCTIFICATION.

REV. C. H. PARRISH, A. M.,
Professor of the Greek Language and Literature, in State University, Louisville, Ky.

"Sanctify them through thy truth."—JOHN 17 : 17.

AT midnight a prayer arose from a solitary chamber in the city of Jerusalem. He who prayed was about to be a victim at the altar of sacrifice. He met death on the following day. Thus, just before the moment of sacrifice, the sufferer himself sends a prayer to the Father above for a special people—"I pray for them," said he, "I pray not for the world, but for *them* which thou hast given me, for they are thine." In the sixteenth verse he says: "They [the them for whom he prays] are not of the world, even as I am not of the world." The sense is: "I myself present a request in respect to my eleven disciples, who have believed my word, dedicated and devoted themselves to me; by so much they are no longer of the unbelieving world, but draw their truest life, their ruling motives from above." At the time Christ offered his prayer the eleven were fully enrolled as disciples of our Lord. Yet he prayed, "Sanctify them." "Make them holy," separate them more and more from the world, and consecrate them to holy service.

If, then, sanctification were either complete or imputed at their regeneration, the Saviour's prayer is thereby rendered absurd. Why such a prayer if they were already and wholly sanctified? Before we answer let us note that in the Old Testament Scriptures the word "sanctify," used about fifty-five times, means set apart for a special purpose; the term "sanctified," used about thirty-five times, for the most part indicates the setting apart for a special use or purpose; the term "sanctification" is not found in the Old Testament at all, and occurs but four times in the New. But throughout the Bible this setting apart or dedication is most frequently for some holy use. The terms describe personal character, whether the holiness be perfect as in God, angels, and glorified saints, or partial, as seen in his people on earth. Now, with the whole Bible before us we can say that the doctrine of sanctification is a setting apart to a holy service, a progressive conformity to the image of Christ, a carrying on of what regeneration begins. Paul reminds his brethren at Thessalonica that their sanctification was "the will of God," therefore they should abstain from "sin and cultivate holiness of heart and life that the will of God might be accomplished in them." In 1 Thess. 5 : 23, Paul makes a fervent prayer for his regenerate brethren, "And the very God of peace sanctify you wholly." It would have been absurd for the apostle to make such a prayer if the sanctification of his brethren were at that time complete. Evidently the believers at Thessalonica needed more personal holiness; hence the prayer of the great apostle: "The God of peace sanctify you wholly." But also the Saviour of the world on the night before his death, lifted up his eyes to heaven, and said: "Holy Father," "O righteous Father," "Sanctify them through thy truth." Without attempting an exhaustive examination of the subject, we shall give such truths as the text furnishes us. Two are expressed by the word itself, viz. : The devotedness of the believer to holy service, and progressive holiness in the believer's character. We shall conclude by noticing the means of sanctification as given in the text.

I. Notice the devotedness of the believer to holy service.

The eleven were already set apart to their work. To them had been assigned the work of the ministry, a holy service. However, their devotedness to that service was imperfect. One may be set apart or assigned to an office, yet be lacking in devotedness to the duties of that office. Evidently the apostles' devotedness to holy service was not what the Master desired it to be. Hence his prayer: "*Sanctify them.*" By saying "sanctify them," Jesus asks for them a will wholly devoted to the task which they would have to accomplish in the world. It was necessary that all their powers, all their talents, all their life should be consecrated to their great work—the salvation of men. After this prayer, the need of greater consecration was more and more clearly recognized by the apostles. A little while after their Master had left the world, they called the multitude of the disciples unto them, and said : "It is not reason that we should leave the word of God and serve tables. . . . But we will give ourselves continually to prayer and the ministry of the word." (Acts 6 : 2, 4.) Some thirty years after this wise step on the part of these apostles to secure to themselves more constant and earnest devotedness to their work, we find Paul instructing Timothy to devote himself without reserve to the duties of the ministry. Give "thyself wholly to them." (1 Tim. 4 : 15.) John, in the fourth chapter of his gospel, tells us how Jesus said of himself, "My meat is to do the will of him that sent me and to finish his work." Godet says: "To carry on that work step by step was his daily devotedness. He sanctified himself by offering to God, step by step, all the elements of his being as they successfully unfolded themselves; all the faculties of his body and of his soul, as they came into play; every domain of his existence as soon as he set his foot in it." In this light we understand his gracious words in the ninth verse: "I sanctify myself," "I devote myself." "All that is natural to common life, all that is within me, I consecrate heartily to the great work which my Father has given me to do."

Such a devotedness he would have in every believer. Hence his earnest prayer: "Holy Father, sanctify them." Believers, what is your office? Is your devotedness to its service imperfect? "I therefore, the prisoner of the Lord, beseech you that ye walk worthy of the vocation wherewith ye are called." (Eph. 4 : 1.) We are called to the office of a Christian. Therefore we should live up to the duties of this high calling. We should act as Christ acted. He has left us an example. At home and abroad there should be devotedness to Christian duty. As servants, we are to abound in the work of our Lord. It is said of him: "He went about doing good." We are required to follow his example. The more faithful the servant the more devoted he is to the Master's service. Serving the Lord is consecration to his cause or devotion to holy ministry. But such devotedness is signified in the word "sanctification." At what period in the Christian's life is his devotion to the Master's interests full and complete? May he not pray at every step of the way, and oftener than that: "Lord, devote me to thy service." Is there not imperfection in his consecration to Christian service? If not, why the Master's prayer: "Sanctify them"?

But there is a difference between devoting one to a holy service and making one holy in character, and thus fit for holy service. In speaking after the manner of men, we may say that bad men are sometimes set apart to holy service. All the Pharisees are not yet dead. The chief priest who serves with great devotion about the holy altar may be a very bad man. But our text is sweeping in its meaning. It does not only signify devotedness to holy service, but also *making one* holy personally and really. This brings us to the consideration of the second blessing expressed in the term "sanctify."

II. Progressive holiness in the believer's character.

The eleven needed a clearer apprehension of Christ and the truth, and a holier character. There was holiness in their heart, a supernatural production effected by regeneration. But this holiness was in its beginning. For the fuller development of this holiness the Master prayed. Holiness was to fill the hearts of the disciples, and mortify the deeds of the flesh, strengthening and developing the new nature, subduing and deadening the the old man and his deeds. "Ye are dead," says the apostle; "mortify therefore your members which are upon the earth." (Col. 3: 3, 5.) Make your death in Christ real in yourself. Let holiness within be seen as holiness without. "Be not conformed to this world, but be ye transformed by the renewing of your mind, that ye may prove what is that good, and acceptable, and perfect will of God." (Rom. 12 : 2.)

Sanctification is not confined to mere outward actions. It is of the whole nature. The spiritual, intellectual, and physical natures are alike the sphere of it. There must be holy, spiritual emotions and affections permeating the heart, influencing the mind, and, reaching the body, controlling all its appetites and powers. All filthiness of the flesh must be put aside. War must be waged, and every Canaanite exterminated. Every sin must be dragged from its lurking place and destroyed. Let us cleanse ourselves from all filthiness of the flesh and spirit, perfecting holiness in the fear of God. (2 Cor. 7 : 1.) "Let not sin reign in your mortal body that ye should obey it in the lusts thereof." (Rom. 6 : 12.) This holiness is real and personal. It is neither by representation nor imputation. The individual is not treated as though holy, but as actually made holy. MAKE THEM HOLY is the prayer of the Master. The entire personality must be sanctified. Sanctification makes true *in* the believer that which is already true *for* him. Christ's righteousness imputed to us by faith justifies us, and this is the believer's title to heaven ; from sanctification arises our meetness for it.

A king's son is heir apparent to his father's crown. Now we will suppose the young prince to be educated with all the advantages of his station, and to be possessed of all the attainments that are necessary to constitute a well-equipped monarch. His accomplishments, however, do not entitle him to the kingdom ; they only qualify him for it. So the holiness and obedience of the saints form no part of that right on which their claim to heaven is founded ; but only a part of that spiritual education whereby they are made meet to inherit the kingdom. Thus, we may see plainly the difference between justification and sanctification. Justification is a single act, and perfect. Sanctification is a continuous process, which goes on throughout the life of the believer. This is manifest from the text, and the frequent exhortation to sanctification addressed to those who were already true believers in Christ. "The flesh lusteth against the Spirit, and the Spirit against the flesh, for they are contrary the one to the other, so that ye cannot do the things that ye would." (Gal. 5 : 17.) This war wages more or less during the lifetime of the believer. At times he yields to sin, and sustains an inglorious defeat. Yet he rises and conquers, and his sanctification progresses, growing from the seed planted in regeneration, which brings forth new leaves and new fruit.

Dr. Boyce illustrates the process of sanctification by the ascent of a mountain. "The temptations and struggles enter into the progress of sanctification; not only these, but even the sins and falls which mar the Christian life; nevertheless, the progress is continuous. It is like the ascent of a mountain. One is always going forward, though not always upward, and the final end of the progressive movement of every kind is the attainment of the summit. Sometimes because of difficulties the road itself descends only more easily to ascend again. Sometimes certain attractions by the way cause a deviation from the route most suitable for ascent. Often it is feared that there has been no higher attainment; often that it has been but a continual descent, until perchance, some point of view is gained from which to look down upon the plain whence the journey was begun, and behold the height which has already been overcome. Often with wearied feet and desponding heart the traveler is ready to despair because of his own feebleness, and the difficulties which surround him. But he earnestly presses forward, and the journey is completed, and the ascent is made, the end is attained."

Our sanctification shall not always be incomplete. We shall not be satisfied until we awake in his likeness. But such likeness involves perfect sanctification, which shall be the believer's portion. "We shall be like him, for we shall see him as he is." (1 John 3 : 2.)

It is evident from what we have said that the author of sanctification is more than man. The text ascribes this work to the Father. Christ pleads, Father, sanctify them. God is the author. "Without me ye can do nothing." Without him there can be no holiness. There may be morality which may resemble it. But be it ever remembered that holiness comes from God, and unless the divine life is within us, we shall ever be without one spark of holiness. But in this work the believer actively co-operates with the divine Author of holiness. He co-operates by walking by the Spirit, by working out his own salvation with fear and trembling. Self-purification is declared to be the work of every one that hath the hope of the likeness of Christ. "And every man that hath this hope in him purifieth himself even as he is pure." (1 John 3 : 3.) Yet "it is God which worketh in him, both to will and to do of his good pleasure." (Phil. 2 : 13.)

III. The *means* which the Spirit uses for our sanctification is the truth of God.

In order to promote holiness, Dr. Channing advised his hearers to read certain books—namely : Humboldt's

SANCTIFICATION.   99

"Cosmos," Mrs. Somerville's "Astronomy," Mrs. Jamison's, Margaret Fuller, etc. We may well note how different the doctor's conception, and that of the Son of God. The whole work both of consecration and cleansing, says Christ, must be accomplished by the word of truth. "Sanctify them in the truth; thy Word is truth." Truth, then, is of transcendent value, because it is God's word. Sanctification grows with an increased and appropriated knowledge of God's truth. "Search the Scriptures; for in them ye think ye have eternal life, and they are they which testify of me." (John 5 : 39.) Christ is the "Word," "the truth." In the Scriptures Christ has been pleased to reveal his heart. Searching the word with the Holy Spirit as teacher, we enter more and more into the very life of Christ. Thus, beholding his heart, we become more and more like him. In the Word we can see the glory of the person, the character, and mediatorial achievements of the blessed Christ. Herein we see him as the chiefest among ten thousand, and altogether lovely. Herein our hearts burn within us, while he talks with us by the way, and opens to us the Scriptures. If we would have the radiance of the sun, we must adjust ourselves to the sun. If we would be holy as God is holy, we must adjust ourselves to the truth of God. More and more we are to fix our eyes on the truth, and walk straight up to it. Walking otherwise than this, we, like Peter, must sink.

"Wherewithal shall a young man cleanse his way? by taking heed according to thy word," says David. (Ps. 119 : 9.) The cleansing power is in the truth. "For the word of God is quick, and powerful, sharper than a two-edged sword, piercing even to the dividing asunder of soul and spirit, and of joints and marrow, and is a discerner of the thoughts and intents of the heart." (Heb. 4 : 12.) It is the truth that produces hatred of sin, and quickens to life. "All things that pertain unto life and godliness," says 2 Peter 1 : 3, have been given through the knowledge of God and Christ. "Thy word," says David, "have I hid in my heart that I might not sin against thee." "Through thy precepts I get understanding: therefore I hate every false way." "Quicken thou me, according to thy word." (Ps. 119 : 11, 104, 25.)

The providences of God, the good works of Christians, Christian association, observance of the Lord's Day, observance of the ordinances, prayer and family worship are not means of sanctification in themselves. They only accomplish the end of sanctification by bringing the believer into connection with the truth of God. It is the appropriation of the Lord Jesus Christ, the "*truth*," the "*Word*" by which our sanctification is promoted. "We all with open face beholding as in a glass the glory of the Lord, are changed into the same image from glory to glory, even as by the Spirit of the Lord." (2 Cor. 3 : 18.) Thus, gazing, and searching, and appropriating, we are transformed into the likeness of the Lord Jesus, from one degree of glorious grace to another, until conformity to the likeness of Christ becomes complete. Christ the truth is the bread of life, and the water of life, and he who would become more and more sanctified must daily eat and drink thereof. (John 6 : 63, 57.) "It is the Spirit that quickeneth; the flesh profiteth nothing. The words that I speak unto you they are spirit, and they are life." "He that eateth me, even he shall live by me." As blood is in all parts of the body, so the life and spirit of Jesus

SANCTIFICATION. 101

Christ are in all parts of the Scripture. "And therefore, All Scripture is given by inspiration of God, and is profitable for doctrine, for reproof, for correction, for instruction in righteousness. That the man of God may be perfect, thoroughly furnished unto all good works." (2 Tim. 3 : 16, 17.) Therefore, sanctify them by thy truth, for thy word is truth.

Sanctification varies in different Christians; we do not find a uniform degree of attainment possessed by all alike. A father may have many sons, but those who stand by him, and seek his interests, are more highly favored than those who are careless and indifferent. The child who clings close to the mother's side has many a morsel in which the distant playing ones do not share. No one need be a *doorstep* Christian; all may come into the holy place, all may enter within the vail.

The Father bids every believer "Come up higher." Many Christians have obeyed the summons. They have entered into such a degree of sanctification as has brought rest, sweet rest, of which other Christians have deprived themselves. Mrs. Edwards, wife of President Edwards, says: "In 1742, I sought and obtained the full assurance of faith. I cannot find language to express how certain the everlasting love of God appeared. The everlasting mountains and hills were but shadows to it. My safety, and happiness, and eternal enjoyment of God's immutable love, seemed as durable and unchangeable as God himself. Melted and overcome by the sweetness of this assurance, I fell into a great flow of tears, and could not forbear weeping aloud. The presence of God was so near, and so real, that I seemed scarcely conscious of anything else. My soul was filled and overwhelmed with light and love, and joy in the Holy Ghost, and seemed just ready to go away from the body. This exaltation of soul subsided into a heavenly calm, and a rest of soul in God which was even sweeter than what preceded it."

Rev. Dr. Payson says: "Were I to adopt the figurative language of Bunyan, I might date this letter from the land of Beulah, of which I have been for some time a happy resident. The Celestial City is full in my view. Its glories beam upon me; its breezes fan me; its odors are wafted to me; its sounds strike my ears, and its spirit is breathed into my heart. Nothing separates me from it but the river of death, which now appears but an insignificant rill, that may be crossed at a single step whenever God gives permission. The sun of righteousness has been gradually drawing nearer and nearer, appearing larger and brighter as he approached, and now he fills the whole hemisphere, pouring forth a flood of glory in which I seem to float like an insect in the beams of the sun, exulting, yet almost trembling, while I gaze upon this excessive brightness, and wondering with unutterable wonder why God should deign thus to shine upon a simple worm." After experiencing this great increase of faith, Dr. Payson cried out, in view of his former distressing doubts, and the great loss he had thereby sustained in his own enjoyment and usefulness, "Oh, that I had known this twenty years ago!"

I do not believe that in this life sinless perfection is attainable. In whatever degree of sanctification one may have attained, there is a feeling of imperfection and weakness. In the New Testament, Christians are not presented as completely pure and holy. The very best of them acknowledge the existence of sinful tendencies, and pronounce any idea of freedom from the presence of sin to be delusive. "If we say that we have no sin we deceive ourselves, and the truth is not in us." (1 John 1 : 8.) But here in this life assurance is attainable. It comes, however, by means of the truth of God. Be it unto you according to your faith. "Sanctification is the process by which, according to the will of God, we are made partakers of his holiness. It is a progressive work. It is begun in regeneration. It is carried on in the hearts of believers by the presence and power of the Holy Spirit, the Sealer and Comforter, in the continual use of the appointed means—especially the word of God, self-examination, self-denial, watchfulness, and prayer."

XI.

FINAL PERSEVERANCE OF THE SAINTS.

REV. A. W. PULLER, A. M.,
President of the Curtis Memorial Seminary, Staunton, Va.

"Who are kept by the power of God, through faith, unto salvation."
—1 PETER 1 : 5.

> "My own dim life should teach me this,
> That life shall live forevermore ;
> Else earth is darkness to the core,
> And dust and ashes all that is."—*Tennyson.*

TO be a saint is the highest attainment to which God has called the highest of his creatures. Wealth, learning, and honor are insignificant, when compared with the blessed reality of being a saint. But to become a saint, in its completeness, means strivings beyond our present imagination. And that we may be encouraged in striving to reach the perfectness of sainthood, our Lord has left us the blest assurance that all who thus strive will certainly attain the desired goal, if they have been "born again." And to a prayerful consideration of this subject we wish to come.

Let us, then, state the question in the plainest words obtainable : Is A CHRISTIAN SURE OF HEAVEN FROM THE MOMENT HE BECOMES A CHRISTIAN ?

This is not the way this question is generally stated. But it is the plain way of stating it. And to this we say, *He is not, and he is.* The Christian may not be always sure of heaven, so far as his feelings are concerned. For all Christians, at times, have their misgivings. Most, at some time or other, have found themselves inmates of John Bunyan's Doubting Castle. At such times we think we have never been born again, and often we say:

> "'Tis a point I long to know,
> Oft it causes anxious thought,
> Do I love the Lord or no?
> Am I his, or am I not?"

Now, in this sense, we say the Christian is not always sure of heaven. But, on the other hand, the Christian is sure of heaven so far as the great plan of redemption is concerned; and just as far as Christians have been firm believers in the everlasting union of God and his church, so far have they been nerved for the great conflicts of life.

I. Our first reason for believing in the doctrine of the final perseverance of the saints is derived from the history of the Church of God.

We mean by this the continuance and security of believers, because of God's purpose and pledged power to keep them. For four thousand years, at least, the world had no Bible, no church, no preacher, according to our understanding of the term, no weekly religious services; yet, according to the eleventh chapter of the Epistle to the Hebrews, God had Christians before Christianity, and the grace of God kept them in all their trials; and to-day they are redeemed around the throne of God. Of the twelve apostles, according to tradition, only one died a natural death; yet all, except "the son of perdition," died Christians.

Look, for a moment, at post-apostolic ages. There is

hardly an acre of ground in Europe that has not been bedewed with the blood of God's saints. Many of the prisons, blocks and stakes are eloquent monuments of the power of God in preserving the souls of his people. They were made lamp posts for Rome. Yet they remained firm to the end, and preached their loudest sermons by their persevering attachment to their Lord and Master. When they were burned at the stake, their ashes were carried by the providential winds, and wherever a grain dropped, a church of the living God sprang up. Their dying shouts were caught up and carried far and near, and men soon learned that it was the planting of God's hand, and could not be pulled up.

Now we ask, if Christians have stood greater trials than we are having, with less advantages than we have, and God enabled them to be faithful to the end, is it unfair for us to believe that the same grace that kept Christians in the days of Abel, Noah, David, Paul and Luther, will keep us to-day? This is the argument used by Paul, when he says: "Ye have not yet resisted unto blood, striving against sin." And may we not to-day, when looking up to the "great cloud of witnesses," exclaim:

> "Once they were mourners here below,
>   And bathed their couch with tears;
> They wrestled hard, as we do now,
>   With sins, and doubts, and fears.
>
> "I ask them whence their victory came?
>   They, with united breath,
> Ascribe their conquest to the Lamb,
>   Their triumph to his death."

Yes, history has its place in this life; and he who reads the future in the light of the past, will be compelled to believe that since God does not change, and since he has kept Christians, he will continue to do so.

II. We believe in the doctrine also because the loss of one soul would be a reflection on God's power.

God made man a free agent. He was free to stand, and free to fall. And when he did fall, it simply showed that Satan is stronger than man. But if one Christian were to be lost, that would show that Satan is stronger than God.

When a man becomes a Christian, Christ tells him to put up his sword, because he has done fighting, and Christ will fight for him. The battle is between Christ and Satan, not the believer and Satan. The Saviour said (John 10: 29): "My Father which gave them me is greater than all: and no man is able to pluck them out of my Father's hand." And as God and Satan are contending for the souls of men, if Satan could get one soul out of God's hand, the finite would triumph over the infinite; which is unthinkable, and would be a gross reflection on the character of God.

III. Our third and strongest reason for believing that a Christian will never be lost, and that a man's destiny is settled at regeneration, and not at death, is that it is the plain teaching of God's word.

Let us here put our view in three statements. We believe that the Scriptures teach—

First, that such only are real believers who endure unto the end.

Secondly, that a special Providence watches over their welfare; and,

Thirdly, that they are kept by the power of God through faith unto salvation.

Let us consider the statements one by one.

1. Do the Scriptures teach that none but real believers continue in the service of God until death? If so, show us chapter and verse. Very well.

Turn to Matthew 13 : 18–23. Our Lord is explaining the parable of the sower. We have here Jesus' explanation of his own word. He has spoken of four classes or kinds of hearers. The first, who received seed by the wayside, was the man who heard, but did not understand the gospel which he heard. Preaching made no visible effect on him. The second class was those upon whom the word of God fell as seed falls upon rocky ground. It came up quickly, and produced a momentary effect. But soon they turn away from the pleasant hills of Zion, and roam on the dark mountains of sin. He who received seed among the thorns was like unto the man who goes to church, but his heart is too full of worldly cares to listen to the gospel. Then there is the man upon whose heart the word fell as seed into good ground. To him the gospel was a reality; and he continued unto the end, bearing fruit to the Master.

The same truth is taught in the parable of the house built upon the sand, and the one built upon a rock. Both men heard the word of God. But the word reached and changed the heart of the one, but did not change the other.

In John 8 : 31, the Saviour said to his disciples: "If ye continue in my word, then are ye my disciples indeed." Keep clearly before you the point to be established, which is, that only the truly regenerate continue until the end. Now, what does this passage teach? Plainly this: that if they were not his disciples they would not continue in his word; but if they did continue in his word, that they would do so only by being his disciples. Or, in other words, the passage teaches that nobody but a real Christian can take what a Christian takes, and yet endure as a child of God. The same truth is taught in John's first letter (2: 19). Speaking of those who had left the church, John says: "If they had been of us, they would no doubt have continued with us." What stronger and plainer language could be asked? In John's mind there was *"no doubt"* about this matter. If they had been of us, they would NO DOUBT have continued with us. May the dear Lord hasten on the time when there will be no doubt in the mind of any Christian upon this point.

2. But let us attend to our second proposition, which is, that a special Providence watches over the lives of Christians. God is an impartial Father. And we do not mean to say that he willingly treats one child better than he does another; but we do mean to say that those who come to him by faith are treated differently from those who do not come to him at all. And Nature furnishes a parallel: You cannot treat the degraded as you do the pure; the man has closed the doors of your approving kindness by his own doings. So we claim that a special Providence watches over those who are Christians. "All things work together for good to them that love God." (Rom. 8 : 28.) The Saviour said, in his intercessory prayer (John 17 : 9): "I pray not for the world, but for them which thou hast given me." The teaching of this passage is so plain that any explanation would be more likely to mystify than help the reader.

3. Let us consider the third proposition, viz., that believers are kept by the power of God through faith unto salvation. And this is in almost the very words of the

statement of the Apostle Paul. (1 Peter 1 : 5.) They are kept—or, as it is in the Revised Version, *guarded*—unto salvation by the power of God. Please observe the statement. Believers are here looked upon as in the passive sense. They are not keeping themselves; they are being kept. And they are not kept by changeable humanity, but by God. They are not kept by his justice and mercy, but by the strongest thing God has—and that is his power.

But how long will God keep us? May he not get tired of keeping us? Let Paul answer (Phil. 1 : 6): "He who hath begun a good work in you will perform it until the day of Jesus Christ." But may not the trials of this life separate us from Christ? Let Paul testify once more. He had tried the power of God—the love of God—and he mentions sixteen of these things by which he had tried it, and concludes by including everything else. These are: tribulation, distress, persecution, famine, nakedness, peril, sword, death, life, angels, principalities, powers, things present, things to come, heights, depths, nor any other creature. (Rom. 8 : 38, 39.) All of these things had tried to separate Paul from the love of God, but all had failed; and those who are kept by the power of God will have a like experience. "Whosoever liveth and believeth on me shall never die," said our blessed Lord. (John 11 : 26.) In what sense did they never die? In a spiritual sense, of course; for we know believers did, and do die a natural death.

Moreover, this covenant is called an *everlasting* covenant in several places in the Bible. And Christ says that he gives "eternal life." Now, if a man sells you a garment that lasts only a month, and warrants it to last a year, he has deceived you. And if God gave us grace for eternity which would give out at almost any time he would deceive us. Hence, we must either cut the words *everlasting covenant* and *eternal life* out of the Bible, and call Christ a deceiver, or believe that believers will never be lost. We prefer to do the latter. The angels of heaven are declared (Heb. 1 : 14) to be ministering servants of the believers, and David says that God thinks so much of us that he has given angels charge over us to keep us from dashing our foot against a stone. (Ps. 91 : 11.) In another place, God is spoken of as taking care of a Christian as the apple of his eye, or his eyeball. Here we may learn that, just as we keep dirt out of our eyes, God labors to keep us clean, and any dirt that gets on us hurts God just as dirt hurts us when it gets into our eyes.

But why more? Paul was "confident," and John had "no doubt." May God help us to live so close to him that we will have no doubt and be confident about our acceptance through his grace.

IV. There are three objections that need to be simply noticed, to be cleared away.

1. The first one is, that this doctrine encourages men to sin. We have two remarks to make upon this: (*a*) If it did not only encourage, but compel them to sin, that is none of our business. All that we want to know is the truth of God's word. (*b*) But this is not true. A Christian may do wrong; but sin is the exception, and not the rule and dominating force of his life. Paul said that, when he wanted to do good, evil was always present with him. No; a Christian *cannot* be encouraged to do wrong. A Christian does not go to heaven because he does right,

but because he trusts in Christ and wants to do right; and God's grace is to keep him in Christ until he comes to where he can do right, and that is, in a large measure, heaven.

2. Another objection is that the chosen people of God have at times been overwhelmed with disaster—destroyed. This objection is offered by those who do not understand the Bible. The Jews have never been destroyed. God has said a remnant shall be left. That remnant is left, and in God's own good time the ransomed of the Lord shall return and come to Zion with songs of everlasting joy upon their lips. Furthermore, the covenant under which they served was defective, so much so that God found fault with it himself, and put us under a better covenant.

3. It is also objected to this doctrine that it leaves the Christian with nothing to do. But instead, it simply prepares him to work by taking away his cares for his own soul, filling his heart with God's rich grace, and sending him to tell the news of salvation.

Let us, dear brethren, bear this blessed truth wherever we go, and though our many faults deface us, and our many mistakes make us slow in coming to a throne of grace, yet let us so live that, when pillars of marble shall have crumbled into common dust, and rolling worlds shall cease to move, we may look up amid the terrors of the final day and the glories of an eternal Sabbath and say—

> "My Lord will own my worthless name
> Before his Father's face,
> And in the new Jerusalem
> Appoint my soul a place."

XII.

HARMONY OF THE LAW AND THE GOSPEL.

REV. J. J. DURHAM A M.,
Corresponding Secretary of the Baptist Educational, Missionary, and Sunday-school Convention of South Carolina.

"Wherefore the law is holy, and the commandment holy, and just, and good."—ROMANS 7 : 12.

IN the moral, as in the physical world, the law of harmony obtains and runs like a golden thread throughout all its parts. "Law, her seat is the bosom of God; her voice the harmony of the world." The moral law of God is the standard of moral rectitude, and has its foundation in, and is in perfect harmony with, his own perfect moral character. We are able to determine what is right or wrong only by the law, "for by the law is the knowledge of sin." (Rom. 3 : 20.) That is to say, we know what is, or is not sin, by what the law approves or disapproves, "for I had not known lust, except the law had said, Thou shalt not covet." (Rom. 7 : 7.) Thus God has left man without excuse for sin, by making known to him what is sin through his eternal law; and whatever does not conform to this in perfect harmony is sin. "Whosoever committeth sin transgresseth also the law, for sin is the transgression of the law." (1 John 3 : 4.) If there were no law, there could be no sin, "for where no law is, there is no transgression." (Rom. 4 : 15.) Since the law is the standard of moral rectitude, and the expression of the moral character of God, it must forever remain unchangeable and what it is, so long as God remains unchangeable and what he is in his moral attributes. "And it is easier for heaven and earth to pass, than one tittle of the law to fail." (Luke 16 : 17.) "The law is holy, and the commandment holy, and just and good." (Rom. 7 : 12.) And when God created man, he made him in his own moral image, "holy, just, and good," in perfect harmony with the law, which was his standard of moral rectitude, and every precept of which he was in every way capable of fulfilling. He was in his finite nature holy as God is holy. But, alas! of his own volition he yielded to the tempter, transgressed the law, ruined his moral nature, lost the image of his Creator, and hence became incapable of fulfilling the law. Here he remains, guilty and helpless, under the threatening penalties and awful thunders of the broken law, until by the gracious act of regeneration he is restored to "holiness, without which no man shall see the Lord." (Heb. 12 : 14.) And this we regard as the one great end of the gospel.

While the moral law of God is the standard of moral rectitude, and has its foundation in his own moral character, the gospel is the expression of the attribute of mercy in the moral perfections that constitute that character. Suppose a man is charged with rebellion against the government of his country; he is tried, found guilty, and is convicted. The penalty is death. Has not the chief executive the right to exercise mercy and commute the sentence, or even pardon the criminal? Man is charged with violation of God's law—rebellion against his moral government. He has been tried, found guilty, and convicted. The penalty is death. But he surrenders, pleads for mercy and pardon. Is it not the prerogative of God to exercise mercy and pardon, through Jesus Christ his Son, who paid the death penalty of the criminal who now seeks mercy and pardon at his throne, without abrogating or antagonizing his moral law? This is the essence and marrow of the gospel; it brings mercy and pardon to guilty man through Jesus Christ, "the propitiation for our sins." The gospel makes known this mercy and pardon to condemned man, and the way by which he may obtain them. There is no conflict, but perfect harmony between the law and the gospel. "What the law could not do, in that it was weak through the flesh, God, sending his own Son in the likeness of sinful flesh, for sin, condemned sin in the flesh. That the righteousness of the law might be fulfilled in us, who walk not after the flesh, but after the Spirit." (Rom. 8 : 3, 4.) Our Lord, who proclaimed and established the gospel among men, and in whose life and character all its doctrines and precepts were illustrated, declared the harmony of the law and the gospel when he said: "Think not that I am come to destroy the law, or the prophets: I am not come to destroy, but to fulfil." (Matt. 5 : 17.) As the law emanates from God, and the gospel from the same source, and as God is consistent and in harmony with himself, so must the law and the gospel be in harmony with each other. As the glory and beauty of the justice and moral rectitude of God are displayed in his moral law, so the glory and beauty of his love and mercy are displayed in the gospel.

XIII.

A GOSPEL CHURCH.

R. DE BAPTISTE, D. D.,
Pastor of the Second Baptist Church, Galesburg, Ill.

"And when they were come to Jerusalem, they were received of the church, and of the apostles and elders, and they declared all things that God had done with them."—ACTS 15 : 4.

IN translating this passage from the original Greek, the words, "of the church," are used to give the meaning of a word which in the common use of the Greek language signifies an "assembly." Coming from a word meaning to call together, it describes an assembly of citizens called together, usually by a herald, the members of which were therefore the elect—the called. Liddell and Scott define the word "ecclesia" as an assembly of citizens summoned by the crier; the legislative assembly. In ecclesiastical (usage) the church: 1. The body. 2. The place.

The ecclesiastical meaning of the word in the New Testament is closely allied to the term "congregation" in the Old Testament, where the word means the body assembled for religious worship, as distinguished from the whole congregation of Israel or any general assembly of the same. "At the bottom lies the idea that the congregation is called together by God himself."

The idea that Christ intended to found a visible organization or church, in distinction from what is by ecclesiastical writers called "the Jewish Church," has been called in question. Some who concur in the view that under Christ and the apostles a visible church or churches were established, assert "that the existence of the church does not depend upon the apostolic forms," while the Roman Catholic idea is, that the Roman hierarchy is "the development of the church of the New Testament."

These theories are at some points in conflict with one another, and both are opposed to the view which we regard as Scriptural—that the New Testament furnishes a true and perfect standard for the constitution and doctrines of a gospel church.

I. Its organic form.

In the text "the church" is understood as denoting the collective body or assembly of believers or disciples of Christ in Jerusalem. The writers in the New Testament have generally (ninety-two times) employed the word *ecclesia*, with its grammatical modifications, in the sense of a local body or assembly for religious worship when speaking of the disciples of Christ in other cities as well as those at Jerusalem: as "the church that was at Antioch"; "the church of God which is at Corinth"; "the churches throughout Syria and Cilicia"; "the churches of the Gentiles." (Acts 13 : 1; Rom. 16 : 1; 1 Cor. 1 : 2; Acts 15 : 41; Rom 16 : 4.)

But by the word "church" we are also, in some few instances, to understand the whole body of God's true people, without restriction as to place or time, as in Heb. 12 : 23, "To the general assembly and church of the first born which are written in heaven," and Eph. 3 : 21, "Unto him be glory in the church by Christ Jesus throughout all ages, world without end." In some instances it denotes the entire company of believers in the world, as in Eph. 1 : 22, 23, "And hath put all things under his feet, and gave him to be the head over all things to the church, which is his body, the fulness of him that filleth all in all," and Eph. 3 : 10, "To the intent that now unto the principalities and powers in heavenly places, might be known by the church the manifold wisdom of God." In these instances its meaning cannot be restricted to any one congregation of believers, or local organization of the disciples of Christ, but evidently embraces all that are truly Christians. The church in the sense indicated by this use of the word is but one universal body. In this amplified sense its meaning is analogous to the term "Kingdom of God," in John 3 : 3, 5, and consists of all who become "fellow-citizens with the saints, and of the household of God, and are built upon the foundation of the apostles and prophets, Jesus Christ himself being the chief corner stone." (Eph. 2 : 19, 20.) But the inspired writings nowhere speak of this universal church as having a visible organization in the world under any one earthly head. It is one body and is of one Spirit, "For by one Spirit we are all baptized into one body, whether we be Jews or Gentiles, whether we be bond or free; and have been all made to drink into one Spirit." (1 Cor. 12 : 13.) But this unity is in no way the result of a form of outward government under the control of a central earthly head, be that head a pope, a bench of bishops, or college of presbyters; nor could it be made more manifest by such a head. Its unity is of the Spirit, its bond is love, which bond of union is formed in the regeneration of the

A GOSPEL CHURCH. 119

soul through the exercise of faith in the one Lord, uniting him and the members of the body in fellowship. So we being many are one body in Christ and members in particular. Christ also is head of the church, being himself the Saviour of the body.

The form of the visible churches planted by the inspired men called and commissioned by Christ was local—companies spiritual, parts of the one spiritual body. Such were the church at Jerusalem, the church at Antioch, and the church at Corinth.

II. Of whom composed.

1. These churches were composed of persons who had been baptized upon a profession of their faith in Jesus as the Christ. The disciples won by the preaching of Christ—the "twelve" and the "seventy"—were baptized. "And after these things came Jesus and his disciples into the land of Judea; and there he tarried with them and baptized." "When therefore the Lord knew how that the Pharisees had heard that Jesus was making and baptizing more disciples than John [although Jesus himself baptized not, but his disciples]." (John 4 : 1, 2, Revised Version.) Of these about an hundred and twenty assembled with the apostles in the "upper chamber" after the ascension of the Lord to wait for the promise of the Father, for he had taught them that they should be baptized with the Holy Ghost "not many days hence." (Acts 1 : 4, 5.) Into this church at Jerusalem, when the Holy Spirit came upon the disciples on the day of Pentecost, "they that gladly received his [Peter's] word were baptized : and the same day there were added unto them about three thousand souls." Paul, writing to the churches he had established among the Gentiles,

refers to their union with Christ and baptism in his name. "Is Christ divided? was Paul crucified for you? or were you baptized in the name of Paul?" (1 Cor. 1 : 13.) To the "beloved of God, called to be saints" in Rome, he says, "Therefore we are buried with him by baptism into death." (Rom. 6 : 4.)

2. It is evident that they associated themselves voluntarily together under this covenant of faith in Christ and fellowship of the gospel.

They had exercised intelligence in the reception of gospel truth that was strongly opposed by the adherents of conflicting doctrines and systems. Paul says of them: "But first they gave their own selves to the Lord, and unto us by the will of God." (2 Cor. 8 : 5.) They were by that very choice compelled to sever long and dearly cherished social as well as religious ties, and often subject themselves to the severest persecutions. To profess faith in Jesus at that early period of the gospel history, whether among Jews or Gentiles, and become the followers of the despised Nazarene, required intelligence, courage, and character. No others could join themselves to the church and endure the tests, both from within and without, by which they were tried. National incorporation into church membership was incompatible with the teachings of Christ, who had said, "My kingdom is not of this world"; and, in fact, impossible in that age, for all the nations opposed Christ and his religion; and hereditary or infant membership formed no part of the teachings of either Christ or the apostles. Baptism and faith were always united in their preaching. "Hence, as at first, all who acknowledged Jesus as the Messiah withdrew from the mass of the Jewish people, and formed themselves into a distinct community, so all who acknowledged Jesus as the Messiah were alike baptized." (Neander.)

3. They were persons whose moral and spiritual life gave evidence of spiritual regeneration. Christ had taught: "Except a man be born of water and of the Spirit, he cannot enter into the kingdom of God." "Except ye be converted and become as little children, ye shall not enter into the kingdom of heaven." (John 3 : 5; Matt. 18 : 3.) Peter preached repentance, faith, and baptism at Pentecost. Paul testifies of the members of the Church at Corinth: "But ye are washed, but ye are sanctified, but ye are justified in the name of the Lord Jesus and by the Spirit of our God" (1 Cor. 6 : 11); and of the members of the church at Thessalonica: "In every place your faith to God-ward is spread abroad; so that we need not speak anything." (1 Thess. 1 : 8.) John, in his Second Epistle, says: "The elder unto the elect lady and her children" testifies (ver. 4): "I rejoiced greatly that I found of thy children walking in truth, as we have received a commandment from the Father;" and in his Third Epistle: "Unto the well-beloved Gaius" (ver. 3): "For I rejoiced greatly when the brethren came and testified of the truth that is in thee, even as thou walkest in the truth." Luke, in Acts 2 : 47, says of the church in Jerusalem: "And the Lord added to the church daily such as should be saved" ["were being saved," Revised Version].

III. The ordinances and worship of a gospel church.

1. The ordinances of the gospel were established by Christ. He delivered them to his disciples, and commanded their observance. He alone has this right. The

church was founded by him, and it is a natural sequence that he alone should determine its ordinances, "as Christ the head of the church and Saviour of the body." The ordinances recognized and observed by the apostles and the churches under their guidance, as of continual obligation for all time, are two—baptism and the Lord's Supper. These were committed by the apostles to the churches. Paul, addressing the Corinthian Church, said: "Now I praise you, brethren, that ye remember me in all things, and keep the ordinances as I delivered them to you. . . . For I received of the Lord that which also I delivered unto you, That the Lord Jesus the same night in which he was betrayed took bread: and when he had given thanks, he brake it, and said, Take, eat: this is my body, which is broken for you: this do in remembrance of me. After the same manner also he took the cup, when he had supped, saying," etc. (1 Cor. 11: 2, 23–26.)

These Christian churches, among both Jews and Gentiles, observed the ordinances of the gospel as commanded by Christ and taught by the apostles; "and they continued steadfastly in the apostles' doctrine and fellowship, and in breaking of bread and in prayers." (Acts 2: 42.) Recorded instances of their observance in the Gospels, the Acts, and the Epistles, show that they were observed in the order in which our Lord instituted them. Baptism being the first, and the initiatory rite admitting into the organized company of believers or church communion, appears in every recorded instance of the observance of the ordinances in the inspired writings to have been administered to all persons seeking union with a church before the admission of such persons to the Lord's Supper. "Jesus made and baptized" disciples before he instituted the "Supper," and at its institution in "the guest chamber" none but baptized persons were present. "And when the hour was come, he sat down, and the twelve apostles with him." (Luke 22 : 14.) In accord with this order was the commission given by the Lord, "Go ye," "make disciples," "baptizing them," "teaching them to observe all things whatsoever I have commanded you." This order of the ordinances of the gospel is an important part of the constitution of a gospel church. These churches were enjoined to "keep the ordinances" as they had been delivered to them. "The church yields her dignity and independence when she gives up the exclusive guardianship and celebration of the Lord's Supper." She must demand that "the seal of Jesus Christ should appear on the forehead of those who are admitted to the Lord's Supper. They should be baptized and become covenant members of the church."

Baptism is a specific act commanded by Jesus Christ. It is not, therefore, a thing of "modes" to choose between. "We who died to sin, how shall we any longer live therein? Or are ye ignorant that all we who were baptized into Jesus Christ were baptized into his death? We were buried therefore with him through baptism into death, that like as Christ was raised from the dead through the glory of the Father, so we also might walk in newness of life." (Rom. 6 : 2–4. Revised Version.) We are given here by the inspired apostle, who is certainly as competent to explain the matter as any uninspired exegete, patristic, mediæval, or modern, what the specific command of Christ comprehends—namely, a symbolical burial in water and resurrection from it, as setting forth our death to sin and rising into new life, through the operation of the Spirit in our conversion.

2. The worship of a gospel church is a thing of very vital importance. It is a part of the organic life of the church. It is the proper exercise of the inward spiritual functions of its organic life. The charisms or gifts spoken of in Eph. 4 : 8, 11, 12 ; 1 Cor. 12 : 4–31, should be regarded, and their proper exercise provided for in the worship and work of the church.

The worship of the church does much toward determining the kind of religious character that will be developed in its members. It was the ground of an impressive address by Paul to the Philippian Church. (Phil. 3 : 1–3.) There are no prescribed forms, or ritual, given to the churches in the New Testament for their invariable observance; but there are references to the exercises in which the disciples with devout spirit engaged when together in assembly for worship. Of these, singing, praying, reading the Scriptures, exhortation, preaching, and the administration of the ordinances are mentioned. It is written that the Judean disciples went daily to the temple, and from house to house, "praising God"; but there is entirely wanting any evidence that the cumbersome system of the Mosaic ritual service was transferred by the apostles of our Lord to the churches they established. To have done so would have been like putting "new wine into old bottles."

The objects to be had in view in public worship are to glorify God and rejoice in Christ Jesus, to edify the church, and to bring the world to believe in Jesus Christ, who is "the Lamb of God that taketh away the sin of the world."

IV. The government, laws, and officers of a gospel church.

1. The government of the churches established by the apostles was lodged in the members of each congregation or church. It was therefore in the strictest sense a democratic form of government, in which all the members of the church participated, and had an equal voice. The majority voting upon any question settled it. This appears (1) from the fact that the churches were composed of members who were voluntarily associated together under a covenant with the Lord and one another, upon terms of mutual love and equality, though not equal in talents, or spiritual attainments, or in the possession of this world's goods. In all these things there was diversity, but all had an equal right to enjoy the exercise of what gift or grace they possessed, and a voice in the decision of whatever came before the body. It would appear also (2) from the instruction given by Jesus to the apostles, that they should neither be "lords," nor have "authority" over one another, as the lords of the Gentiles did, who ruled over them; for one is your Master, even Christ, and all ye are brethren. This was also taught by Paul to the Gentiles, among whom he established churches. "Ye are all the children of God by faith in Christ Jesus," and "there is neither Jew nor Greek, there is neither male nor female, for ye are all one [man] in Christ Jesus." (Gal. 3 : 28, Revised Version.) Recognizing the headship of Christ alone over the body, the members exercised their governing power under him.

(a) In the reception of members. "Him that is weak in the faith receive ye, but not to doubtful disputations." (Rom. 14 : 1.) On this, commentators say that "receive ye" means to cordial Christian fellowship—the communion of the church.

(*b*) In the discipline of members. They were so instructed by Christ. (Matt. 18 : 17.) "Tell it to the church." "If he will not hear the church let him him be unto thee as an heathen man and a publican." They were so instructed by Paul (1 Cor. 5 : 4, 5, 9), to discipline the violators of moral purity among them, and "not to keep company with fornicators"; and at Thessalonica to withdraw from every brother that walked disorderly.

(*c*) In the election of an apostle in the place of Judas. (Acts 1 : 25, 26.) "This was the first assembly convened to transact the business of the church; and the vote in so important a matter as electing an apostle was by the entire church. It settles the question that the election of a minister and pastor should be by the church, and that he should not be imposed on them by any right of presentation by individuals, or by any ecclesiastical body." (Barnes on Acts 1 : 25, 26.)

(*d*) In the election of deacons. (Acts 6 : 2–6.) "Then the twelve called the multitude of the disciples, and said, . . . "brethren, look ye out among you seven men." "They chose" seven, "whom they set before the apostles; and when they had prayed they laid their hands on them."

(*e*) In the ordination of elders. "Ordained them elders in every church." (Acts 14 : 23.) The word rendered here "ordained" is also rendered "chosen" elsewhere, denoting primarily to vote with uplifted hands. Alford says: "There is no good reason for departing from the usual meaning of electing by show of hands." "The apostles may have admitted to ordination those presbyters whom the church elected." (Harvey.)

2. The laws of a gospel church are those given by Christ and the apostles, and found in the New Testament. No church has a right to alter, or add to any ordinance or law for the constitution, government, or doctrines of a church, that may be found in the New Testament. Neither has Christ, nor have the apostles left anything on record giving to uninspired men an authority belonging to Christ alone, who is "head over all things to the church." He said: "Teach them to observe all things whatsoever I have commanded you." "If ye love me, keep my commandments." He cannot suffer intervening legislative authority to intercept the allegiance due from the disciple to himself only. A gospel church has no legislative authority in itself as to matters established by Christ; its prerogatives are executive only, and it must govern itself by the laws which Christ gave. It is independent of all other ecclesiastical bodies, or authorities, but is under law always to Jesus Christ. In new and perplexing questions that may arise and cause divisions among members, and hinder the spread of the gospel, the counsel and advice of sister churches may be sought to aid in settling the difficulty; but such counsel or advice is not law, and cannot have the force of command, and may be rejected by the church. This was the course pursued by the church in the Gentile city of Antioch, when the question of circumcision was raised by "certain men from Judea," and the church "determined that Paul and Barnabas, and certain other of them should go up to Jerusalem, unto the apostles and elders about this question." (Acts 15: 2.) This was a case of advice and counsel sought by the church at Antioch from the church at Jerusalem and its ministry, particularly the inspired

apostles. The whole church took part in the deliberations, and joined in the letters of advice. (Acts 15 : 4, 23.)

3. The officers of a gospel church must be determined by the New Testament. The apostles completed the organization of the church, and they have left us in their writings all the necessary information on the subject. The permanent officers are only two, pastor, variously called bishop and elder, and deacon.

(*a*) The apostles are the first named in the earliest history of the church; but they had a special work for which they were called, endowed, and sent. The apostles' office ceased at their death. No successors were appointed; nor from the nature of the qualifications as indicated in Acts 1 : 21, 22, could any be appointed. The other seventy (Luke 10 : 1) appear as evangelists.

(*b*) The "seven" who were deacons are the first permanent officers. (Acts 6 : 2–6.)

(*c*) Bishops or elders are named as permanent officers, who, with the deacons, are spoken of as such in connection with each other. (Phil. 1 : 1; 1 Tim. 3 : 1, 2, 8.) Bishop and elder are used interchangeably in Acts 20 : 17, 28; Titus 1 : 5, 7. From these and 1 Peter 5 : 1, 2, it is quite evident that both names refer to one and the same office—elder expressing the dignity, and bishop the duty of the office. From Eph. 4 : 11, and from the meaning of the word (Jer. 3 : 15), pastors are regarded as permanent officers in the church, and identical with elders and bishops. The various other ministerial gifts bestowed upon the church as "prophets," "evangelists," "teachers," "governments," do not necessarily represent officers, but ministerial endowments.

XIV.

BAPTISM.

REV. M. W. GILBERT, A. M.,
Pastor of the First Colored Baptist Church, Nashville, Tenn.

"And Jesus came and spake unto them, saying, All power is given unto me in heaven and in earth. Go ye therefore, and teach all nations, baptizing them in the name of the Father, and of the Son, and of the Holy Ghost."—MATTHEW 28 : 18, 19.

ALL the precepts of Jesus rest upon his power to command. He is king. We owe him allegiance and obedience because he is God manifested in the flesh. His authority is derived from the Father. His rule is spiritual; and his power to command is beyond question.

"All power is given unto me in heaven and in earth." Does this absolute authority of Jesus mean anything to the redeemed church? Does it signify anything to humanity at large? The great commission and the foundation of the Christian Church rest upon the authority of Jesus as our Supreme Lawgiver. All missionary enterprises are undertaken because Jesus commands it. We preach his commandments, we follow his precepts, we obey his mandates, because he so bids us. The Lord says in our text: "Inasmuch as all authority is given unto me in heaven and in earth, by reason of this authority, I, your Master, your Lord, and your Redeemer, bid you make disciples of all nations, baptizing them in the name of the Father, and of the Son, and of the Holy Ghost." Our

Lord, by his own words, commands us to make disciples of all nations, and to baptize those thus made disciples.

Observing the order of the text, we are—

I. To make disciples of all nations.

Our text places the discipling of the nations before their baptism. It first says: "Go and teach, or make disciples, of all nations." First convert the nations of the earth, turn them to God, persuade the people everywhere to accept Christ as a crucified, risen, ascended, and living Saviour; then, after these things are done, after these conditions are fulfilled, baptize them in the name of the Father, and of the Son, and of the Holy Ghost.

Does any one ask why the Baptist churches condemn infant baptism? It is because their Lord commands them first to make disciples. "He that believeth and is baptized shall be saved." Here the believing comes first; then baptism follows, as effect follows cause. John the Baptist preached repentance before baptism. Surely infants cannot experience repentance. John the Baptist further required confession of sin in those baptized. "Then went out to him Jerusalem, and all Judea, and all the region round about Jordan, and were baptized of him in Jordan, confessing their sins." (Matt. 3 : 5, 6.) Can infants fulfill this condition? Philip told the eunuch he would baptize him, if he believed on the Lord Jesus with all his heart. It is said of the Corinthians, in Acts 18: 8, that "many of the Corinthians hearing, believed, and were baptized." Notice the order: hearing, believing, being baptized. In Acts 2 : 41, we learn that "they that gladly received his word were baptized." Here we see the necessity of first receiving gladly the word before baptism ensues. When the Samaritans "believed Philip preaching the things concerning the kingdom of God, and the name of Jesus Christ, they were baptized, both men and women." The jailer at Philippi first believed, then he was baptized. First of all, then, we learn that only persons who can exercise saving faith in Christ ought to be baptized; and, secondly, that where there is no exercise of faith, there is no baptism. "Without faith it is impossible to please God."

II. Our text teaches the duty of all believers to be baptized.

"Go ye into all the world, and disciple all nations, baptizing them in the name of the Father, and of the Son, and of the Holy Ghost."

"Yes, but what is baptism?" says one. "I was baptized when I was an infant. I was sprinkled." Do you you remember anything about it, then? "No." Did you believe when you were in infancy? "No." Then you were not baptized. "He that believeth and is baptized shall be saved." "But," says another, "I was baptized or christened—*i. e.*, sprinkled, when I was grown up, and was conscious of the fact." Did you believe on Jesus then? "Yes, most emphatically. And was I not baptized?" No, emphatically *no!* "Then what is baptism? Can it not be sprinkling, pouring, or immersion?" Not *all* of them. Baptism can no more mean sprinkling, pouring, and immersion all at once than eating means sleeping, drinking, or hearing.

What, then, is baptism? or, What is it to baptize? In answering this question, we must not consult the ordinary mind, but we must take the words of the best scholars on this subject. But what kind of scholars? Shall they be Baptist scholars, or Pedobaptist scholars? I shall take the testimony of Pedobaptist scholars—those who practice sprinkling and christen their infants. For the most conclusive proof of the truthfulness of anything is found in the concessions of its opponents. We shall only mention as authorities men who love truth too well to attempt to lessen its teachings, though they do not practice it.

The word "baptize" is an untranslated word from the Greek. It was simply transferred into our language. Liddell and Scott, in their standard Lexicon, say that *baptizo* means "to dip in or under water." They add that in the case of ships this word means "to sink them." In not one place does this Lexicon speak of *baptizo* as meaning sprinkling or pouring. Noah Webster, who was not a Baptist, says in his Unabridged Dictionary that the word "baptism" is from the Greek *baptisma* or *baptismos*, which is further derived from *baptizein*, meaning "to dip in water."

Dr. Cunningham Geikie, of the Church of England, in his "Life of Christ," says of Christ's baptism by John: "Baptism was an ordinance of God, required by his prophet as the introduction of the New Dispensation. It was a part of righteousness—that is, it was a part of God's commandments, which Jesus came into the world to show us the example of fulfilling, both in the letter and the spirit. Moreover, he had not received the consecration of the Spirit, abiding in him, and had not yet assumed the awful dignity of the Messiah, but had hitherto been only the unknown villager of Nazareth. No subject is more mysterious than the 'increase in wisdom' which marked the Saviour, as it does all other men, nor can we conjecture when it was that the full realization of his divine mission first rose before him. As yet there had been no indication of its having done so; for he had not yet manifested his glory, or appeared at all before men. Is it too much to believe that his baptism was the formal consecration which marked his entrance upon his great office? John resisted no longer; and, leading Jesus into the stream, the rite was performed. Can we question that such an act was a crisis in the life of our Lord? His perfect manhood, like that of other men, in all things except sin, forbids our doubting it. 'Holy and pure,' mark his words before sinking under the waters; he must have risen from them with the light of a higher glory in his countenance. His past life was closed, a new era had opened. Hitherto the humble villager, veiled from the world, he was henceforth the Messiah, openly working among men. It was the true moment of his entrance on a new life. Past years had been buried in the waters of Jordan. He entered them as Jesus, the Son of man; he rose from them the Christ of God."

Dean Alford, of the Church of England, says: "The baptism was administered by the immersion of the whole person." Kurtz, who belonged to the Lutheran Church, says in his "Church History": "Baptism took place by complete immersion." Dr. Philip Schaff, of Union Theological Seminary, New York, says: "Respecting the form of baptism, the impartial historian is compelled by exegesis and history, substantially, to yield the point to the Baptists, as is done, in fact, by most German scholars." Krause, another Pedobaptist scholar and church historian, says: "Baptism was performed by immersion in the name of the Trinity." One fact must impress us, and that is, that the scholars of Germany—that land of scholars—sustain the position maintained by Baptists. Guericke, in his "Church History," translated by Shedd, says: "Baptism was originally performed by immersion, in the name of the Trinity." Dr. Bunsen says, in his "Letters to Arndt," on the "Signs of the Times": "As regards their form of government, the Baptists are, as every one knows, Independents, who perform the rite of baptism, like the primitive Christians, by immersion."

Pope, in his Greek-German Dictionary defines *baptizo*, "to dip in, dip under." Chamber's "Encyclopedia," declares: "It is, however, indisputable that in the primitive church the ordinary mode of baptism was by immersion." Professor Whitney, a professor in Yale University, says that the word "baptize" is translated into German by the verb "taufen." Now, what is Professor Whitney's own definition for "taufen"? He says it means "to dip, immerse, plunge." Dr. Robinson's "Greek-English Lexicon of the New Testament," which was considered the most authoritative on New Testament Greek until Thayer's appeared, defines *baptizo* by the expression "to dip in, to sink, to immerse." He clearly makes the admission that the meaning of *baptizo* from the time of "Plato onward is everywhere to immerse, to sink, to overwhelm." The Greek language is not a dead language, as some suppose. It is still spoken by the modern Greeks. Surely they ought to know their own language, and the meaning of their own words. The modern Greeks declare that *baptizo* always means dipping, or immersing, and can mean nothing else. In corroboration of this fact, the Greek Church (in Greece and Russia), although it practices infant baptism, nevertheless always immerses or dips infants three times, for the Greek Church does not hold that its children can be baptized, according to the import of the word, without immersion. Stourdza, a native modern Greek, in a work published in 1816, declares that *baptizo* has but one signification. It signifies literally and invariably to plunge. "Baptism and immersion are therefore identical."

Professor E. A. Sophocles, of Harvard University, a native Greek, in his "Lexicon of the Greek, Roman, and Byzantine Periods," defines *baptizo* as signifying to "dip, immerse, sink, with figurative uses derived from this"; and he further declares that "there is no evidence that Luke and Paul, and the other writers of the New Testament, put upon this verb meanings not recognized by the Greek." A common complaint of the Greek Church against the Latin or Roman Catholic Church is that the Catholic Church must be held accountable for substituting sprinkling for immersion.

The reformers were convinced that a change ought to be made in the form of baptism. Luther said more than once: "Baptism is a Greek word, and may be translated immersion, as when we immerse something in water that it may be wholly covered. And it is almost wholly abolished (for they do not dip the whole children, but only pour a little water on them); they ought nevertheless to be wholly immersed . . . for that the etymology of the word seems to demand." He also declares that baptism "is rather a sign both of death and resurrection. Being moved by this reason, I would have those that are to be baptized to be altogether dipt into the water, as the word means, and the mystery signifies." Calvin also spoke as freely in commenting upon the baptism of the eunuch, as follows: "They descended into the water. Here we perceive what was the rite of baptizing among the ancients, for they immersed the whole body into the waters; now the custom has become established that the minister only sprinkles the body or the head." Baptism in the original cannot mean sprinkling or pouring, for the words "sprinkling" and "pouring" occur many times in the New Testament, and they are not once translated thus from *baptizo*.

We have thus the testimony of some of the most eminent among scholars and reformers, conceding the Scripturalness of the Baptist position as to the ordinance which gives them their name. No Baptist is among them. Truth compels these men to pronounce against their practice, as in this matter it does all Pedobaptists whose scholarship entitles them to respect. The list could be multiplied many fold did not lack of space forbid. Our common English Bible, our King James' Bible, translated by seventy eminent men, not one of whom was a Baptist, will lead one aright, though he know not one letter of Greek. Thousands of men and women have joined the Baptist churches by their own unaided reading of the word of God. And thousands more will join it thus. Oh, that we could get everybody of every church to read the word of God for himself! Read the word of God for yourself. Read it with a view to discover truth and unearth error. Read it to find out your duty. Read it for instruction. Read it for your sanctification. "Search the Scriptures, for in them ye think ye have eternal life, and these are they which testify of me," Jesus said.

Let us notice for those who read nothing but their English Bibles that the expressions, circumstances, and places connected with the administration of baptism in the New Testament prove it to have been immersion. Beginning with Matt. 3: "In those days came John the Baptist preaching in the wilderness of Judea, and saying, Repent ye: for the kingdom of heaven is at hand. For this is he that was spoken of by the prophet Isaiah, saying, The voice of one crying in the wilderness, Prepare ye the way of the Lord, make his paths straight. And the same John had his raiment of camel's hair, and a leathern girdle about his loins; and his meat was locusts and wild honey. Then went out to him Jerusalem, and all the region round about Jordan, and were baptized of him in Jordan, confessing their sins."

We notice that John baptized where there was an abundance of water, and that he baptized *in* Jordan. Lieutenant Lynch, of the United States navy, who traversed this river, says that "its width varies at different points from seventy-five to two hundred feet, and its depth from three to twelve feet." At the traditional spot of our Lord's baptism, in the week preceding Easter, about seven or eight thousand pilgrims come, according to Dr. Broadus, "from all parts of the East, and there these thousands, men, women, and children, do actually immerse themselves and one another in the river—not as baptism (for they have received that in infancy), but as a sacred bath at that holy spot." This same event occurs at the same spot every spring.

In Matt. 3 : 13, and following verses, we read : "Then cometh Jesus from Galilee to Jordan, unto John, to be baptized of him." The Lord Jesus went, it seems, about seventy miles for the express purpose of being baptized. "But John forbade him, saying, I have need to be baptized of thee, and comest thou to me? And Jesus answering, said unto him, Suffer it to be so now: for thus it becometh us to fulfil all righteousness. Then he suffered him. And Jesus, when he was baptized, went up straightway *out of the water*; and lo the heavens were opened unto him, and he saw the Spirit of God descending like a dove, and lighting upon him: and lo a voice from heaven, saying, This is my beloved Son, in whom I am well pleased." No one can read this passage carefully and not decide that our Lord was baptized *in* the river Jordan.

Notice now Mark 1 : 4–11 : " John did baptize in the wilderness, and preach the baptism of repentance for the remission of sins. And there went out unto him all the land of Judea, and they of Jerusalem, and were all baptized of him *in the river of Jordan*, confessing their sins. And John was clothed with camel's hair, and with a girdle of skin about his loins; and he did eat locusts and wild honey; and preached, saying, There cometh one mightier than I after me, the latchet of whose shoes I am not worthy to stoop down and unloose. I indeed have baptized you with water: but he shall baptize you with [or rather, *in*] the Holy Ghost. And it came to pass in those days, that Jesus came from Nazareth of Galilee, and was baptized of John *in* Jordan. And straightway *coming up out of the water*, he saw the heavens opened, and the Spirit like a dove descending upon him. And there came a voice from heaven, saying, Thou art my beloved Son, in whom I am well pleased." John 3 : 23, reads : " And John also was baptizing in Enon, near to Salim, *because there was much water there;* and they came and were baptized." John the Baptist required an abundance of water for baptism. In the Acts, eighth chapter, we have the baptism of the eunuch. Begin with the thirty-sixth verse: "And as they went on their way, they came unto a certain water: and the eunuch said, See, here is water; what doth hinder me to be baptized? And Philip said, If thou believest with all thine heart, thou mayest. And he answered and said, I believe that Jesus Christ is the Son of God. And he commanded the chariot to stand still: *and they* went down both into the water, *both Philip and the eunuch;* and he baptized him. And when they were *come up out of the water*, the Spirit of the Lord caught away Philip, that the eunuch saw him no more: and he went on his way rejoicing."

Can any one deny the fact of immersion from so plain an account? Read also the account of the conversion and baptism of the jailer and his house at Philippi, when Paul and Silas were so mercifully delivered. Turn to Acts, sixteenth chapter, and read from the thirtieth to the thirty-fourth verse: "And brought [*i. e.*, the jailer] them out, and said, Sirs, what must I do to be saved? And they said, Believe on the Lord Jesus Christ, and thou shalt be saved, and thy house. And they spake unto him the word of the Lord, and to all that were in his house. And he took them the same hour of the night, and washed their stripes; and was baptized, he and all his straightway. And when he had brought them into his house, he set meat before them, and rejoiced, believing in God with all his house."

What now are the facts in this case? First, the jailer took Paul and Silas to his house, where the apostle preached the word of God; secondly, the jailer took them out the same hour of the night, "and washed their stripes; and was baptized, he and all his, straightway"; thirdly, after the baptism, it is stated that the jailer again "brought them into his house," and "set meat before them and rejoiced in God with all his house."

The symbolical meaning of baptism indicates immersion. Ananias said to Paul: "Arise and be baptized and wash away thy sins, calling on the name of the Lord." Sprinkling would imply here the use of too small an amount of water to be adequate for a washing.

In Rom. 6 : 3–4, we read : "Know ye not, that so many of us as were baptized into Jesus Christ were baptized into his death? Therefore we are buried with him by baptism into death : that like as Christ was raised up from the dead by the glory of the Father, even so we also should walk in newness of life." Here baptism is spoken of figuratively, symbolically, as a burial, "buried with him by baptism"; hence, when there is no burial, there can be no baptism.

Bloomfield, who is not a Baptist, says of these two passages of Scripture : "There is here plainly a reference to the ancient mode of baptism by immersion, and I agree with Koppe and Rosenmüller, that there is reason to regret that it should have been abandoned in most Christian churches, especially as it has so evidently a reference to the mystic sense of baptism."

Read now Col. 2 : 12 : "Buried with him in baptism, wherein also ye are risen with him through the faith of the operation of God, who hath raised him from the dead."

Lightfoot, a Pedobaptist commentator, says of this verse: "Baptism is the grave of the old man and the birth of the new. As he sinks beneath the baptismal waters, the believer buries there all his corrupt affections and past sins; as he emerges thence, he rises regenerate, quickened to new hopes and a new life." Bishop Wilson, another Pedobaptist commentator, says: "The expression 'buried with him in baptism' alludes to the ancient form of administering that sacred ordinance of the immersion or burial, so to speak, of the whole person in the water, after the example of the burial of the entire body of our Lord in the grave." We have then the authority of God's word for what baptism is. The opinions of learned men confirm this authority. It is, moreover, worthy of note, that while these scholars are Pedobaptists, no Baptist can be found who will concede the validity of sprinkling or pouring as New Testament baptism.

When Jesus was on earth, he said to one and another: "Follow me." Let all who would be truly enrolled among his disciples, follow him in baptism.

> "To Jordan's stream the Saviour goes,
>   To do his Father's will;
> His breast with sacred ardor glows,
>   Each precept to fulfill.
>
> "As from the water he ascends,
>   What miracles appear!
> God, with a voice, his Son commends:
>   Let all the nations hear.
>
> "Hear it, ye Christians, and rejoice,
>   Let this your courage raise;
> What God approves, be this your choice,
>   And glory in his ways."

"If ye love me," Jesus says, "keep my commandments." "But," says some one, "if sprinkling is not and cannot be baptism, how do you account for its beginning?" Luther, the great reformer, says it was not practiced in the beginning. Calvin says the church felt authorized in instituting a change. The scholars of the Church of Rome declare that the church had the right or authority to change an ordinance, and has changed the original rite for convenience. The church has the right to change an ordinance of God. Think of it! We hold that no church, or bishop, or pope, or principality, or power under the canopy of heaven, is authorized to change a mandate of Almighty God. " Heaven and earth shall pass away, but not one jot or tittle of my word shall fail till all be fulfilled." "And if any man shall add unto these things, God shall add unto him the plagues that are written in this book: and if any man shall take away from the words of the book of this prophecy, God shall take away his part out of the book of life, and out of the holy city, and from the things which are written in this book." (Rev. 22 : 18, 19.)

"Is baptism important after a man is converted?" exclaims some Christian. All of God's commandments are important. The least of them are essentially important. "Believe" and "be baptized" are the two commands which our ascended Lord left behind him for his church. Who shall say the one is essential and the other is not? Obey both. Obedience is better than mutilation. "Behold to obey is better than sacrifice, and to hearken than the fat of rams."

XV.

THE LORD'S SUPPER.

WM. J. SIMMONS, D. D., LL. D.
District Secretary of the American Baptist Home Mission Society for the South.

"For I have received of the Lord that which also I delivered unto you, that the Lord Jesus the same night in which he was betrayed took bread: and when he had given thanks, he brake it, and said, Take, eat; this is my body, which is broken for you: this do in remembrance of me. After the same manner also he took the cup, when he had supped, saying, This cup is the new testament in my blood: this do ye, as oft as ye drink it, in remembrance of me. For as often as ye eat this bread, and drink this cup, ye do shew the Lord's death till he come."
—1 Cor. 11: 23-26.

LIKE all good Jews, Christ was observing the passover which they had been ordered to keep as a memorial. (Exod. 12: 21-29.) The table was supplied with unleavened bread, wine, the bitter herbs, and the paschal lamb. The bread was unleavened as a symbol of their afflictions in Egypt. (Deut. 16: 3.) And also because it commemorated their speedy exit from the land of the Pharaohs, as it is remarked in Exod. 12: 39, that "the dough was not leavened, because they were thrust out of Egypt, and could not tarry." For this same reason the feast was eaten standing, to typify the fact that they were in a hurry to depart, and had no time to sit.

The wine was an emblem of rejoicing, and was mingled with water, which was drunk after the following thanks: "Blessed be thou, O Lord, who hast created the fruit of the vine; blessed be thou for this good day, and this holy convocation, which thou hast given us for joy and rejoicing. Blessed be thou, O Lord, who hast sanctified Israel." Herbs were to symbolize to the Jews the bitterness of their lives as well as to indicate that in their haste they had no time to select better seasoning; to this they afterward added a sauce of dates, raisins, and other ingredients, mixed to the consistency of mustard, to indicate the clay in which they labored. The lamb was to be a male without blemish; it was to be roasted, to avoid eating raw or boiling, as was the manner of the heathen. This mode of cooking the lamb indicated the fires of persecution. It should be eaten without breaking a bone, in private, each family having a lamb, and all must be eaten. This was an offset to the great public feasts of the Egyptians and Syrians, who carried around the sacrificial victims with great show and pomp, and then devoured them, carrying away some portions as relics. These preparations for the feast of the passover being made from year to year, kept in the Jewish mind the great passing over of the angel, when he saw the blood on the lintels of the doorposts.

Christ observed the passover, and at the end thereof instituted "The Lord's Supper." The one ceremony was a fitting introduction to the other. The one was the symbol of the fading shadow of Christ as foreseen in the slain lamb, while the other is the new feast of saints in a new dispensation, and Christ himself the Paschal Lamb. Hence, we read that Paul calls Christ our Passover. (1 Cor. 5 : 7.) In examining the conditions, and the figures, it will be seen that there are many points of agreement between the Jewish passover, and "The Lord's Supper"; between the emblems of the one and the other;

the lessons to be taught by the former and the latter. Yes, remarkably true is it that the "Person of Christ," "the suffering and death of Christ," "the fruits of Christ's death," and the manner in which we are to be made partakers of the rich and glorious fruits of his sacrifice are boldly, vividly, and strongly typified in the Jewish passover, and the Lord's Supper. The former is of the old dispensation, the latter of the new.

Yet another thing to be impressed upon us is this, that "Blood is the price of liberty." "Born in iniquity and in sin," there is no escape from the thraldom thereof till "the blood of Christ cleanseth us from all sin." (1 John 1 : 7.) "For if the blood of bulls and of goats, and the ashes of an heifer sprinkling the unclean, sanctifieth to the purifying of the flesh, how much more shall the blood of Christ, who through the eternal Spirit offered himself without spot to God, purge your conscience from dead works to serve the living God. And for this cause he is the mediator of the new testament, that by the means of death, for the redemption of the transgressions that were under the first testament, they which are called might receive the promise of eternal inheritance. For where a testament is, there must also of a necessity be the death of the testator. For a testament is of force after men are dead: otherwise it is of no strength at all while the testator liveth." (Heb. 9 : 13–17.) Now Matt. 26 : 26–29; Mark 14 : 22–25; Luke 22 : 19, 20; and 1 Cor. 11 : 23–26, all give accounts of the introduction of this the second ordinance of Christ, baptism being the first. John is silent on this subject. Paul alone tells us that it is to be observed "till he come," even as the passover was to be kept till Christ came the first time.

K

I. The elements.

We have briefly spoken of the elements used for this Supper, and desire now to speak more specifically. There are two elements, bread and wine, which were in olden times brought by the members of the church, each bringing some. What was necessary was used in the administration of the ordinance, and the balance was gathered and appropriated for the benefit of the poor. How deep an interest the members must have had when in this way they prepared these offerings ! No doubt it is from this beautiful custom of individual contributions that a collection is generally taken for the poor saints at the Lord's Table. For the most part now the elements are provided by the deacons. It should be recalled here that Christ sent his disciples to prepare the passover wherein also offerings for the Supper were also prepared. There were no deacons to prepare the " Lord's Supper," but they were afterward appointed, apparently to attend to the poor in the distribution of what was left after eating. It was because of this the apostles declared : " It is not reason that we should leave the word of God, and serve tables."

The reasons for using bread are perhaps as follows: 1. To harmonize with its uses in the passover. He took the loaf and broke it. So he was broken. 2. To symbolize Christ as the great food for the spiritual system. (John 6 : 51.) 3. Because it is easy to get, and is commonly understood as containing the results of the divine energy in nature, being produced from the earth by the rain and the sun. 4. To remind them that he had given the Jews manna in an unaccountable way ; and as it came down from heaven, so did Christ himself. 5. As no one can tell how bread enters the system and produces life, strengthens bones and muscles, etc., so there is a mystery in that Christ becomes our strength and life. Bread produces strength in the body, so does Christ in the soul.

Baptists believe the matter of little moment whether the bread be leavened or unleavened, and hence both are used. Now as regards wine. It is well to notice that the word "wine" is not used by the Master, but the "fruit of the vine." When this idea is of itself brought in contact with the word itself in the original, it is evidence that no violence is done by using the word wine. Much controversy has obtained as to fermented and unfermented wine, but no one disputes that the "fruit of the vine" is wine; and indeed scholars tell us that the word generally used is the one for unfermented wine. (Matt. 9: 17; John 2: 3–10; Rom. 14: 21; 1 Tim. 3: 8; Titus 2: 3.) Wine is used: 1. To call to mind the fact that the Lamb was slain. That he gave his life for us. "The life is the blood." (Gen. 9: 4.) That his blood caused God to pass over us as the blood of the lamb did on the Jewish doorposts. 2. It is a reminder of Jesus' pains and sufferings, and that he was wounded for our transgressions; yet it is an emblem of joy. 3. As the fruit of the grape is crushed to secure wine, so was he bruised to secure grace for transgressors. Other analogies might be suggested, but these will suffice.

II. The name.

The most common and most acceptable term for this ordinance known to intelligent Baptists is the Lord's Supper. Other terms are applied to it, as "the Sacrament," "the Communion," "the "Eucharist"; but the term "Lord's Supper" seems the most appropriate, and as in every way meeting the demands of the case. It is the term which the Apostle Paul in 1 Cor. 11: 20

uses to designate the ordinance. It is the term, moreover, which most fully recognizes our Lord's relation to that which is pre-eminently his in its institution and symbolism. It is the term which most generally, if not always, should be used. It was on Thursday night that the Lord's Supper was instituted, but to emphasize the relation of the Christian Sabbath to the resurrection of our Lord, the early Christians celebrated the ordinance on that day. (Acts 20 : 7.)

Says Rev. J. Newton Brown, in his "Encyclopedia of Religious Knowledge," "Much has been said respecting the time of administering the Lord's Supper. Some plead for the morning, others for the afternoon, and some for the evening; which latter indeed was the time of the first celebration of it, and is most suitable to a supper. How often it is to be observed has been a matter of different opinion. Some have been for keeping it every day in the week, others four times a week, some every Lord's Day, which many think nearest the apostolic practice, a practice which was long kept up, and only deviated from when the love of Christians began to wax cold. Others have kept it three times a year, and some once a year; but the most common custom for its observance is once a month. It appears, however, both from Scripture and from the nature of the ordinance, that its observance ought to be frequent."

One word more as to the posture in taking the Supper. The passover was first taken standing, but after the Israelites had entered Canaan they took it in the position which Christ and his disciples assumed in the upper room. This custom of reclining showed signs of equality and strict union. For is not Christ "our Elder Brother"?

His Father our Father? We see many Pedobaptists kneeling at the Lord's Supper. This method was introduced by the Roman Catholic Church. It was intended to be an act of worship. The Roman Catholics believe the elements to be the body and blood of Christ; hence in kneeling they are worshiping him, as recognized in the bread and wine.

III. The significance of the ordinance.

Let us somewhat in detail, though briefly, notice the significance of the Lord's Supper:

1. It is commemorative of the blessed Saviour. He commands his disciples thus: "This do ye, as often as ye drink it, in remembrance of me." What glorious memories! How grand!

2. It is emblematic, teaching his will and an acknowledgment thereof. A sign of acceptance of his doctrines. "This cup is the new testament in my blood." The old testament replaced by a new one.

3. It is a type of that which is to come. Recalling the past and suggesting the great future. "But I say unto you, I will not drink henceforth of this fruit of the vine, until that day when I drink it new with you in my Father's kingdom."

4. It is demonstrative, showing that his disciples are to meet to vindicate their belief in the Lord and the Lord's death, and to testify to his second coming, as well as to exhibit faith in his having come. The Jews reject Christ.

5. It exhibits the love of his disciples, not only for the Master but for each other; establishing the fact that all can unite in Christ and form one family. Remember, the Jewish passover was a family institution, and was confined to one family or two small families united. In

the time of Josephus not less than ten nor more than twenty persons were allowed. Here we see Christ and his twelve disciples, though it is commonly believed that Judas ate the passover, but not the Lord's Supper. This was Christ's family. Is not he the Bridegroom of the church? He had no other family. His was a household of faith. This gives splendid evidence of the social character of his church. With one accord around his table they met, and lovingly they meet to-day. Accepting the rendering of Dr. A. N. Arnold: "Because there is one loaf, we the many are one body; for we all partake of the one loaf." Is not this a union of blessed import, Christ's body food for all?

6. It is a bond that holds us together. While it was not probably the Master's intention to hold the church together by this ceremony, yet it is a bond that tightens around his disciples. Indeed, to the soul that loves Christ, this is a precious season. It crystallizes our sentiment and openly publishes the fact that this rallying time is a season for cementing us together. One has only to recall his feelings when he has changed his relations from one church to another. How gladly you can sit down with entire strangers and feel that indeed you are drawn by invisible yet irresistible bonds to "love the brethren."

7. It advertises to the world that we are keeping intact, faithfully and surely, the very simple, plain ordinance he gave us through his disciples. It portrays truly that the ministry are faithful and that through all these ages there have been those who have delivered it just as he gave it; and that there are myriads who are willing to still do so. Aye, more; when we consider as Baptists what opposition we encounter to be able to deliver it as we received it, we

grow proud of our position. But none of these things move us. Not a single heresy is traceable to Baptists. It is our pleasure to keep from the table all whom we believe are not disciples, or who, if they are, do not live free from following after "strange doctrines." Yes, Lord, we will, aided by thee, deliver this glorious Supper, just as thou gavest it to us! It never grows old.

IV. The prerequisites.

This leads us naturally to consider the prerequisites to this table of the Lord. Mind our language: not *our* table, but the Lord's table. Not *our* supper, but the Lord's Supper. We must surely find the conditions in his teaching or that of the teachings and practices of the apostles.

The three requisites admitted by the creeds and most of the members of all denominations are repentance, baptism, and church membership. Christ ate with disciples. Do not forget this; for "Jesus took bread, and brake it, and gave it to his disciples." Christ drank with disciples. Do not forget this: "And he took the cup and gave thanks, and gave to them, saying, Drink ye all of it." They had repented, been baptized and united with Christ. Yet we see a host of people, who profess to repent and will not be baptized. How can they justly claim that we thrust them from the table when we believe that baptism is immersion. This is the Lord's Supper, not ours. Does any man work for another and act according to his own will? If the master of the house bids his servant invite certain guests who fulfill certain conditions, how dare he invite others, who not only fall short of these conditions, but who, on the contrary, have violated these very conditions? Nor does it make a difference how much one may claim to have fulfilled these conditions; it is my duty and yours to satisfy ourselves, as the Master's servants, that the person bidden has observed the conditions. No one doubts the fact that "repentance, baptism and church membership" are prerequisites to the Lord's Supper. The Lord Jesus, when he gave the great commission, plainly showed this: "Go ye, therefore, and disciple all nations, baptizing them in the name of the Father, and of the Son, and of the Holy Ghost, teaching them to observe all things whatsoever I have commanded you." Here we have:

1. Discipling. 2. Baptism. 3. Observing commands. Now read in connection with the great commission, Acts 2 : 38–41; 8 : 12, 35–38; 9 : 17, 18; 22 : 16; 10 : 47–48; 16 : 14, 15; 16 : 29–33; 18 : 8. From the above, baptism is seen to be a grand essential.

Some one congratulates himself that John and the apostles were not baptized. While the Scripture is silent on that point, it is a more just inference that they were baptized than that they were not. Even if they were not, to them was given the charge to baptize; and it came from high authority and was of the nature of those things to which Paul refers in the text, when he says: "For I have received of the Lord that which also I have delivered unto you."

But lest some one may accuse me of teaching Baptist doctrine, forgetting in the charge that all Bible doctrine is Baptist doctrine, or that I may be charged with wresting the Scriptures, I will put here the convictions of a few Pedobaptists. My aim will, I trust, be seen in the quotations themselves. But I will state it plainly. Baptists reject from the Lord's Supper such as have not been baptized. They do not believe any one baptized except he is immersed. Should one be immersed and unite with a Pedobaptist church,(?) then we reject him, as by his course teaching error, and thereby failing to practice and teach the truth.

We are not keepers of the consciences of such, but our own. The coming to the table depends on repentance, baptism, and union with a church. If we do not acknowledge a man's baptism, he cannot get to our Lord's table. Pedobaptists are consistent in inviting us, for they believe we are baptized, while we do not believe they are.

We have a baptism accepted throughout the world, by even those who practice sprinkling and pouring, while these last-named are rejected by millions. This is all there is to what is called "close communion." It is a question of baptism and holy life. I pass over the question of "church," as to whether these great Pedobaptist organizations are a "church," etc., as it is not material to this present argument. Suffice it to say, that Baptists and Pedobaptists disagree as to what is a church, but do not disagree on the fact that a man must be baptized and join a church, no matter how widely they may differ as to what that baptism is.

I take these extracts from a pamphlet by Rev. Henry F. Colby; Dr. Pendleton's "Doctrines," and Hiscox's "Baptist Short Method."

Dr. Wall, in his "History of Intant Baptism," p. 2, chap. IX., says: "No church ever gave the communion to any persons before they were baptized. Among all the absurdities that ever were held, none ever maintain that any person should partake of the communion before he was baptized."

Dr. Dick, in his "Theology," says: "None have the right to the holy table but those who have been previously purified by the washing of water and the word."

Justin Martyr says: "This food is called by us the Eucharist, of which it is not lawful for any to partake but such as believe the things taught by us to be true, and have been baptized."

Dr. Cave says: "The communicants in the primitive church were those who had embraced the doctrines of the gospel, and had been baptized into the faith of Christ. For, looking upon the Lord's Supper as the highest and most solemn act of religion, they thought they could not take care enough in the dispensing of it."

Baxter says: "What man dare go in a way which hath neither precept nor example to warrant it, from a way that hath a full current of both? Yet they that will admit members into the visible church without baptism do this."

Doddridge says: "It is certain that as far as our knowledge of antiquity reaches, no unbaptized person received the Lord's Supper. How excellent soever a man's character is, he must be baptized before he can be looked upon as completely a member of the Church of Christ."

Dr. Dwight, a Congregationalist, says: "It is an indispensible qualification for the ordinance that the candidate for communion be a member of the visible Church of Christ in full standing. By this I intend that he should be a person of piety; that he should have made a public profession of religion; and that he should have been baptized."

Dr. Hibbard, a Methodist, says: "Both Baptist and Pedobaptist churches agree in rejecting from communion at the table of the Lord, and denying the rights of church membership to all who have not been baptized. Valid baptism they consider essential to visible church membership. This also we hold. The only question then that divides us is, What is essential to valid baptism?"

Dr. Hodge, the Presbyterian, says: "The Christian Church requires of those whom it receives to membership in visible communion nothing more than a credible profession of faith, the promise of obedience to Christ and submission to baptism as the initiatory ordinance."

V. The benefit of the ordinance.

I wish to ask now what benefit is bestowed by the observance of this ordinance upon the individual himself, and what really is the character of the elements when partaken of? There are four views held touching this matter.

1. Transubstantiation. This is a big word that explains the Roman Catholic belief, and means that the substances, bread and wine, are changed to the actual body and blood of Christ.

2. Consubstantiation, a word to represent the views of the Lutherans, and means that the actual body and blood is really mingled with the bread and wine.

3. The Calvinists believe that through the bread and wine, by some mysterious spiritual power Christ's life is made common to us, and that we feed upon him as spiritual food.

4. Baptists believe with Zwingli, that these elements are only emblems, and this view is sufficient to call to remembrance the word and works of the Lord Jesus. Let us consider a few practical lessons:

In eating the Lord's Supper, we are commanded to examine ourselves, for many become worthless, benumbed, useless, sleepy Christians from eating unworthily, and are not approved of God. (1 Cor. 5 : 1–8 ; 1 Cor. 2 : 27–32.) "Ye are my disciples if ye do whatsoever I command you." He has commanded us to love one another; also, to do this in remembrance of him. As often, therefore, as we do so, we show our love for our brethren, and obey the Lord's command.

We owe to our Master to make this constant protest against the evils of sprinkling, pouring, and the like, for God needs us to preserve that which has been committed to us. It makes us stronger and stronger as often as we please Christ by a ready compliance with his will. It tests our title to discipleship.

Again this is a church ordinance, given to a church, for a church, and should be kept in the church. So long as the church stands, just so long will we lovingly remember Jesus around the table. The scenes of the cross will grow brighter and brighter, and our duty to preach our distinctive views grows none the less obligatory. As we practice so shall we preach; and the great God who made us prosper the word! In the language of Dr. Thomas Armitage, in his "History of the Baptists":

"When men are willing to return to the gospel order of regeneration and baptism, their obedience to Christ will remove all controversy on these subjects by restoring things to the gospel status, and then there must of necessity be again one Lord, one faith, one baptism, and one table. Until then there never can be, and what is more, there never ought to be, except on this apostolic church principle."

XVI.

THE CHRISTIAN SABBATH.

REV. G. H. JACKSON, B. D.,
Pastor of Emmanuel Baptist Church, New Haven, Conn.

" Upon the first day of the week when the disciples came together to break bread, Paul preached unto them.—ACTS 20 : 7.

IN beginning a discussion of so great a subject as the Christian Sabbath, it may be well for us, by way of introduction, to distinguish between the legal Sunday and the Christian Sabbath. They are two distinct institutions. The only point of resemblance between them is that they occur on the same day of the week. The legal Sunday is an institution prescribed by law, and guarded by the same. It cannot be said, however, that Christianity has nothing to do with this observance, for at once it is evident, were there no legal Sunday, the worship of the Christian Sabbath would be in a greater or less measure interfered with. The legal Sunday is instituted by law, and its observance is maintained by the authorities. There is more or less agreement between the commands laid down for the observance of this legal holiday, and those mentioned in the commands of Moses concerning the Sabbath to be observed by Israel; but the observance of the Christian Sabbath is in no sense compulsory. Here lies the great difference. The Christian observance is one throughout of love to God, and is of a spiritual nature. The other is compulsory, and consequently there can be no real union between them. The law can properly make no prescription for the Christian observance of the day in work and worship.

We have neither time nor place to speak of the necessities which demand the observance of one day in seven. They are many and obvious, however, alike from a physical, economic, and moral point of view. We do not claim, moreover, that one day's rest in seven is something modern, but quite the opposite; for the Assyrians, and doubtless other ancient nations, recognized the needs of nature in this particular. The Sabbath instituted during the Mosaic administration was more peculiarly a legal than a religious institution. Let us consider now :

I. The Sabbath as a religious institution.

1. The Jewish and the Christian. The Jewish Sabbath of to-day has lost much of its former significance. While the Jews were a nation, their Sabbath, as has been mentioned above, was in the fullest sense a *legal* holiday, which was also observed as a day of religious worship in the synagogues. These people made no distinction between the legal and religious sanctions of this day, for Israel was church and state, inseparable; sometimes her kings were prophets of the Most High, sometimes her kings' actions were wholly governed by the direction of prophets. The day to them was one of rigid observance, fulfilling the letter of the law if not the spirit of it; not only being careful that their own celebration was righteous, but also that no one else committed an unholy act. To-day such jurisdiction is over, and the Jews observe the Sabbath as a religious sect.

(1) They worship on the seventh day, Saturday, as of old; this is according to the command given unto their

ancestors, with which day we can raise no objection, since it is the legitimate Jewish Sabbath according to God's ordainment.

(2) They observed the day by resting from their labors, by meditating upon the "Law and the Prophets," and by hearing them expounded by the scribes in the synagogues. They were over scrupulous concerning work on the part of man or beast; and even that which had the semblance of toil was condemned.

(3) This day was instituted in the wilderness by the command of Moses, and was appointed as a day of reverence to God, on which no work should be done, and the the people should not go beyond their tents. Beyond a doubt, the Jewish Sabbath on its religious side was intended as a day of worship and sanctity; yet in the time of our Lord we find its observance had degenerated to a formal and ritualistic one.

(4) The Christian Sabbath is the ideal of the Mosaic intention, the substance of the Hebrew shadow. The Christian Sabbath is the first day of the week. It is not for me to attempt to show by what authority this first day was observed by the apostles in preference to the seventh. We have evidence that the thing was done, and we quote our text in proof: "Upon the first day of the week, when the disciples came together to break bread, Paul preached unto them." The inference is fair that not any particular week was meant in which they came together, but that they were accustomed to come together on the first day of every week, and on one of these first days Paul preached to them. This is more evident by the words of John 20: 19–23, where the appearance of Jesus was to his disciples in the upper room on the evening of the first day in the

week, the same being the day on which he rose from the dead. We are told that on this occasion, Thomas was not present. The establishment of the first day still further appears from the time and occurrence of the second visit of Jesus to the disciples when they had assembled. And after *eight days again* his disciples were within, and Thomas with them. Then came Jesus, the doors being shut, and stood in the midst of them, and said: "Peace be unto you." Here we have a stated day mentioned, the first day of the week, the eighth day after the first visit. It also implies that this was the day of religious convocation. The fact that the disciples met for worship on the first day of the week is still further proven by Paul's first letter to the Corinthians (16 : 2): "Upon the first day of the week let each one of you lay by him in store as he may prosper." This command had also been given to the churches of Galatia ; signifying a universal custom of coming together on the first day, at which time the collection for the saints was to be taken.

In these passages the *facts* are clearly set before us, and we can draw such inferences as are permissible. For my own part, in studying the characteristics of these two religious systems, I cannot possibly see anything illegal in making a time distinction between the Jewish and the Christian day of worship. From a Christian standpoint, how could it be otherwise? If the Jewish Sabbath was a part of the law under which these people lived, and no one will dispute it, then why should it remain? Christ was the fulfillment of that law. Christianity abrogated the law, by bringing a better in its place. Christianity demands a spiritual worship; and its Sabbath requirements cannot be fulfilled by self-conscious prayers, prominent seats in the synagogues, boastful almsgiving, and an obedience to the letter of the law only. Jesus said to the woman of Samaria (John 4 : 23): "But the hour cometh, and now is, when the true worshipers shall worship the Father in spirit and in truth; for the Father seeketh such to worship him." The Jewish Sabbath was associated with formalism and self-righteousness, and with a spirit that would separate men from God. Now since a new era in every other particular had dawned, it seemed fitting that a new Sabbath should come associated with the central vitalizing idea of that era.

II. The spiritual significance of the Sabbath is heightened, not diminished, by the change from the seventh to the first day of the week.

The Jewish Sabbath was not devoid of spiritual significance, but to a very great extent it had been lost. That is evident when we remember that "he came to his own and his own received him not," although the Messiah was expected and he answered the description of him of whom "Moses and the prophets did write."

1. That the true spiritual significance of the day is not changed but only restored, and so heightened, will be seen when we compare the idea of it which the prophets tried to impress upon the people with the meaning that it had to the disciples as the Lord's Day. Moses' words were: "To-morrow is a solemn rest, a *holy* sabbath unto the Lord." Jehovah's words are: "Remember the sabbath day to keep it holy." True holiness can never come from any act on our part, any outward manifestation; but it is an unseen, inward condition of the heart. It is this condition that invites God's presence, and it was to aid in securing such a state that the holy Sabbath of God was

instituted; a day when the business cares and the worries and anxieties of everyday life should be forgotten, and the soul should, undisturbed, commune with its Maker. I have been told that some coal mines that are left dismal and gloomy on Saturday night by the workmen, when they return to labor on Monday morning, have the black coal covered with a calcareous deposit of almost dazzling whiteness. It is called "Sunday stone" by the miners, because it has been accumulated during the Sabbath, when the sound of the pick and the voice of the driver were not heard. Even so was the Sabbath made for man, that something of the white holiness of the Almighty might fall on his soul during its quiet meditations, and cover by expunging something of the staining sin that might have accumulated during the preceding week, thus producing a period of greater spiritual aspiration when God's Spirit might reign supreme.

2. The spiritual significance of the Sabbath does not change with day, because the seventh day has not the spiritual significance to the Christian that it had to the Jew. As we have said, to the Jew it was a part of his law, a part of his worship, a direct command to his people at Sinai. The command to observe the seventh day was particularly to the Jew. If Christianity were a continuance of Judaism, then we would be justified in accepting its day of worship as ours; but Christianity breaks away from the old dispensation of the law and establishes a dispensation of grace. The law calls for a just condemnation of those that break it, grace pardons the transgressor. One is full of justice, the other is full of mercy; and these distinctions are so great as to entirely separate the two religious systems. If these differences do exist, it

is because God has designed to have it so, and if we do not make the distinction between the Sabbaths of these two systems, we fail to recognize the mission of the Messiah. The Christian Sabbath is the Lord's Day; the day on which the Son of God proved his Messiahship and manifested the truth of his word: "Destroy this temple, and in three days I will raise it up." This day, then, had a powerful and tender significance to the faithful few for whom Jesus had prayed in the upper room, just before the agony in Gethsemane and on the cross. It also means much to the Christian of to-day. If Jesus had not risen from the dead, then is our preaching vain, and men who have confessed Christ are yet in their sins. The Christian Sabbath is an advance on the Jewish. That is prophecy, this fulfillment. That is more legal, this more spiritual. That is crayon, if you will, more or less imperfect from the nature of the case, this the painting, with the added lifeness and tone the speaking colors alone can give. Let us value it according to the meaning the unfoldment of God's purposes has put into it.

III. What constitutes the observance of the Christian Sabbath.

1. It consists in abstaining from all labor and sinful recreation. "Six days shalt thou labour and do all thy work" were the words of Jehovah to Israel in the wilderness. These have never lost their significance. They were expressive of the needs of man and beast. "In it thou shalt not do any work, thou, nor thy son, nor thy daughter, nor thy manservant, nor thy maidservant, nor thy cattle, nor thy stranger that is within thy gates." By abstaining from labor man has a day on which he can meditate upon the wonders of his Creator, and hold spir-

itual communion with him, when the cares of the world and thoughts of its deceitful promises can be forgotten for a time. He also, by his religious condition, gives the world-busy mind the needed rest. Men's minds need rest as well as their bodies. The Sabbath also gives man's physical nature, and his animals, the cessation from labor that both alike demand; and if the demand is not met, man is the sufferer.

By abstaining from sinful recreation. "If thou turn away thy foot from the sabbath, from doing thy pleasure on my holy day, and call the sabbath a delight, the holy of the Lord honourable, and shalt honour him, not doing thine own ways, nor finding thine own pleasure, nor speaking thine own words, then shalt thou delight thyself in the Lord; and I will make thee to ride upon the high places of the earth, and I will feed thee with the heritage of Jacob thy father; for the mouth of the Lord hath spoken it." (Isa. 58: 13, 14.) It is an injury to the churches in our day that men who are Christians are beginning to favor Sunday recreation outside of the prescribed limits set forth in God's word.

2. The Christian Sabbath should be observed by profiting by all the means of grace. Quiet meditation, in which the soul draws nigh to God, turning from its sins meanwhile, should obtain. The associations of the day will in themselves furnish an abundance of subject matter for meditation. It is the Lord's day, the resurrection day, the day when Christ presented himself alive to his own after his passion. This of itself should arouse the spiritual nature.

The Sabbath should be observed by private prayer. The time on this day is all the Lord's; and in our closets we can talk to him, the ever living God. Yes; even if in agony of spirit, we may there wrestle with him alone till the blessing come, as Jacob did with the mysterious visitor by the brook Jabbok.

We should also profit by the public means of grace—the prayer service, the public worship, and the preached word. The ability of the soldier in battle depends much upon the drill. The church is the place in which Christian soldiers may drill; but the battle field is the world in which he lives six days of the week, and which his drill should prepare him to take for Christ.

In our observance of this holy day, we should keep constantly in mind that we are preparing to enter into that blessed rest which the Sabbath typifies. Israel, in her journeyings, ever remembered the promised Canaan, and longed for its rest. Our Sabbath pictures a land of heavenly rest; and it is nearer now than when we first believed. Its pleasures are beyond the power of man to conceive. Its glory cannot be expressed in human words. Its blessedness will satisfy, and its joys are never ending.

> "When we've been there ten thousand years,
> Bright shining as the sun,
> We've no less days to sing God's praise,
> Than when we first begun."

A true observance of the Christian Sabbath will enable us, by faith, to see the land that is very far off, and something of the King in his beauty who dwells there.

XVII.

THE RIGHTEOUS AND THE WICKED.

HARVEY JOHNSON, D. D.,
Pastor of the Union Baptist Church, Baltimore, Md.

"Then shall ye return and discern between the righteous and the wicked ; between him that serveth God, and him that serveth him not."—MALACHI 3 : 18.

THAT there are two such classes of mankind as the righteous and wicked I think the text clearly teaches. And that there is a radical and essential difference between them other passages of Scripture prove. That there are righteous and wicked persons is proven not only by the plain declarations of the Scriptures, but from the facts connected with the individual lives of people of all ages. We are early informed, in the word of God, of a righteous Abel and a wicked Cain ; of a righteous Noah and a wicked world in which he lived ; also, of righteous Lot and the wicked inhabitants of Sodom and Gomorrah ; and Malachi, in the text, informs us that there is a righteous and a wicked class, and that there is a difference between them, and that the difference is a discernible one ; for he says : "Ye shall return, and discern between the righteous and the wicked."

In what, then, does this essential difference consist ? The difference is to be seen in the fact that the wicked are born once only, but the righteous are born again, and are therefore removed from the natural sinful state into a state of holiness and righteousness. It is a state of holiness because they are born of God. (See John 1 : 13.) This passage reads: "Which were born, not of blood, nor of the will of the flesh, nor of the will of man, but of God." And being born of God, the Apostle Paul, in Rom. 8 : 17, says they are "heirs of God, and joint heirs with Christ"; and they are therefore partakers of the holiness of God. There is indeed a radical and essential difference, for it is more than the idea of a simple imputation to us of Christ's righteousness, which is the placing of his righteousness over against our sins ; or, in other words, God taking the righteousness of Christ and counting it as our own. Yes, it is all of that, and more, far more, for there is an impartation as well as an imputation. The imputation is a legal act, and is essential to Christ's fulfillment of his agreement with the Father to make whole the divine law, which man had broken, and to thus make possible the way back to God for poor fallen man. But I do not understand that that act of itself would make man any better *in himself*, but as simply opening up a way for his return to God. So there must be something else done, in order that we may see God and dwell with him in happiness and peace. Our first parents had not an imputed righteousness, but an indwelling righteousness, and it was essential to their remaining in the garden of Eden. They had it, for it was one of their endowments when God created them, and they retained and enjoyed it until they disobeyed their Creator. That single act produced a twofold effect : it broke the divine law, and transformed the violators into sinners.

Now I hold that imputed righteousness, or Christ

righteousness, counted to us, being a legal act, prepares the way for us to God; and by the impartation of his righteousness,—or, in other words, we being partakers of his divine holiness,—we become fit subjects to dwell with him in heaven.

The writer to the Hebrews (12 : 10) says that it is the purpose and will of God that we be partakers of his holiness. Of course, I mean his communicative holiness, which we get through Christ, and by the operation of the Holy Spirit. And Peter also tells us that it is the purpose of God that we be partakers of the divine nature. (See 2 Peter 1 : 4.) This holiness and this new nature are made ours by faith in Jesus Christ, because the new birth is ours, by faith; for no man is born again until he exercises faith in the Son of God. Hence, all men who remain in an impenitent and unbelieving state are wicked, and therefore under condemnation. (John 3 : 18.) "He that believeth on him is not condemned; but he that believeth not is condemned already, because he hath not believed on the only begotten Son of God."

Another difference between the righteous and the wicked is that the righteous hath hope in his death, say the Scriptures; for Solomon, in Prov. 14 : 32, uses these positive words : "The wicked is driven away in his wickedness, but the righteous hath hope in his death." What a vast difference is here stated to exist between the righteous and the wicked! The expectation of the one is cut off, but the hope of the other continues—the hope of a blessed immortality and resurrection of the body, its final reunion with the soul, the hope of heaven, joy, peace, and happiness. But to none of these do the wicked expect to come.

I have thus far been aiming to show the difference

that exists between the righteous and the wicked, by pointing out the nature and character of the righteous; and hence stated before that the wicked were born once only, but that the righteous were born again, thus removing them from a lost and ruined state into that of being saved. This cannot be said of the unconverted and unregenerated; they remaining in the state of their old birth, or old nature, are of necessity in a state of sin, and are therefore sinners, and because sinners they are wicked. They are in sin because they are born into it. It unfits its possessor for the enjoyment of heaven; for Jesus told Nicodemus that "except a man be born again he cannot see the kingdom of God."

This sin is twofold. It is that of which we become possessors because of the first sin, and that which comes to us by actual personal transgression. There is no doubt as to the corruption of humanity by Adam's fall. The spring became vitiated, and the stream flowing therefrom became impure. It matters not how long the stream may be, nor how winding, the impurity is transmitted therewith. Such is the declaration of Scripture, such the verdict of human history. As a corroboration of this, read Gen. 6:5: "And God saw that the wickedness of man was great in the earth, and that every imagination of the thoughts of his heart was only evil continually." The period to which this relates is quite far removed from Adam, and yet God says that every imagination of the thoughts of the heart was only evil continually. Original sin, the sin of Adam when he broke the divine command by partaking of the forbidden fruit, severed as it were the union between him and God, and when the tie that had bound him to God since his creation was once broken, man was left in an awful and deplorable condition, for he was then exposed to the influence of that Satanic power, that poisoned and utterly corrupted his nature; and then sin, corruption, and death entered into our world. For God had said in " the day thou eatest thereof, thou shalt surely die," and the Apostle Paul in Romans tells us that man did die, for he says: "Death passed upon all men, for that all had sinned." So sin, corruption, and death come to us through Adam's transgression. The word of God says: "Death reigned from Adam to Moses, even over them that had not sinned, after the similitude of Adam's transgression." Death reigned over them because it reigned in them, and it was in them through transmission from Adam. That we cannot explain the transmission of this evil nature and its consequences does not militate against the fact of its being so. We cannot explain how traits, physical, mental, and moral are transmitted from parent to child, but no fact of social science is more widely recognized than that. Just as a fountain transmits along all the reaches of its stream the water pure or impure, as the case may be, of which it is the source, so the fountain head of humanity sent forth its stream corrupted by the fall.

As to the goodness and justice of God in suffering this to be, it may be said that man went astray from God, and that he did it without any act on the part of God, either to prompt or compel him to do so; but, on the contrary, he was carefully warned of his danger, and told just where it lay, and a positive law was given, and a bound of safety set for him, and he was also told what the penalty of disobedience would be. (Gen. 3: 2, 3.) It will also there be seen that man accepted the advice of another rather than God,—obeyed another rather than him,—and God simply let him eat of the fruit of his ways as the result of this voluntary and willful disobedience. (Prov. 1 : 31.) "Therefore shall they eat of the fruit of their own ways"; and what else could have been done since man was endowed with the prerogative of freedom of will? He could obey or disobey. He chose to disobey, and there could be no injustice in leaving him to the consequences of his choice.

But God did not so leave him. Let those who think otherwise, and are inclined to charge God with injustice, contemplate his goodness and mercy in providing a way for the restoration of man to his love and favor, and to more than his lost position. This God has graciously done by giving his only begotten Son, to expiate our guilt on the cross of Calvary. He died, the just for the unjust; the righteous for the unrighteous; and God, in his goodness, accepted the death of Christ as a satisfactory atonement for our sins. This, I say, is God's remedy; and it is a sufficient one too, as is proven by the word of God. "The blood of Jesus Christ, his Son, cleanseth us from all sin." (1 John 1 : 7.) And it is said in Rom. 3 : 24, 25 : "Being justified freely by his grace through the redemption that is in Christ Jesus, whom God hath set forth to be a propitiation through faith in his blood, to declare his righteousness for the remission of sins that are past." Now in order to receive the benefits of this grand and glorious provision, man must believe in the efficacy of the blood of Christ to save him from his sins. He must also believe that Jesus is the Son of God, and the Sent of the Father. "If ye believe not that I am he, ye shall die in your sins," Jesus said. John the Evangelist, as recorded in John 3: 36, says: "He that believeth on the Son hath everlasting life; but he that believeth not the Son shall not see life; but the wrath of God abideth on him," because he not only sins by breaking stated and positive laws, but by refusing the remedy that God has prepared for the restoration of the broken law, and the reinstatement of man himself to his gracious favor. Yes, the wrath of God abideth on him; and, without repentance and faith in the Lord Jesus Christ, will continue to abide upon him until the day of his death, and also in the hour of death, and after death. "He that is unjust, let him be unjust still; and he which is filthy, let him be filthy still; and he that is righteous, let him be righteous still; and he that is holy, let him be holy still." (Rev. 22:11.) These are the words of John, in speaking of Christ's second and final coming, and of the end of the world.

This brings us to the thought of the future state and condition of those who continue in sin until they are called by death to meet the judgment. And here we will note another difference between the righteous and the wicked; and that is, they are to have different places of abode in the future state. Turn to Matt. 25: 34, and read these words: "Then shall the King say unto them on his right hand, Come, ye blessed of my Father, inherit the kingdom prepared for you from the foundation of the world." Now read the forty-first verse of the same chapter: "Then shall he say also unto them on his left hand, Depart from me, ye cursed, into everlasting fire, prepared for the devil and his angels." Here we have mentioned not only two different places of abode for the righteous and the wicked, but the nature of them both. One is a *kingdom* prepared, and the other is *everlasting fire* prepared. We also have their state and condition mentioned; one is blessed, and the other cursed. The passage quoted shows that the state of the wicked is perpetual; for they are commanded to depart "into everlasting fire." There are those who stop to quibble over the words "everlasting" and "eternal." They say that the word "everlasting" does not mean without end, but that the word "eternal" does; and that God, when speaking of the punishment of the wicked, uses "everlasting" instead of "eternal." Therefore they argue that the punishment of the wicked is not perpetual; but that after they have been subjected to a remedial and refining process, they will at last escape, and get to heaven, because, as is held, the word "eternal" means perpetual, and the word "everlasting" does not. But the word in the original is the same; and so this reasoning fails. If the blessedness of the righteous is perpetual, as indicated by the word eternal, so is the woe of the wicked. If the one is limited, so is the other.

Let it be remembered in this connection that God is not only good and merciful, but he is just also. His goodness and mercy may not trespass upon his justice, to forbid him to punish the wicked. But with God, goodness and mercy have their place and their time of operation. When, however, men sport away the day of mercy, and abuse his goodness, and worse than waste the time allotted for repentance and a change of life, what else could we expect than that a just God would then let justice do its work? And what could be the work of justice to a criminal but to let him suffer the full penalty of his crime? Crime must be punished until expiated. How can the unrepentant make expiation, when repentance and pardon are the means that

God has provided by which they may be saved, and they slight these?

If we grant that God has the right to punish at all, who shall set the limit to that punishment? And that he will punish for sin, we have two very striking examples: In his bringing the flood upon the world, and the destruction of Sodom and Gomorrah. Who can question, after reading such examples of his divine judgments, that he will continue to visit punishment upon those whom death finds in an unsaved state?

In conclusion, hear the admonition of Isa. 55 : 6, 7 : " Seek ye the Lord while he may be found ; call ye upon him while he is near. Let the wicked forsake his way, and the unrighteous man his thoughts ; and let him return unto the Lord, and he will have mercy upon him, and to our God, for he will abundantly pardon."

XVIII.

THE WORLD TO COME.

REV. S. W. ANDERSON, A. B.,
Pastor of Mount Zion Baptist Church, Nashville, Tenn.

"And these shall go away into everlasting punishment; but the righteous into life eternal."—MATTHEW 25 : 46.

SOMETHING may be learned from this Scripture touching the world to come, or heaven and hell. That both these exist, no believer in revelation will deny. A future existence in appropriate abodes for the righteous and the wicked is taught in many places in the Scriptures. In both the Old and the New Testament is many a passage that speaks of heaven. It is represented as a beautiful home, in which the righteous will dwell, surrounded by conditions fitted to their redeemed state. There will be no pain, sickness, sorrow, or death where they live. There are sufficient reasons to prompt us to believe that there is such a blessed home somewhere, though we know not, nor can know, its location. But we can find it by following Jesus; for "he is the way," we read in the Bible. The Psalmist says: "Thy word is a lamp unto my feet, and a light unto my path." (119 : 105.) No traveler will lose the way if he follows reliable directions.

Some have said "heaven is a place," while others say "it is only a state." The two combined, in my judgment, most nearly gives the truth; it is both a place and a state. It must have a location, as from many considerations we cannot do otherwise than conclude. Jesus said: "I go to prepare a place for you," and the word he uses indicates location. He had a material body,—changed, but material,—which could be seen and touched. To accept Jesus as the Christ is to accept his teaching, which was that there is a heaven, a place of abode, where we are to lay up eternal treasures. Jesus said to his disciples, at one time: "Rejoice, because your names are written in heaven." (Luke 10 : 20.) In 1 Cor. 15 : 40, we read: "There are also celestial bodies, and bodies terrestrial." This would seem to teach that heaven must be a place for the celestial body, as earth is for the terrestrial. God first provides the place, and then the thing. As surely as there is a body, so surely there must be a place. He never formed an order of beings without preparing for them a place to live. When he gives us "celestial bodies," he will provide a place called "heaven" for them. When God made man, he had long before made and ornamented the earth for him. Whether "bodies" are in heaven or earth, there is location for them, and the place is suited to the body. Earth is fitted for the mortal bodies we have here, and heaven will be for the immortal sanctified bodies we dwell in there.

Having pointed out the fact that heaven exists, and is a place, we proceed to consider the kind of place it is:

I. It is a place of true love, a place where all is pure.

Perfect love is not in this world. Here hatred, malice, envy, deception, hypocrisy too frequently prevail; too often, hearts are filled with the spirit of wranglings and covetousness. Brother is arrayed against brother, parent against child, child against parent, nation against nation. This world presents a fearful condition of affairs. Here the wrong spirit fills so often the human heart and crowds out every thought of love. Love is the supreme word of our language. God has commanded that we should love him supremely and our fellow-men as ourselves. Creation, the plan of salvation, the Bible—in fact, all of God's mercies and goodness and providences, if summed up in one word, would be love. In the doctrine that "God so loved the world that he gave his only begotten Son, that whosoever believeth in him should not perish, but have everlasting life" (John 3 : 16), we can see the very image of love. And such love is found only in heaven. Love is the first command : love God ; love is the second command : love your neighbor—in truth, love is the foundation of all the commands. Strip the Bible of the love there is in it, and we have no Bible. Lift from earth the glory of love that crowns it, and it becomes clothed in sackcloth. Withdraw from the universe the love that cements its bonds, and the whole fabric falls in pieces. Separate love from heaven, and no inducement remains to the saint to make it his home. But heaven is the place of love, the only place of complete love, the very source of true, pure, and unmixed love. "Thou shalt love thy neighbor as thyself" is a command given to be continually broken here ; but there it is kept, and will be kept to the letter. Every creature is full of holy love for every other creature. In heaven alone does such obtain.

II. It is a home of rest and joy.

Since our parents' fall, earth has been a place of incessant labor and fatigue. God said to Adam : "In the sweat of thy face shalt thou eat bread, till thou return unto the ground." (Gen. 3 : 19.) God's word will stand, though heaven and earth pass away. Earth ever since has been a field of continual toil and sorrow. We all have experienced this truth, but to the careworn believer there are joy and consolation in these words: "There remaineth therefore a rest to the people of God." (Heb. 4 : 9.) That rest is not here, but in the bright mansions above. The other side of the grave it is found; nowhere but in heaven. John heard these words on the Isle of Patmos: "Blessed are the dead which die in the Lord from henceforth : yea, saith the Spirit, that they may rest from their labours." (Rev. 14 : 13.) Christ says: "I will give you rest." (Matt. 11 : 28.) He no doubt mainly refers to heaven; for no perfect rest comes in this world. Again: "Ye shall find rest unto your souls." (Matt. 11 : 29.) Tired, weary souls, seek and obtain heaven, and you will enjoy this rest. The weak and heavy laden should run for heaven. It is a place of rest—rest for the soul; and with rest comes joy. There is joy in heaven among the angels, and also joy for the saints. "There is joy in the presence of the angels of God over one sinner that repenteth." (Luke 15 : 10.) If they rejoice when he repents here, how much more will they rejoice when he goes up to live with them in heaven? In Matt. 25 : 23, by way of reward to the faithful servant, the Lord said: "Enter thou into the joy of thy Lord." These, and like passages, prove beyond a shadow of doubt that heaven is a place of rest and eternal joy. It would not be complete joy otherwise. It would not be joy if there were the possibility of its termination. In heaven there is no end to joy. It is eternal.

III. A place of perfect life.

Perfect life is unending, unfettered being. It is called life to live here a few swift years. The creature of time from experience knows nothing of real life. So soon as he begins to live he begins to die. *All* time is not a minute in eternity; in fact, eternity is not measured, it has neither beginning nor end. John 1 : 4 tells us that "in him was life." This life fills heaven; it is brighter than the sun. Heaven's host enjoys its fullness. This old world breeds death; in every vein death comes. All things are either dead or dying. Man and beast, fowls of the air and fish in the sea, insects and mammoths, are all under the ban of death. "In the midst of life we are in death." Trees, grass, herbs—in fact, whatever this sin-cursed world produces—must come to naught. On the other hand, God in unity and trinity is a being of eternal life. "From everlasting to everlasting thou art God." (Ps. 90 : 2.) Angels, saints, and every inhabitant of heaven are full of life. The holy city is ever green with God's glory. Saints eat, drink, and rest under the balmy shades of the tree of life; and while listening to the sweet, low ripple of the crystal stream, they give glory to heaven's King, and cry, Holy! holy! holy! art thou Lord God Almighty, King of heaven and of earth! In heaven all is life; every hint of it is suggestive of life.

IV. We shall know each other there, and shall have the best associates.

Paul says: "For now we see through a glass darkly; but then face to face: now I know in part; but then shall I know, even as also I am known." (1 Cor. 13 : 12.) What Paul says of the Corinthian Christians will apply to other Christians as well. On this earth we can know but a little, but in heaven we shall know even as we are known. Angels could ask no more. It is wonderful knowledge to know as one is known. To see clearly and know perfectly is perfection. We are also to have the best associations. "None but the pure in heart enter heaven; neither fornicators, nor idolaters, nor adulterers, nor effeminate, nor abusers of themselves with mankind, nor thieves, nor drunkards, nor revilers, nor extortioners, shall inherit the kingdom of God." (1 Cor. 6 : 9, 10.) Seek heaven for knowledge and purity; make it your home. We shall know each other there, and shall have pure, clean, honest associates. In heaven we shall have for our associates angels, principalities, powers, cherubim, seraphim, and those who have come up through great tribulation, having washed their robes and made them white in the blood of the Lamb. And, above all, we shall be with our Father, God, and our Brother, Jesus, and our Comforter, the Holy Spirit. Color, poverty, adverse circumstances, weigh nothing. Doors stand ajar night and day to the pure in heart.

V. Heaven will be a place of peace and holiness.

Earth is over-burdened with sin and wickedness. Peace, universal peace, is not known. Discord, wrangling, confusion, and disagreement reign. Vice too often unblushingly walks the land. But God is a God of virtue. The heavenly choir, on that beautiful night, to that audience of shepherds sang: "Glory to God in the highest, and on earth peace, good will toward men." (Luke 2 : 14.) The song was an echo of what was, and is, in the home from whence the singers came. Perfect peace cannot exist where sin is. Heaven is the home of peace, because no sin is there. If you would have universal peace, make heaven your home; no other place affords it.

Heaven is also a place of holiness. As the Scriptures

teach, it is a place without sin; the angels are pure and the redeemed have been cleansed by the blood of the Lamb. Our sinful bodies must be purged of sin before heaven will be ours in full. The carnal man must be torn down and the new man made complete. The terrestrial, full of sin, gives way to the celestial, which is holy and fitted for heaven. God wishes us to be "partakers of his holiness" (Heb. 12 : 10); hence he chastises us here, that we may reach heaven, the place of holiness.

VI. Heaven is a place of knowledge.

A thirst for knowledge is a distinguishing feature between man and beasts. Man is governed by knowledge and wisdom, while the beast is guided by instinct. He who seeks perfect and complete wisdom and knowledge will fail on this side of heaven, and yet heaven's knowledge may begin here. He who had all knowledge said: "I thank thee, O Father, Lord of heaven and earth, because thou hast hid these things from the wise and prudent, and hast revealed them unto babes." (Matt. 11 : 25.) God reveals unto his children the things needful, and conceals them from the wise and prudent, even in this life. This being true, how much more will he reveal to us when we get to heaven? No limitations will be imposed on our development there. There no weak and sinful mortality will impede our progress. Our celestial bodies will help the soul to fully develop, to increase in wisdom, and to become more and more like God. Our teacher will be Jesus, our school the universe, and the term of our tuition eternity.

VII. Heaven will be a place where we can know God more completely, see his glory, and conform to his nature.

We must be separated from sin in order to know God,

take in his glory, and be conformed to his nature. Upon one occasion, Moses dared to ask God to show him his glory. (Exod. 33 : 18.) God exhibited only one attribute of his glory, namely: his "goodness." To see this Moses had to be hid in the cleft of a rock, and there could bear to see only the hinder skirt of God's garment. If man were adamant, and had eyes like the sun, he could not behold all the "goodness" of God; it is too great. God withheld from Moses a full view of his glory. God himself, his glory and his nature, are veiled in mystery. We cannot behold them this side of heaven. The Psalmist says, "the heavens declare the glory of God." So does the earth, and even the abyss; but they do not declare all; they give us but meagre hints of it. The greatest manifestation of God's glory is in his plan of salvation. See his Son as he is, and you behold the greatest embodiment of God's glory. We read of the "glory of God in the face of Jesus Christ." (2 Cor. 4 : 6.) Had you seen Jesus on earth, you could have seen God's glory; and yet you would have seen it veiled. If you would behold it perfectly, you must go to the home on high, where it will shine forth in its beauty. *There* is a combination of all the manifestations of God's glory. There our Lord and king will reveal and explain many mysteries not understood here. Believers should live close to the cross and rejoice "in hope of the glory of God." (Rom. 5 : 2.) Jesus prayed: "Father, I will that they also, whom thou hast given me, be with me where I am; that they may behold my glory." (John 17 : 24.) All who belong to Christ will be with him, and will also behold his glory. Time is too short to see God's glory; when ten thousand centuries have passed, God's glory will have just begun.

Eternity cannot be sufficient to make all its fullness known.

VIII. Heaven will have for the redeemed a full assurance of divine approval.

We feel, in a measure, at peace with God here. We possess a degree of boldness, because we have "access" to him through Christ. But we can never have full, complete assurance of divine approval until we reach heaven. Our feet must first walk the streets of the New Jerusalem, and we must be rid of the dust stains of earth. We must enter the heavenly portals to know perfectly that God is ours and we are his. Here on earth we have "hope of the glory of God." (Rom. 5 : 2.) We also have "faith and patience." (Heb. 6 : 12.) But when we reach heaven, there will be no longer need of "hope," "faith," "patience," for we shall have the full fruition of grace and know we please God. And there will be no cessation of this approval, because there can be no falling from the condition of spiritual completeness in which it is bestowed. Redeemed in heaven, we shall be redeemed forever, with the perpetual favor of God forever resting upon us.

In our text we are taught that the wicked "shall go away into everlasting punishment." The future of the wicked is unknown to us, only as is revealed in God's word. Unaided, we can know nothing. The Bible is our light on this subject; we are wholly dependent on it for knowledge. There is neither space nor need for discussing the authority of the Bible. Men far abler than I have again and again treated this matter, and their results have been accepted and the vast majority of men to whom the Bible is known acknowledge it divine.

What, then, is the doctrine of the Bible as to hell, the home of the lost?

"These shall go away into everlasting punishment." Upon its very face this tells us there is a hereafter, a future existence, and that in this future life some are to go into everlasting punishment. These are such as reject God; those who failed to feed Christ when he was hungry; give him drink; take him in; clothe him or visit him. If they did not see him thus in need, they saw those of his in want, and he says: "Inasmuch as ye did it not to one of the least of these, ye did it not to me." It is a very solemn duty to speak or write of hell, but duty demands it. Our knowledge of it is meagre and our pleasure in speaking of it is less. We much prefer to speak of the glories of heaven, and spend our time in sounding the praises of him who secures our redemption therein.

But there is a hell, and we cannot shun the duty of sometimes declaring the fact. The arguments used to prove heaven a place will prove hell a place also. God has provided a place for those who love him, and also for those who are his enemies. Heaven is for the just, and hell for the unjust, whether men or angels. How solemn are the words of the Bible to whose authority we appeal! "Fear him, which after he hath killed hath power to cast into hell." (Luke 12 : 5.) "Ye serpents, ye generation of vipers, how can ye escape the damnation of hell?" (Matt. 23 : 33.) "And if thy hand offend thee, cut it off; it is better for thee to enter into life maimed, than having two hands to go into hell, into the fire that never shall be quenched." (Mark 9 : 43.) "And fear not them which kill the body, but are not able to kill the soul; but rather fear him who is able to destroy both soul and body in hell." (Matt. 10 : 28.) The imagery is fearful and prompts to eagerness in seizing the means proffered for escape therefrom. So urgent is the Scripture on this point that we are told in the words of Jesus that it is better even to mutilate the body than to suffer it to incur the pains of hell. Terrible indeed it is. No brush could paint its horrors, no tongue describe its wretchedness— wretchedness without alleviation, wretchedness without hope.

This dark and fearful abode was prepared for Satan and the angels that followed him, and thus kept not their first estate:

"And the angels which kept not their first estate, but left their own habitation, he hath reserved in everlasting chains under darkness unto the judgment of the great day. Even as Sodom and Gomorrah, and the cities about them in like manner, giving themselves over to fornication, and going after strange flesh, are set forth for an example, suffering the vengeance of eternal fire." (Jude 6 : 7.)

I. Hell is a place without pleasure, even in sin.

The drunkard, the liar, the adulterous, will find their pleasures ended. The sun of pleasure never rises in hell, nor will there be enjoyment of any kind there.

II. It is a place where there is no longer hope in the efficacy of the Redeemer's blood.

In this life the vilest man hopes to be saved. He in a measure finds consolation in the hope that some day he will be a saved man, will be washed by the blood of Jesus. But in hell he is sensible of the fact that hope no longer remains. Not a ray of light will illumine hope there. The day of grace will be merged in the day of doom.

III. It will be a place whose inhabitants are eternally separated from the holy angels and the glorified saints.

"Go away," says the text, "into everlasting punishment." God's angels will not be there, neither will the loved ones who have come up through great tribulations. The loss of heaven is the loss of all that is dear in this life, and the life to come. Hell means an eternal separation from God, and the loss of all in which the soul can find delight. The loss of heaven will be terrible from these considerations:

(*a*) The understanding will be enlarged and active and clear. Men will see more clearly than they see here their mistakes and sins and losses.

(*b*) The affections will be keener. The power to love and hate will be at its highest. Keen affections with nothing to satisfy them is misery itself.

(*c*) The memory will be retentive. Nothing forgotten, the past will be as though it were the present. A rejected Christ, a neglected gospel, and slighted prayers will stare men in the face.

IV. It is a place of fearful punishment, both positive and negative, at which with averted gaze we are looking.

God will, God must, punish the transgressor; to believe otherwise is folly. "The soul that sinneth it shall die. The wages of sin is death." (Rom. 6 : 23.) How terrible this death is as to the finally impenitent, let this word bring anew to our minds:

"He that overcometh shall inherit all things; and I will be his God, and he shall be my son. But the fearful, and unbelieving, and the abominable, and murderers, and whoremongers, and sorcerers, and idolaters, and all liars, shall have their part in the lake which burneth with fire and brimstone: which is the second death." (Revelation 21 : 7, 8.)

Oh, that all men would praise the Lord! Oh, that all would try to overcome, that they might inherit all things! Oh, that all would hear and heed these words addressed to God's people of Israel! "I have set before you life and death, blessing and cursing; therefore choose life, that both thee and thy soul may live."

> "While God invites, how blest the day,
> How sweet the gospel's charming sound!
> Come, sinners, haste, oh, haste, away,
> While yet a pardoning God is found."

Then shall the Lord say, "Come, ye blessed," instead of "Depart."

XIX.

BAPTISTS AND BIBLE WORK.

REV. S. T. CLANTON, D D.,
Missionary of the American Baptist Publication Society for Louisiana.

"To the law and to the testimony: if they speak not according to this word, it is because there is no light in them."—ISAIAH 8 : 20.
"But the word of God grew and multiplied."—ACTS 12 : 24.

ISAIAH the inspired prophet, and Luke the inspired evangelist, give utterance in the above to words that assure us of the expansive power of the gospel, and inspire us to earnest and genuine loyalty to God's word. They are suggestive too as to the duty of organizing and perpetuating efforts for its circulation. By that word, everything in morals and religion must be tried, and its enlarged circulation increases human advancement and civilization. This indicates its unique importance, and urges to effort in employing it for the extension and upbuilding of the kingdom of Christ. As the days of antagonism and controversy are largely over, and the era of pure translation, revision, and wise circulation has set in, let us devoutly rejoice, and, at the same time, remember how dearly it cost our spiritual ancestors, who believed in and suffered for the Bible as the only standard of doctrine and duty, and by our fidelity to our sacred legacy, show ourselves their worthy sons and successors in Bible labors. They could not, nor can we, do otherwise and be true to ourselves, to the world, and to our God.

A survey of agencies for the supply of Bibles to mankind will show the position of Baptists, and their liberal gifts for this cause. History says "they were leaders in the European Bible movements," since the "British and Foreign Bible Society owed its origin to a Baptist minister." For many years they co-operated with their brethren of other denominations in sustaining the American Bible Society. In 1836, however, they formed the American and Foreign Bible Society, such formation being brought about by the refusal of the older society to sanction the translation of the Greek terms respecting baptism in missionary versions, rather than transfer the same. The American Bible Society started with this principle: "To disseminate the Scriptures in the received versions where they exist, and in the most faithful where they may be required." But in February, 1836, "the Board decided to appropriate money, for such versions only, on the foreign field, that could be consistently circulated by all religious denominations in their several schools and communities." A comparison of these two resolutions makes a decidedly unfavorable impression upon one, and fills him with aversion at acts so inconsistent.

How did this strike the patrons of the Society? We answer that they were horrified; for it was sectarianism, which was surely contrary to its constitution, contrary to the law of Christian courtesy, contrary to all instincts of honor and right, and contrary to its own special resolution of May, 1834: for the speedy distribution of the Bible to all the accessible people of the earth. The glaring injustice of this policy was keenly felt as an imposition and a violation of a sacred trust, which demanded and received a sharp rebuke. The protest against this action of the Bible Society, drawn up by Baptists, impressed not only that society, but the world, by the vigor and courtesy of its expressions. It appeared in fourteen elaborate theses, as radical in tone as Luther's in the sixteenth century. This is the *cause* of the Baptists withdrawing from the American Bible Society.

Does one inquire what followed? The answer comes: The American and Foreign Bible Society. Numerous conferences in all parts of the country, and a unanimous determination was exhibited to stand by our own translation, undisguised and unmutilated. These enthusiastic meetings and vigorous discussions of the crying need of men for the unadulterated word of God, which saves human souls, and builds up men, races, and nations in character, industry, the arts of peace and modern living, hastened the organization of the American and Foreign Bible Society, May, 1836. As at the first prayer meeting in the Acts, so here, one hundred and twenty persons were present. Fidelity in translation and wide circulation of Bible were its object. Its character was approved and Baptists were urged to contribute for its maintenance. It distributed fifteen thousand dollars for the rejected Bengali Scriptures (rejected by the American Bible Society), Judson's Burmese Version, for reprint of Marshman's Chinese Versions, and others. Each mission had every possible requisite for printing, translating, and distributing Scriptures. And such were their facilities and accuracy that others sought their services in the publication of books and documents. Various questions of policy arose, such as, Shall the society confine its work to foreign fields or at home? shall it co-operate with the American Bible Society? and, as to English Scriptures, shall translation or transferring be applied? Their protest forever committed them to translating all Greek words referring to baptism as a principle into every human language. To this the logic of events inexorably held them. In it the Baptists of both continents rejoiced and toiled.

Things went on with comparative smoothness and prosperity, till the Board expressed a doubt as to the expediency of undertaking the correction of the English Version. This created new difficulties and extraordinary interest at the anniversary. Beware of the man, not only of the one book, or who thinks he has a mission or a great idea, but beware of the man who has an amendment to the constitution! The society decided that, in its issues and circulation of English Scriptures, it shall restrict itself to the Common Version, without note or comment. This, then, gave birth to the American Bible Union. We turn to a brief notice of it.

It was organized in May, 1850, at the home of Wm. Colgate, Esq. It was composed of the friends of English translation who believed in the faithful and accurate translation of the Bible into every living language. Its catholic and organic law, and its rigid rules of translation, were such as to secure purity, fidelity, and accuracy in all its Bible work in every tongue in the world. Its new line of untried work was pushed with energy and gratifying success. It sought the education and confidence of the people by extensively scattering its effective literature. It received for its work little, if any less than one million dollars. It completed the revision of the New Testament, and much of the Old. Its Versions, like the mission of Baptists among Christians, influence every translation made by Protestants in Europe, Asia, Africa, and America; its work prepared the way for the favorable examination and candid acceptance of Revised Versions; its work praises it in the gates! The Civil War so reduced the Union that it sought consolidation with the American and Foreign Bible Society. In this it failed. Its costly library passed into the hands of the latter body. Thus ended the useful career of this institution.

We pass to the Bible Convention of 1883. We shall glance at its preliminary arrangements and its plan of amicable solution, the present needs and fruit of Bible work, and the reason for Bible Day. Note the origin of the movement. Dr. Benjamin Griffith, the untiring General Secretary of our Publication Society, read the following, passed May 29, 1882:

"*Resolved*, That we instruct the Board of this Society to invite the committee of nine recently appointed in New York, the Executive Board of the American Baptist Missionary Union, the Board of the American and Foreign Bible Society, the Board of the American Baptist Home Mission Society, and the two Boards of the Southern Baptist Convention, to appoint committees of conference for the purpose of issuing a united call to the denomination in the several States and Canada, asking for the appointment of messengers to a general meeting to consider and advise as to the best methods of conducting the denomination's Bible work."

The duty imposed was promptly and faithfully performed. All responded except the South and Canada. In briefest statement, the Baptist Bible Convention, of that conference, was its grand result. Its decision was regarded binding upon the several bodies represented by carefully selected delegates. Each society was entitled to five, and each State missionary organization one for every one thousand members or fraction thereof. Saratoga, N. Y., was the place, and May 22 and 23, 1883, the time, of this great Baptist assembly.

Conformably to instruction and agreement, the call to the Baptists of America went forth. The question of methods and agencies in the past had been a source of anxiety to the churches and a restraint upon them in many ways. All, however, felt the utmost importance of a right answer to this question to our denominational prosperity and progress. And, accordingly, four hundred and thirty-six accredited delegates met in the convention, on the like of which the American sun had never shone. There you saw the faithful secretaries, the model pastors, the great preachers, the learned theologians, the scholarly professors, the able editors, the eminent jurists, the heroic laymen, the untiring missionaries, and the saintly and fair "Daughters of the King"; there in that immortal gathering, and in the great discussion of methods and agencies, the young ministry and the honored veterans, the East and the West, alike shared, with such masterly effort and eloquence, and in such a beautiful spirit, that of it Dr. G. D. Boardman was led to exclaim : "Let not the skeptic henceforth underrate the peace-speaking power of the blood of Christ!"

Ponder for a moment on the plan of Baptist Bible work. It is as our polity—full, free, and comprehensive; it covers translation, revision, and circulation at home and abroad; it champions the Baptist position of 1833, and reaffirms it as sound and obligatory; it declares that as these principles are divine, it is our duty to circulate Versions made upon them, in all languages, as far as possible; it concedes that as there are differences of opinion in our denomination, touching the several Versions in English, as to fidelity, it is the right of every Baptist to use that Version which best commends its faithfulness to his conscience in God's sight; it requires the society selected for home Bible work to circulate the Common Version, the New Version, with the corrections of American Revisers incorporated in the text, and the translation of the American Bible Union, according to demand, and that all moneys specially designated shall be applied according to the wish of the donor; it names the American Baptist Missionary Union for the foreign Bible work of American Baptists; it requests the Union more fully to recognize the necessity of accurate translations and wide distribution of the Bible in foreign lands, and to urge distinctly and effectually the duty of more liberal giving by the churches, and that whatever additional agencies may be required to secure this result, the Union should employ. It provided that the Publication Society should maintain a Bible Department, under a secretary of equal authority with the Missionary Secretary, whose duty it shall be to collect and expend funds for home Bible work; that, as a guarantee of satisfying the chief current views among us, and as a measure of securing Baptist unity in the prosecution of our home Bible work, the American and Foreign Bible Society be requested to dissolve, and thenceforth cease to exist as a separate organization; that the Publication Society and the Home Mission Society maintain such intimate and close relations as that the very large missionary force of the latter society, among people of many languages and on our frontiers, may be effectively employed in the practical work of Bible distribution.

The great Baptist Bible Convention met, did its work, and has passed into history. On its decision, Dr. Thomas Armitage spoke. He was at his best, and beyond. It was a great day in America for the people of "one Lord, one faith, one baptism." His was the voice echoing, in no uncertain sound, the proud satisfaction and the cordial unanimity of the denomination over the result of that illustrious Bible Convention. The sight, oh, how beautiful! The spirit manifested by all, oh, how magnanimous! To my latest day, never shall I forget it. It is another page added to the literature of our great Historical Society.

This, then, is the plan of Baptist Bible work. Its acceptance by the denomination was formally declared by appropriate resolutions, by Dr. T. J. Morgan. How did it strike the laymen who are, in a sense, the bone and sinew of the work? Judging by remarks made, most favorably. For Hon. C. W. Kingsley, of Massachusetts, in an eloquent address, pledged his church for one thousand dollars for Bible work that year, and himself to be one of one hundred men to raise an endowment fund of one million dollars for Bible work? Did he *represent the sentiment of the Baptist laity?* Time alone will tell. Mr. Slater and Mr. Hand each gave one million dollars for education of the Negro race South. Did God, through Mr. Kingsley, call one hundred stewards to the aid of Bible work, that his Word may run and be glorified? One has answered; but *where are the ninety-nine?*

I pause a moment here, on the question of Bible revision. It is important, and elicited unusual interest and thought at the Boston anniversaries in May, 1889. The will of the denomination, and the interpretation of the

Saratoga Bible Convention of 1883, on *this point*, were declared by the following, by Dr. Hoyt:

"*Resolved*, That until the Board shall receive further instruction from the Society, it shall be understood that the Board be directed to prosecute the work of revision only so far as concerns the improvement of the translation of the New Testament and the further improvement and translation of the books of the Old Testament, commonly known as the Bible Union Version, and in so far as money is donated for this purpose." This enactment was adopted with enthusiastic unanimity, and great relief and comfort came to all hearts.

The lessons of the occasion, and the things that should touch our hearts regarding Bible work, are these: First, its present needs. They are, according to crying appeals and reliable statistics, exceedingly great and growing rapidly. The late Dr. Isaac C. Wynn, of New Jersey, in an address on this subject, said, among other things, this: " Baptists should do more in circulating the Bible over our land, because more needs to be done; because they can do more; because their faith and history commit them to it." There are ten millions of American citizens without a Bible, whose destitution is the more to be deplored because they do not appreciate it. Such a presence among us, is it cheering or alarming? The men on the mission fields, laboring amid darkness and desolation, moral, intellectual, and otherwise, tell you that they find in their ramblings family after family without the Bible. One among the Black Hills says: "It is nothing strange to find individuals and families without a Bible." Such too generally is the moral condition of many in every town; a condition eating as a cancer at the life of the community. If this is so on our Western frontiers, what must it be among the Negroes South, whose inherited poverty, ignorance, and oppression, of many kinds, are too well known for repetition. I need not lift up the curtain on their disordered cabins and cottages, their destitute Sunday-schools and churches, and their worthy and struggling ministry. Already the imagination of my reader has done that. An intelligent minister in the mountains of Kentucky said, what we have seen in Louisiana, and doubtless what others have seen elsewhere in the South, that six persons were seen reading from one Bible, and as many from one Testament. The people are hungry for the word. Such a starving set of men for Bibles I never saw before as I saw in Louisiana, near the Arkansas line. A big trunk was emptied in a little while. But what were they among so many? This is the sad refrain of workers as they face the piteous cry of the multitude for the bread and water of life. As they lift their eyes to you for this bread entrusted to you, will you give them a stone?

Look now at the influence first of Bible work thus far. Without any controversy, great is its effectiveness. It has made us, in an eminent sense, what we are. In its effects we rejoice, for it is our most precious heritage. It is our joy, our crown, and our strength. Its fruit is read of all men, in the love of home, in the honor of parents, in the order of society, in the conduct of the churches, and in the moral grandeur of the missionary enterprise. Do you regard the influx of a foreign population from the lowest of European society a peril to our Republic and our Sabbath? Do the evils of Romanism and socialism trouble you? Do the problems of Mormonism, divorce, and other national evils stare you in the face as eyesores in our fair land, and stagger your faith as to the fulfillment by America of its mission to itself and the world? Do these and such as these annoy you? They clamor for the Bible. It is the tree whose leaves are for the healing and education of the nations. Rev. Mr. Wheaton and five others, who were liberally educated for the Roman Catholic priesthood, by reading a Greek New Testament were led to Christ for light and salvation and into the Baptist Church as a field of labor. As the Bible triumphed gloriously here, so it will do against everything that exalts itself above God. Its pathway is known, for wherever it goes its fruit is seen, on the isles of the sea and in portions of our own land. In one of these in North Carolina a zealous worker writes: "I distributed Bibles and Testaments." What followed? A religious awaking. Scores testified promptly that the Scriptures distributed did the work. Churches, Sunday-schools, and prayer meetings followed in quick succession, and soon the whole character of the region was changed, so that it could hardly be recognized as the same country. Time would fail to multiply cases, call up witnesses, or use elaborate arguments. Nor is it necessary; for so much has already been said, and eloquently written and stored away.

Linger awhile at "Bible Day," and anew take in its significance and breadth. Evermore let it be remembered that the day is not for the Publication Society alone, but for all American Baptist Societies, agents, and agencies, local, State, and national, at home and abroad. The Society acts as the mere collecting agency, with all the work and worry implied in such a term, which business men keenly appreciate, but divides the proceeds of the day, on principles of equity and mutual agreement, among all societies. English history has its Magna Charta, and our America has its Declaration of Independence. There are Marathon, Waterloo, Bunker Hill, St. Bartholomew, and Canossa. As you meditate on each name, instinctively volumes of history flash upon you. If these things, that recount past events of a secular nature largely, have their day, shall we not perpetuate the glory and result of the greatest Bible Convention by a hearty observance of Bible Day, on second Sunday in November of each year? It holds interests dear to earth and heaven. Its celebration looks to the world's good. It is a church effort, peculiar to us. The cause, the occasion, our watched declaration to God and men, urge us in tender and solemn tone to "sow bountifully on each recurring Bible Day, in order that we may reap bountifully." This is the law here as unalterably fixed and certain in its operation as any "natural law in the spiritual world." Some one asks, Is there not a good deal of sentimentalism about this? Was there in Samaria or India, or Ireland when the famine reigned there? Was there during the days of the Christian Commission, or at the Saratoga Bible Convention in 1883? Observe the day, therefore, as "unto the Lord." Bring to it the charms of speech, the fragrance of prayer, and the golden eloquence of cheerful and liberal New Testament giving. Thus observed, the day will be glorious, and the results magnificent.

XX.

BAPTISTS AND PUBLICATION WORK.

REV. R. J. TEMPLE, B. D.,
Missionary of the American Baptist Publication Society for Mississippi.

"The work is great and large."—NEHEMIAH 4: 19.

THIS is the day of the printing press; and the printing press, in this country of free schools, is a tremendous power; the printed page is already a sentiment-moulding machine of immense proportions. Through the capacity of the printing press, the words of the Preacher: "Of making many books there is no end," are more applicable in our day than ever before. That the sentiment of these books is not always pure, and sometimes not even patriotic, is a cause of no little anxiety on the part of the religious and thoughtful; and therefore many efforts are made, from time to time, to give the public a pure and profitable literature. In aid of this effort, the publication of religious books, papers, tracts, and periodicals, is a Christian necessity. Hence the publications of the various denominational societies.

Of our own I am to write, and upon the special subject: "The Publication Work of the American Baptist Publication Society."

This Society is among the oldest and best established publication houses in our country, and is without a rival as an agency for the publication of Baptist literature; and in giving to the world a pure New Testament literature, it is one of the greatest, if not the greatest, in the world.

In 1824, in the city of Washington, the American Baptist Publication Society was organized in a private room, by twenty-five persons, although at first it was called by another name. That which gave the Society birth was the impression that grew out of the conviction in the minds of those then present, with many others, that we, as Baptists, and a growing denomination, had much more to do than we had yet attempted, as our share in giving religious reading to the world. Those sainted ones in that room at Washington—like those in that upper room at Jerusalem—interested in bringing into existence one of the greatest societies for religious work of our own, or any other denomination, have passed away; but the work of that February evening remains. The Society still lives on, has grown and is growing, has more friends, and is stronger in the confidence of the people to-day than ever before. It presents a stature of magnificence, of grandeur and goodness seldom witnessed anywhere.

It is said of the first Napoleon that the secret of his success, and his consequent greatness, was his power of concentration, of fixing his mind upon a central idea, and becoming oblivious to all else besides. Many would find the key to the success of the great "Apostle to the Gentiles" in the words: "This one thing I do." So, I believe, the growth and greatness of our Publication Society can be traced directly to its singleness of purpose, and the religious boldness with which it has been held.

The entire function of the Society, from the first until now, in one direction, and its unified object, is to spread religious literature far and wide, to lift men up to a better life here, and prepare them for the life to come. This is done through Bibles, commentaries, hymn books, library books, periodicals, of grades from young to old, helps to study the Sunday-school lesson, and a generous assortment of denominational and evangelical tracts. From its origin until now, myriads of thousands of pages have been printed, and still the one object has ever been kept in full view.

Though it has grown from penury, comparatively, to prosperity enjoyed but by few similar institutions, yet its purpose has remained the same. In its publications, the Society follows three lines: Sunday-school literature, standard religious works, and denominational literature. Of the first there are two kinds—the library book, and "lesson helps." Early in its history a prime purpose of the Publication Society was to provide such books for our Sunday-school children as would form in them a taste for good reading, and aspiration for true Christian character, and thus prepare the way for the reception of the gospel at an early age, into good and honest hearts. These books always receive the closest scrutiny; so that whether biography or history, they shall not only be true to life, but also to the story of the gospel.

Says the excellent Secretary, now more than thirty years in the service of the Society: "I grow solemn and still when I think of the library book. More than any other it is read and re-read in perhaps fifty homes a year, doing its mission for good or evil steadily all the time. No one can estimate its power, as it moulds the growing minds of the countless thousands of children who take such books to their homes and hearts. Library books, of all books, ought to be the best. And when we contemplate publishing a new work of this sort, I am always anxious about its tone and its teaching. So great is the caution in this regard, that committees of intelligent laymen and bright ministers are chosen to read and select the books the Society offers in its library list."

Of the Sunday-school lesson helps published by our Society, one who has used them for years, indeed from boyhood, and has witnessed many marked steps forward, says: "I am puzzled for words suitable to express my high appreciation of their excellence. It was no surprise nor over-statement to find this sentence in the Report of Board of Managers made at the anniversary in Washington: 'We publish what many excellent judges pronounce the best series of graded Sunday-school helps in the world.'"

Witness, now, how under the fostering care of the Society by whose agency 8,418 Sunday-schools have been organized, Baptist Sunday-school periodicals have progressed. Starting in 1857 with a single publication— "The Young Reaper"—that had in the first year a circulation of 50,000 copies monthly, this enterprise has steadily grown until now the Baptists have the most admirable and elaborate series of graded Sunday-school helps ever known. These embrace thirteen different periodicals, ranging in adaptation from the infant class child to the superintendent. Of these, over 31,000,000 copies were published during the last year. When we consider that the circulation of these papers was several millions greater last year than any year previous, who can calculate the influence upon the millions of minds and hearts of those using them?

Men and women of national reputation for scholarship,

the ablest in our denomination from every section of our country, are secured to prepare these lesson helps, adapted to the wants of our schools wherever located. And wherever used, these lesson helps and Sunday-school papers are realizing, in much larger measure than can ever be accurately known here, the purpose—the regeneration and sanctification of those into whose hands they come—for which they are sent forth. But a single instance from the pen of a New York City pastor will sufficiently illustrate the saving power of what might be termed the weakest of these periodicals: "If every one of them could do what one did in the hands of one of my little girls, the world would be speedily turned over. The school had closed. A young lad came to me and said: 'A well-dressed stranger wants to speak with you; he is in the vestibule.' And the man was shown to the study. In his hands he held a copy of 'Our Little Ones,' just given to the infant class. He was silently weeping, and endeavoring to master his emotion. 'I was standing on the corner, debating where I should go. Last night I was in a gambling hell, see here!' —exhibiting a roll of money—'and I was thinking, Shall I go home, or go on a spree? We had a little girl in our house, about four. She died three months ago. The light in my life went out. I have spreed it a good deal since then. My wife has begged me to go to church with her. But I have told her the church was a sham; though when I was small, my mother used to believe in it and take me. Well, while I was debating, a little girl, with this paper in her hand, stepped up to me and said: 'If you only went to my Sunday-school, see what a pretty paper they would give you! Don't you want mine?' 'Oh, sir,' said the man through his sobs, 'it was so unexpected, that it seemed to me, for the instant, that my own little girl was looking me in the face, and I heard her sweet voice again. I took the paper, and my eyes fell on the words: "He died for you." My pride is broken; my heart is sore. Won't you tell me about Jesus?'"

The Society's list of standard religious works is constantly increasing in quantity, but especially in quality. Among these it now catalogues its new American Commentaries, many volumes of which the public has already seen. Its corps of writers are the strong men of our denominational Israel—men whom we delight to honor, and who will cause coming generations to say of our time: "There were giants in those days." In this series of commentaries we have models. Mechanically, they are the best we have ever seen; theologically, they are sound to the core. To the study of the studious and thoughtful preacher they are indispensable. They open the word of God anew to the learned and unlearned. They are more than simply reference books; they are volumes consecutively arranged, that can be perused with ever increasing taste and profit. These books of the Society are steadily increasing in sale. Of this list of standard works, should be mentioned also a few others of prominence: "Christian Doctrine"; "Baptist Principles"; "The Church"; "Harmony of the Gospels"; "Words and Works of God"; "Perfect in Christ"; "Baptist Hymnal"; "Baptist Hymn Book."

During the past year the Society has added to its catalogue ninety-one new publications, and 382,100 have been printed. The total number of copies of books, pamphlets, tracts, and periodicals, new and old, printed during the year, is 33,000,000. This exceeds the number of copies printed the year before by 2,273,850. Suppose this printing done during the year to be in book form, with pages 16mo size, and there would be 728,946,523 such pages; being an average of 2,000,000 for each of the working days in the year. This is a very large increase over any previous year.

The total issues since the organization of the Society, February 25, 1824, until now, is over 423,000,000 copies of books, tracts, and periodicals; equal to 8,569,026,278 16mo book pages. Of these, many are denominational, setting forth in the strongest manner the distinguishing principles of Baptists. For these principles the Society has always stood, and for their promulgation has labored most abundantly. And the result is, that from its lists of books on distinctive denominational views, it would be impossible to raise a question that has not been anticipated and answered by some one of the many capable writers whose views have been published by the Society.

The remarkable advantages afforded by the Society for information on distinctive Baptist principles, in its books, pamphlets, and tracts, make ignorance of these principles almost unpardonable. Why should there be found in one of our churches members whose only reason for being Baptists is that they believe in immersion, or that their parents were Baptists, when for eight or ten cents they can have such statements of our views as are published in the little pamphlets: "Restricted Communion," "Why I am a Baptist," "Baptists and Religious Liberty," and many others. It is these principles, accepted by the regenerated heart, that make Baptists.

The Society having never lost sight of the purpose that gave it its first name, still does a large amount of tract work, both in printing and distributing. There is not in the world another tract list of the same extent of equal merit. These tracts, many of them printed on the most attractive colored cards, are pleasing to the eye, as they are profitable to the heart.

Of the power of one of these "little books," as Luther called them, I have just read the following testimony in a private letter from a minister in the Northwest, a former classmate at Morgan Park, who knew nothing of my writing this paper; nor have I his consent to use, nor has he the knowledge that I am using the contents of his letter. He writes: "A part of our forty members were a burden rather than a help, and we were seriously thinking of strengthening ourselves by prunings. But there is a brighter and bigger side to the situation. Spiritually, we have of late taken a new turn, a new leaven has manifestly begun to work. Some of our members begin to breathe a new atmosphere, and speak of it to others. A fresh vigor begins to shine through all our services; a new hope, and new love, and a new faith, are beginning to possess us. The reason is so simple, I wonder we had not found it long ago. We have ceased to ask God to reward our faithfulness, and are beginning gratefully to accept his gifts. . . . We are not trying to *earn* God's chief blessing—it's too big. . . . Not our work for Christ, but his work for us, is our hope, and there is no flaw in that. Not what *we* are, but what he is, is the ground of our faith. Not our resolves for the future, nor work of ours, but our belief in his promises, is our confidence.

"I write all this because I worked hard at the self-renunciation idea, but from the wrong side. It is the result, not the cause, of the new life. God's grace has delivered me, and I am now rejoicing in him. All this glorious change came through reading a little tract, 'The Blood of Jesus,' which most vividly presents the gist of the gospel, but the part that the natural heart is likely to miss in reading God's word. Hereafter I preach, by God's grace, not *our* work, but *his*."

The extent of the Society's publications entitles it to the name it bears so worthily. It is the Publication Society of American Baptists, and also in a sense of the Baptists of the world. Its field of operation is the United States and Canada, and in foreign countries—Sweden, Germany, France, Spain, Denmark, Norway, and China. It was a book from its shelves that gave us Oncken and over 31,000 souls in Sweden. In addition to the 400,000,000 copies of books, tracts, pamphlets, and periodicals published, its influence has been exerted through other agencies. Through the Society's missionary work, 776,072 Baptist sermons have been preached, 92,444 prayer meetings held, 1,055,341 families visited, 21,756 baptized, 886 churches organized. In property acquired, in business standing attained, to what extent has the Society proven itself a great work? During the first ten years of its history, its receipts were less than $35,000; during the last ten years the immense sum of $4,324,000 passed through the treasury. From no home sixty-six years ago, it has in its progress acquired a magnificent domicile, well located in Philadelphia, besides five branch houses in as many leading cities, East and West, North and South. The total cash receipts of the first year amounted to $373.80; to-day the total receipts of the Business Department alone amount to more than $500,000 annually, and this department, moreover, like all other departments of this great organization, is conducted with so much consecration and ability, that up to 1887 there had been accumulated $70,000, as a reserved fund for the purchase of machinery and the better equipment of the Society for its great work in every direction. What, moreover, could better attest the business qualities of the Society's managers? The Society, like Nehemiah, is engaged as a Baptist organization, in building a mighty wall of conviction and intelligent defenses about the truths of the New Jerusalem— the New Testament, the centre and sun of this sacred gospel.

For more than a half century of steady advancement this Society, the oldest, greatest, most necessary and helpful, of our Baptist societies, the pride of many of the best men of the denomination, and indispensable to all, has labored nobly. In its life of sixty-six years, who can say it has not wrought faithfully? Yet its usefulness can be increased, its work more generously sustained and enlarged. When Nehemiah began the work of rebuilding the wall of Jerusalem, he was enabled to carry it to a grand completion in spite of opposition, because upheld by two mighty supports—a royal commission and the cordial co-operation and support of his brethren. We too have the King's signet for our work in these words: "Teach them to observe all things whatsoever I have commanded you." What has been done has been accomplished through faith in God, and the sympathy and support of the Baptist churches of the land. And to-day, with every branch of its great work growing, the resources of the Society are not in its growing work, except to a limited extent, but still in the voluntary annual contributions of members of Baptist churches; offerings made in the Bible Day and Children's Day collections, and the legacies of those whom the Lord has made able and willing to help in the work. Hear what Dr. Griffith says: "Baptists have never yet begun to use the press as an evangelizing agency."

If this be true, what say the more than *three* millions of Baptists in the United States? Shall we not begin? The Society needs the support of the churches, and is entitled to it, and the churches need a strong society. Their interests are mutual; the success of the one in a large measure is the life of the other.

There is need of money with which to prosecute the growing work, and to answer the increasing demands coming in upon the Society almost daily. To the $700,000 of assets of the Business Department, and the $300,000 in the Missionary and Bible Departments, we need to add two-thirds as much again before the Society will be in possession of funds sufficient to meet present demands. There is need of more money to enlarge the tract work of the Society, to extend the denominational literature, to furnish needy ministers and students with books necessary to their usefulness and progress. There is need of more money with which to employ more men to carry the blessings of the Society into the neglected neighborhoods. To fail in this is to go backward. Can we afford to do so? In spite of those who say we cannot do more, in honor of our royal commission, we must "Go teach all nations." And to those who would deter us from helping the work, we have but one reply: The work is great and large, a work for God and man. Why should the work cease?

XXI.

BAPTISTS AND COLPORTAGE.

REV. R. T. POLLARD,
Missionary of the American Baptist Publication Society for Alabama.

"And daily in the temple, and in every house, they ceased not to teach and preach Jesus Christ."—ACTS 5 : 42.

OUR text belongs to that period in the history of Christianity when the church was struggling against contending foes, to pass the crisis which would determine its control over the world. On the one side, the priests and the captain of the temple were displeased because the apostles taught the people and preached through Jesus the resurrection of the dead (Acts 4 : 2); and on the other, there was Saul of Tarsus, who, with great rage and a bloodthirsty spirit, was so completely blind to his own wickedness, that he compelled many to blaspheme. Then Herod, desiring to become more popular, "stretched forth his hands to vex certain of the church. And he killed James, the brother of John, with the sword." (Acts 12: 1, 2.) The sudden death of the two hypocrites, Ananias and Sapphira, caused great fear in the church, and resulted in the rapid spread and advancement of the new religion. This created envy on the part of the Jewish leaders, which resulted in the imprisonment of the apostles. But God has never presented to his children the dark side of a providence but that he afterward presented the bright side. He never saddens us with " In the world ye shall have tribulation," unless he also gladdens us with "In me ye might have peace." He will not command Simon to let down the net, unless there are fishes to be caught. The obstacles thrown in their way made the believers more persistent in their efforts to carry to men the news of a dead and risen Saviour; and thus, in the language of our text, " daily in the temple, and in every house, they ceased not to teach and preach Jesus Christ."

The term used to denote this "house to house" teaching and preaching is colportage, from the Latin words meaning "neck" and "to carry," and is used to signify that kind of missionary work which is done by those who carry books, tracts, and other religious literature, going from house to house teaching and praying and preaching.

I. This kind of missionary work is one of God's appointed agencies for bringing the world unto himself; for—

1. The apostles employed it.

The Apostle Paul said unto the elders of Ephesus: "Ye know . . . how I kept back nothing that was profitable unto you, but have shewed you, and have taught you publicly, and from house to house." (Acts 20 : 18, 20.) I would not say that the apostles, in the prosecution of their work, carried books and tracts for distribution; but I dare say that had such been accessible then as now, they would have gladly carried them. But the words of Paul to the elders of the church at Ephesus show that he regarded this house to house missionary work as a sure way of reaching the hearts of men; and thus they ceased not to teach and to preach. They regarded the opportunity to work in this way as a great and useful one, particularly in view of the fact that they had already suffered disgrace by imprisonment, and the eyes of the people were turned upon them to see success or failure. They felt that "precept must be upon precept, precept upon precept; line upon line, line upon line; here a little and there a little." (Isa. 28 : 10.)

2. This method of work has the peculiar advantage of bringing one into personal contact with those who need to be impressed.

It seems that men are so constituted that when they are singled out, a stronger appeal can be made to their sensibilities, judgment, and will. Humanly speaking, had the woman of Samaria heard a sermon delivered by the Saviour on the "well of water," she would doubtless not have been impressed; but being addressed personally, his words went to her heart, and she repented.

Thus the apostles went from house to house, presenting the gospel personally to men. Imagine them in the act! What a picture they make! Filled with love for the Master, they are toiling on in the face of adverse criticism and scoffs and stripes. Their very success will add to their unpopularity and danger; for they are teaching and practicing things which are contrary to the Jewish law and ritual. But the burden of the work is upon them, and Satan's agents are active, and the Redeemer's kingdom must be established. Then, as now, the servants of the Lord must not sit still and wait for the people to come to them, nor must they wait to meet the people in some public place; they must go to the people.

"Deny thyself and take the cross,
　Is the Redeemer's great command;
Nature must count her gold but dross,
　If she would gain this heavenly land."

II. Baptists have been the pioneers in colportage work in this country.

When one has been made to understand the work done along this line by the American Baptist Publication Society,—the great agency of American Baptists for the distribution of religious literature,—he will doubtless agree with this statement. Take a few facts. A book entitled " A Story of Six Decades " has this to say about the Society's work in colportage: " Nearly a year before the American Tract Society held its first informal meeting to discuss the question of employing colporteurs, the Baptist Publication Society had announced, in 1840, its purpose to employ 'traveling agents'; and in the 'Annual Report' for 1841, the technical term, *colporteurs*, appears for the first time in any regular American document in the record given of such 'traveling agents upon the colporteur system.' "

Colportage was one of the main objects of the Society, as it is even now, as is shown by the Society's constitution. Then, as now, there were hearts full of the love of Christ, waiting and hoping to be called upon to engage in such work, though they could scarcely get a support out of it.

The first plan of the Society for prosecuting this work was the employment of itinerant ministers and missionaries without salary, but to whom a commission on the sale of books was allowed. A subsequent plan was to pay a moderate salary, with traveling expenses. The report for 1845 showed that Rev. A. B. Harris, whose field was Illinois, Missouri, and Kentucky, was employed to do colporteur work at a salary of seventy-five dollars a year. For one half year's work his report was: Miles traveled, 2,486; churches visited, 40; sermons preached, 66; addresses made, 28; religious visits, 275; volumes sold, 644; pages of tracts distributed, 9,000.

The demands for such work in foreign fields were frequent and urgent; and the Society saw that the seed sown in these places would not be lost. It was, therefore, encouraged to enlarge its borders. Oh, how true are these words: "He that goeth forth and weepeth, bearing precious seed, shall doubtless come again with rejoicing, bringing his sheaves with him." (Ps. 126 : 6.) Notice in some of the following incidents the willingness of the Holy Spirit to use men to promote his kingdom, even though they are engaged in their own secular affairs. Take the work in Germany. In the winter of 1830–31, Captain Calvin Tubbs, of Philadelphia, master of the brig "Mars," who was a Baptist, became icebound with his vessel in Hamburg. For some time he found shelter in the family of Rev. John Gerhard Oncken, then a member of the English Independent Church at Hamburg and a missionary of the Edinburgh Bible Society. Through the instrumentality and faithfulness of Captain Tubbs, Mr. Oncken was led to accept Baptist principles. Soon after this some tracts were sent to reinforce this personal presentation of the truth as made by this, perhaps, fireside preacher. As an acknowledgment of the good work done by the reading of the tracts, especially those on baptism, Mr. Oncken said: "They were quite new to me, and have tended not a little to establish me in my purpose to comply with this part of my Saviour's command as soon as possible. With Captain Tubbs' small beginning—the presentation of Baptist principles to an individual—Mr. Oncken and six others were baptized by Barnas Sears, D. D., on April 22, 1843. A church was then organized, to which Mr. Oncken was called as pastor. More tracts were sent to him by the Society, and means to publish others and to employ colporteurs.

This was but the beginning of a great work, which spread with magnificent results into Switzerland, Denmark, Norway, Sweden, Russia, and Austria. Baptist churches were established in many of the larger cities of Europe, and much was done to revolutionize public sentiment there on the subject of religious liberty. This great work was not accomplished, however, by a single effort, but through persecutions and all but death to the faithful workers. Notwithstanding all this, the work moved on, and resulted in the conversion of twenty-six thousand persons and the organization of one hundred and thirty churches. About one thousand two hundred preaching stations comprised what was styled the "German Baptist Union." The work grew so fast and showed so conspicuously the hand of God that there was started a publication concern, owned and controlled by Dr. Oncken. Persecution and oppression continued during this whole period. Finally from infirmity and age this earnest worker and servant of Jesus Christ had to give up the work.

But, thanks be to God, when one falls by the way, another is raised up to take his place. Moses may be commanded to ascend Mount Nebo to view the promised land and die, but Joshua will be spoken to by the Lord, saying: "Moses my servant is dead; now therefore arise, go over this Jordan, thou and all this people, unto the land which I do give to them, even to the children of Israel." (Josh. 1 : 2.) It may be well for David to give up the kingship, for Solomon will arise to take his place. The Publication Society, in 1878, secured the services of

Philip W. Bickel, D. D., at the request of brethren in Germany, to fill the position made vacant by the resignation of Dr. Oncken. This brother's support was assumed by the Society for three years. This benevolence on the part of the Society was both auspicious and timely, for it was evident that the brethren in Germany could not have succeeded alone. By special contributions the Society sustained Dr. Bickel in Germany a second term of three years, in which time, as is shown by Dr. Bickel's report for 1884, great good had been accomplished. The report showed that two thousand nine hundred and sixty-seven persons were baptized during the year 1883. Twenty-seven colporteurs were employed, and Bibles and other literature in abundance were scattered over Germany.

The results of the Publication Society's colporteur work in Germany were not confined to the limits of that country. They were felt in Sweden. The beginning was made by one small book, called "Pengilly on Baptism," which the Society had sent to Germany at the request of Dr. Oncken. This book came into the hands of Rev. Andreas Wiberg, a converted Lutheran minister, and made him a Baptist. "In the morning sow thy seed, and in the evening withhold not thine hand: for thou knowest not whether shall prosper either this or that, or whether they both shall be alike good." (Eccl. 11 : 6.) He became "an engine of power" in Sweden, translating tracts and books, and preparing a plan for colportage. In 1855, he was employed by the Society as a missionary colporteur. At that time, those who left the State church and became followers of the "way," suffered severe persecution; but the Lord gave the word: great was the company of them that published it. In 1866, when this work was transferred to the American Baptist Missionary Union, there were one hundred and seventy-six Baptist churches, with a membership of six thousand six hundred and six, in Sweden. In addition to this, great good was done in adjacent countries.

In 1883, Turkey received aid through this Society. Rev. John Baptist Haygooni, M. D., was supported in that country as a missionary colporteur and evangelist, and he accomplished a good work. He had come to this country without knowing of the existence of the Baptist denomination. After studying the New Testament, and comparing Baptist views with it, he became a member of a Baptist church. He was duly commissioned by the Society, and sent back to his home. Others, from the same and adjacent countries, are also under commission; so that the Society, in its colportage work, is preaching the gospel in the very places where those, in the early days of Christianity, first heard the story of the cross.

Besides the places already mentioned, the Society has supported colporteurs in France, Italy, Mexico, British Columbia, Manitoba, and Armenia, besides those in all sections of our own country. Hence it is clearly seen that the Society is awake to its duty, both as a religious and a denominational organization. As a religious organization, it spreads everywhere the common evangelical doctrines; it seeks, in the language of the Apostle to the Gentiles, "to make all men see what is the fellowship of the mystery which from the beginning of the world hath been hid in God, who created all things by Jesus Christ" (Eph. 3 : 9); and, as a denominational Society, it seeks to spread abroad those special doctrines wherein we differ from other Christians.

III. The magnanimity and faithfulness of the Publication Society have opened up greater possibilities for doing colporteur work in the future.

In this, and other countries where the Society has conducted this work, the denomination has learned to look at it with profound interest. The millions of pages of tracts and books that have been distributed by the Society through its colporteurs and Sunday-school missionaries have done no little in laying a strong denominational foundation and in presenting convincing proofs for the doctrines held by us. This has, therefore, made more, and stronger, supporters of the work.

And yet, although so much has been done, we cannot help remarking that so much more remains to be done. There is great religious destitution almost everywhere. If the Society had the money with which to do it, it could profitably sustain a colporteur *in every county of the United States*. As this cannot now be done, the practicable thing to aim at is to have a Baptist colporteur in every Baptist association in our land. This could easily be done, if the associations were willing to have it so, and would generously assist in supporting the work.

This work appeals strongly to all of us; especially does its claims rest upon our churches. The Saviour's command, "Go ye therefore and teach all nations," rests with binding force on all of us. Local churches are not organized to procure the salvation of believers; they are already saved. They are organized because by organization and the concentration of our forces, the great commission can more effectively be carried out. The church is God's great agency for bringing the world to himself. About the time of the great persecution following the day of Pentecost, when the disciples were scattered abroad, it is said that they preached as they went; and in Acts 11 : 22, these words are found : "Then tidings of these things came unto the ears of the church which was in Jerusalem : and they sent forth Barnabas, that he should go as far as Antioch"—to preach, of course. Notice the fact that the *church* sent Barnabas. So the churches must now support missionary laborers.

But there is also a *personal* obligation. Sometimes our churches fail to do their duty. This failure does not relieve any individual from his personal obligations. He must do something. It was never intended that any man's individuality should be completely lost in that of his church. Each man must bear his burden and do his part. He must give something for his work. His whole duty will not have been discharged until he has done what he could to send the gospel even to the cottage of the humblest and poorest man in our land.

XXII.

BAPTISTS AND SUNDAY-SCHOOL WORK.

BY THE EDITOR.

"Gather the people together, men, and women, and children, and thy stranger that is within thy gates, that they may hear, and that they may learn, and fear the Lord your God, and observe to do all the words of this law."—DEUTERONOMY 31 : 12.

DR. H. C. TRUMBULL defines a Sunday-school as "an agency of the church, by which the word of God is taught interlocutorily, or catechetically, to children and other learners clustered in groups or classes under separate teachers; all these groups or classes being associated under a common head." This department of religious work is not new. From the time when Moses gave the command found in the text, up to the present, under varied conditions and surroundings, with more or less of effectiveness, Sunday-school work in some form has been substantially done. There probably was a time during the dark ages, the true Israel of God being persecuted and scattered, when but little formal Sunday-school work was attempted; but even then it is not likely that those who loved Christ sufficiently to endure persecution for the truth's sake, would fail to impart to their children a knowledge of the way of life eternal.

It is but little more than a century since what is called the modern Sunday-school came into existence; and it is an interesting fact that Robert Raikes did not revive the

Sunday-school idea, and shape the work after the Jewish model found in the Old Testament; and that the farther we get from the time of Raikes, and the more our work is developed, the nearer we really are in the thing taught, in the manner of teaching and in the people taught, to the original and primitive model. The evolution of the Sunday-school work has brought us to the point where gathering our children and our church members together on the Lord's Day for the study of the Scriptures, we are in the true position for obeying the command which, though given to the people of ancient Israel, is in spirit, at least, equally binding upon us to-day who love the Lord.

Baptists were foremost in this modern Sunday-school work. Contemporary with Raikes was William Fox, a prominent Baptist of London, who, about the year 1780, organized a Sunday-school. Through the efforts of Mr. Fox the Sunday-school Society of England, an organization which still exists, was created. In our country the Baptists of one hundred years ago undertook the work. Schools were organized in a number of places, which, no doubt, largely contributed to our growth and prosperity. Some of our most prominent Sunday-schools were organized early in the century, and can trace an unbroken history through all the intervening years: the Sunday-school of the Second Baptist Church of Baltimore was organized in 1804; that of the First Baptist Church of Philadelphia in 1815, and several others in 1816. And the subsequent history of the denomination in this line of Christian work is not unworthy of so excellent a beginning.

Baptists early began Sunday-school *mission* work, so that the present work of our American Baptist Publication Society in that line is but the natural outgrowth of what was long ago undertaken. Brief mention only can be made of this work. To show of what value it was to the West, and the bravery of the men who undertook it, and the persecutions they endured, as well as the great results achieved, I quote from the address of welcome, delivered by Rev. T. E. Welch, D. D., to the First National Baptist Sunday-school Convention, which met at St. Louis, Mo., November 2, 1869. Dr. Welch had then been preaching fifty-eight years :

"Perhaps I have been selected to deliver this address of welcome because I had the honor, in company with the Rev. John M. Peck, of organizing in this city the first Sunday-school ever formed west of the Mississippi. And, sir, when I think of the circumstances under which that school was organized, and the opposition it met with in this village, then of fifteen hundred inhabitants ; when, sir, the very spot where we are now assembled was in the woods and among the bushes—one-half of the population French Catholics, and the greater portion of the other half wicked sinners, infidels, and atheists, some of whom I heard repeatedly say that the Sunday-school would never cross the Mississippi ; sir, when I think of these circumstances, and then look over this audience, and recollect that these are Sunday-school workers, that have come from the far distant parts of our wide-spread country for the very purpose of promoting the cause of Sunday-schools, I am almost ready to ask, 'Am I in a trance, or do my eyes deceive me?'

"Sir, that the audience may have some evidence of the opposition that school had to encounter, I hold in my hand the paper—the very identical paper—addressed to Brother Peck and myself in relation to that school. It is directed, 'Rev. Messrs. Welch and Peck, Present,' and indorsed upon the communication, 'From Mr. Justice,' of which no notice was ever taken execept to read it. But God protected that school. And he made it eminently useful, for out of that school grew the first colored Baptist church, of St. Louis, of which Brother Berry Meacham was one of the first pastors.

"About fifteen years ago I unexpectedly spent a Lord's Day in this city, and in the morning visited the colored church, to see how they prospered. I sat, sir, in the pulpit of the Second Church. Brother Anderson, the father of the present pastor, was then pastor. He said to me: 'Brother Welch, do you know, sir, I was one of the first scholars in that first Sunday-school you and Brother Peck formed in this city, and it was there I learned my first A B C?' In the evening of the same day I preached for the First Colored Church, of which Brother Cartwright is now the worthy pastor. A strange brother was sent, I suppose, to keep me company, and to aid me in the service, to whom, while the church and congregration were singing, I related the conversation I had with Brother Anderson. 'Why,' said he, 'I was a scholar in that very first Sunday-school myself, and there I learned my A B C, and there I received my first religious impressions.' Perhaps, Brother President, you may be able to imagine what the feelings of my heart were that Sunday night, when my head reached its pillow, to think that here were two Baptist ministers, and at least three Baptist churches, that had grown out of that Sunday-school. I felt like exclaiming, 'My soul doth magnify the Lord, my heart doth rejoice in God my Saviour.'"

On February 25, 1824, the American Baptist Publication Society was organized. It was designed, originally, as a tract society; but in 1840 its work was enlarged to embrace colportage, a method of work which the Society originated. The work was further enlarged, until the Society has now become the distinctive Sunday-school Society of American Baptists. This can best be shown by the following extract from a pamphlet published by the Society, entitled "Sixty-one Years":

"There remains to be noticed still another, and, perhaps, the greatest feature in the Society's missionary work—namely, its *Sunday-school work*. The colporteurs have always given special attention to the organization of Sunday-schools. But in 1867, the Society determined to enter more fully upon this great work; and from that time they have been appointing strictly Sunday-school missionaries.

"The present aim of the Society is to put, as it may be able, into each State and Territory of the Union a first-class Sunday-school missionary, fitted by nature and grace for this special work. These brethren are not merely charged with a general interest in Sunday-schools, but give their entire energy to this *one* work. In prosecuting it, every other interest may be incidentally promoted; but the kindling of Sunday-school fires is the great mission on which they are sent. They aim, under God, to accomplish three things: 1. To organize all the Baptist Sunday-school forces of the State for efficient work. 2. To form a new school wherever one is needed and can be sustained. 3. To improve the instruction now given in all the existing schools.

"The Society's Sunday-school missionaries differ from all other missionaries in two things: 1. They devote *their whole time to this one work*, taking a State for their field. 2. They not only organize new schools in needy places, but they devote a large part of their time, as just stated, to efforts for the improvement of schools already organized."

In some of the States—North Carolina and Alabama, for example—the Society has two missionaries.

But the Publication Society not only causes new schools to be organized and old ones to be developed; its unequaled Sunday-school publications, as is shown in the chapter on "Baptists and Publication Work," provide the soundest evangelical and strictly Scriptural instruction for all grades of children and adults; and when it is remembered that the child's mind is pliant and receptive, that the purpose in view is the conversion and training of the scholar, well and truly may it be said that "the necessity of this Sunday-school mission work cannot be overestimated. Of all the mission work in which the Lord's people can engage, there is none so influential and far reaching as that of leading children to Christ."

P

1. This Sunday-school work has special value. It has been, and must always be, a great blessing to our churches. It has caused many a church to exist. Hundreds of instances can be given where from a feeble Sunday-school a strong one has grown, which ultimately led to the organization of a church. But it is helpful to the churches also in this: that it gives to the churches its most intelligent and energetic members. From its ranks the strongest men in the ministry have always come.

2. The Sunday-school has also blessed our homes. In too many instances home religious training is practically nothing. Many homes have not a family altar. To such homes, who can estimate the value of the Sunday-school's influence? And to all homes, even though there be religious instruction and family worship, the Sunday-school is a positive helper. Hear the words of that eminent Sunday-school authority, Dr. H. Clay Trumbull:

"In short, I believe that whatever we have in America of satisfactory home religious instruction, is largely due to the Sunday-school, and that our still existing lack in this direction, in the home, is to be reached and supplied through a wise use and a wise improving of the Sunday-school, as the divinely-appointed complement of the family for the religious teaching of the young. And as in America in modern times, so everywhere and always, the brightest days of family religion have been coincident with, and have been consequent upon, the efficiency of church-school work in the community. It stands to reason, as well as accords with revelation, that this should be so." ("Yale Lectures on the Sunday-school," pp. 175, 176.)

3. The Sunday-school is helpful to the community. It gets its material from all ranks in the community. It converts this raw material of ignorance and sin into enlightenment and a Christian life. We need not fear

any evil results coming from the thousands of ignorant foreigners who flock annually to our shores, bringing with them ideas hostile to American institutions and the Christian religion, if only we can get their children into the Sunday-schools. For the power of the gospel which is preached and taught in our Sunday-schools is sufficient to uproot infidelity and Romanism, and every other agency of Satan, and plant in their stead the religion of Jesus, which is that of peace and liberty and righteousness.

4. The Sunday-school powerfully affects our denominational growth. Wherever you find a church that has no Sunday-school, you will find it to be as a candle that is burning at both ends. The days of its existence are numbered. A strong and vigorous Sunday-school of to-day means a strong and vigorous church ten or twenty years hence. Baptists are in our country (in 1890) more than three millions strong; but if all our Sunday-schools were closed our decline would soon be apparent. On the other hand, if we vigorously maintain our existing schools, and plant others in the churches yet without them, and, going beyond, occupy mission stations, our denominational growth in the next ten years will surprise us all. For, let it be remembered, we have what no other Christians have—namely, a safe and solid platform of Scriptural doctrine upon which to stand. The Bible, and the Bible alone, is our guide. Repudiating all human creeds and doctrines, we have no excuses to make for anything we teach or practice. We do not, therefore, have any defensive warfare to wage, but one that is thoroughly aggressive. We can then with all our heart call upon God to bless us in our teaching, and, praying for the Holy Spirit's help, we may take as our battle cry, "The

sword of the Lord and of Gideon," and march on to victory.

5. The Sunday-school exerts a great influence upon our denominational strength. I do not mean *numbers*, but vigor and integrity. Mere numbers do not necessarily mean strength. Many of our churches are very large, but for practical service they are of no more use than was Gideon's army before he began to discharge his men. A church is strong in proportion as every member fully counts as one. So our denomination will become stronger as the years go by, only as we give to the people a well-rounded, symmetrical development in grace and knowledge. Our ability to promote the cause of a pure Christianity is in proportion to our knowledge of the Bible. The doctrines of the New Testament are not philosophical opinions, but living truths. Regeneration, justification, adoption, sanctification, final perseverance, mean something. Back of these living truths stands the Holy Spirit, their Author, who uses them to save men and lift them up to a higher life.

When every Baptist shall fully know the doctrines of his church, and shall go forth in the power of the Spirit to teach men the same, then may we expect such a revival of our churches as we have never yet had. Now, in our Sunday-schools our doctrines are taught. In our Bible lessons on Sunday, the various truths, as we come to them, are explained and illustrated and enforced. The Baptist catechism supplements this lesson, and gives briefly, clearly, and forcefully all the truth. So that as our scholars come up from the ranks of the Sunday-schools and go into the churches, though they may then be at the beginning of the Christian life, they are certainly not at the beginning of

Christian knowledge. They enter the churches not as untaught babes who must be fed upon the milk of the word, but as those who are prepared to eat and digest the strong meat of doctrine. Such members make us strong as a denomination, and, being strong, they cannot be "tossed to and fro, and carried about with every wind of doctrine, by the sleight of men, and cunning craftiness, whereby they lie in wait to deceive" (Eph. 4 : 14), and hence our denominational integrity is preserved.

6. The Sunday-school is of value as a missionary agency. The unregenerate heart is desperately wicked. It is opposed to the teachings of the Bible. There are forms of belief which some men set forth which are so unlike the true teachings of the gospel that the sinner is not displeased to hear them, and he may even profess a ready acceptance of them. Such are not *the truth*. Our beliefs, conforming as they do to the Scriptures, are not acceptable to the sinful heart, and do not rock men to sleep in carnal security. And so it happens that to enter a wicked community with the gospel, it is often more expedient to begin with Sunday-school work. This not only gives the preacher a place to preach, but often secures for him a more favorable hearing. It always has been true, and yet is, that the shortest road to a parent's heart is through his child. By planting Sunday-schools in this way, and for this purpose, gospel fires have been lit all along our Western frontier. Wicked settlements have been converted into peaceful communities. Where once there was no God or Sabbath, there is now the church, the Sunday-school, and all the elements of a Christian civilization.

This is not theory. The value of the Sunday-school as

a missionary agency has been proven hundreds of times by the missionaries of the American Baptist Publication Society. The story of the labors of these missionaries as they went beyond the Mississippi to the Rocky Mountains, and then farther still until the banner of the Cross was lifted high on the Pacific coast, is thrilling. Many a place has been held by the itinerant Sunday-school missionary until the missionary pastor could come and hold it; and many another place has been first invaded by the Sunday-school because that way was seen to be more practicable.

This great work has been going on for many years, and much land has been conquered for the Lord, but "there remaineth yet very much land to be possessed." Our country is favored. God has wonderfully blessed us. It must all be taken for Christ. Such work as is advocated in this chapter is not only Christ-like, but also eminently patriotic.

> "Where is the man, with soul so dead,
> Who never to himself hath said,
> This is my own, my native land?"

And where is the Baptist who does not, or should not, want to see the whole country serving our Lord the Christ as he desires to be served?

This great Sunday-school work of the American Baptist Publication Society, which ought to be doubled at once, is supported in several ways. First of all, the Society has a large amount of money,—trust funds, aggregating nearly four hundred thousand dollars, the gifts of benevolent Baptists,—the interest of which is used to support missionaries. Then the Book Department of the Society appropriates annually a large sum, which is also used to support missionaries. A third source of revenue is formed by the churches. Every Baptist church in the land is expected to take a collection once a year, at least, for this Sunday-school missionary work. Wealthy individuals frequently make large donations to it. But there is one form of support which is most inspiring of all: that is the money received once a year from the observance of Children's Day. The second Sunday in June is that day. At that time, our entire Sunday-school army, from the extreme North to the extreme South, and from the Atlantic to the Pacific, has a general muster. All the Sunday-school people, young and old, bring their special contributions then to aid in supporting this great Sunday-school work, and the amount received is counted by thousands. But large as have been the aggregate offerings, they are not by any means what they should be; and the total amount received is painfully inadequate. Cries are constantly coming to the Society for more laborers from people who are spiritually hungry and destitute. They need the men, and the men are ready to go; but they can go only as the Society has the means to support them. And this increased demand for more men and money will continue for very many years to come. What Christian who loves his Lord can refuse to aid this great and glorious work?

This Children's Day service for the denomination's Sunday-school missionary work is eminently appropriate. What can be more so than that they who have been, and are being blessed by Bible instruction in the Sunday-school, should aid in having others similarly blessed? Let us all, then, enter the Sunday-school ourselves, and bring all others we can into it. Let us do all we can to make our own schools more efficient; and, taking enlarged views of the kingdom of our Lord, do what we can to increase the missionary work of this great Baptist power, which God has so signally owned and blessed,—the American Baptist Publication Society,—that thus we may fully obey the words of the text: " Gather the people together, men, and women, and children, and thy stranger that is within thy gates, that they may hear, and that they may learn, and fear the Lord your God, and observe to do all the words of this law."

XXIII.

COLORED BAPTISTS AND JOURNALISM.

W. H. STEWARD,
Editor of the American Baptist, Louisville, Ky.

"Lift up a standard for the people."—ISAIAH 62 : 10.

LET us consider:
 I. The origin of the colored Baptist newspaper.

Like many other things, the colored newspaper came because there was an imperative demand for it. The soft notes of progress among colored people were hushed amid the boisterous tones of prejudice and the mighty din of greater improvement elsewhere. The press, generally heavily burdened with theories of that whereby the nation might recover from the stroke of war, had little time to deal with things directly concerning the Negro. Even when his condition wrung from it some comment, there seemed to be a desire hastily to dismiss it. A discussion of any phase of his condition begat the intensest passion, and indignation grew to white heat. The abolition press had done its work. The Northern press felt the victory won, and there was much hesitation as to the direct course to pursue. Fearing misdirection and unwise suggestions, the Negro saw that if he could first get the ear of his race and inform his own people, it would not be difficult to reach the whole public. Religion, however crude and emotional, however unsystematic and superstitious, has been the guiding star of his people. Along this line heavy blows were struck. The easy simple faith of Baptists did not confound his untrained understanding. Rituals, creeds, and liturgical displays attracted his attention, but distracted his sense. His idea of religion was rather emotional than visual. Out of this condition sprang the colored Baptist newspaper.

II. Its growth.

The limited information as to letters among the Negroes was unfavorable for such an enterprise. Cold calculation was against it. But the earnest desire to read outweighed all calculation. So great was this desire, that many families, of which not a single member could read, subscribed for papers; other instances are mentioned to the effect that Negroes were often seen sitting in public places and riding in public conveyances with papers and books in their hands, but inverted. Reading upside down is the expression. Many of them, led on by this fierce desire for information, learned to read without instruction both papers and periodicals. The time is not far back when Baptist newspapers could be counted upon the fingers of one hand, among a constituency approaching a million and a quarter members. The rapid growth among these people intellectually, spiritually, and otherwise is due largely to the splendid educational institutions of our denomination. To-day not less than forty-five newspapers, to say nothing of the great mass of publications in books, pamphlets, and other periodicals, are printed, circulated, and read.

III. What colored papers have done.

When it is said that three-fourths of all doctrinal information among this race has been furnished by newspapers, the proportion is not overdrawn. Conventions of all kinds, associations, special meetings of all sorts, are dependent almost wholly upon these papers for the publication of their announcements and proceedings. The position which the Baptist churches have gained is due largely to this instrumentality. The rapid and positive steps toward placing themselves upon the vantage ground where their positive principles and numerical strength would properly place them, have been made possible through the guidance of the colored press. In this great conflict, for which we have been forced to contest every inch of ground, the most effective weapon has been the press. Mighty as has been the influence of the ministry among our people, with the simple principles of our faith and practice, yet their work in presenting the claims of our denomination for recognition outside of the portals of the church would have been slow and largely unfruitful but for the potent agency of the press. Here warm and uncompromising allies have faced doctrinal opposition with unflinching courage. Whatever of interest has been created, whatever of intelligence has been disseminated, whatever of advocacy inaugurated and sustained, that the press has satisfactorily achieved.

IV. What the colored press ought to do.

Grave and heavy are the responsibilities of this race. The many theories suggested concerning what the Negro would be, have in a measure been disposed of. The result in every case has been beyond the most sanguine expectations. Whether this progress shall keep the pace set in its onward march will depend upon what it considers its duty, both radical and national. The press has clearly outlined a policy of keeping before the people issues and doctrines of important moment. People read more closely and critically; more dangerous opponents, with keener and sharper judgments, come to the front with vile shafts of destruction. The press, if it does not wish to shrink from its mission, should meet determinedly the vanguard of the opposition. It should attempt as well to purify and elevate the standard in accordance with current and progressive tastes.

V. What the press can do.

Scarcely any factor of public benefit can bring about so many permanent and effective changes as the press. Eloquence, with its passionate appeals, cannot reach the masses. The press has a hold on every home, and makes demands upon every thinker. If its methods are systematic, if its arguments are convincing, nothing less can follow than a high, stanch, and intelligent Christianity.

XXIV.

BAPTISTS AND GENERAL EDUCATION.

BY THE EDITOR.

" Go through, go through the gates; prepare ye the way of the people; cast up, cast up the highway; gather out the stones; lift up a standard for the people."—ISAIAH 62 : 10.

"The people that walked in darkness have seen a great light; they that dwell in the land of the shadow of death, upon them hath the light shined."—ISAIAH 9 : 2.

IF these two passages had been written concerning the Negro race in our country, they could not more truly set forth two great facts in our history.

The one is the command which came to the Baptist denomination of the North with reference to the colored people of the South, in the dark days of a quarter of a century ago, when civil war, with its desolations, sat brooding over our land. The spirit of this command was, that these Baptists should go through the gates of war and slavery, prepare the way of the people, cast up the highway, and lift a standard for those whose bonds were being broken.

The other text would tell of our condition after the lapse of twenty-five years, during which this command of God was faithfully obeyed. Well and truly can it be said of us to-day: "The people that walked in darkness have seen a great light; they that dwell in the land of the shadow of death, upon them hath the light shined."

Glorious command; and still more glorious the sublime faith and zeal and obedience which have wrought such magnificent results! The spirit that has animated Baptists in all ages and countries has been that of absolute freedom of mind and soul. Hence the demand for soul liberty, and the sufferings heroically endured when it was denied them. Hence also the efforts put forth everywhere by them, not only for the education of those who were to preach, but also for that of the masses. It is our proud heritage, that while we have never set a bound for any man as to how much or how little education he should have before he should be allowed to follow the leadings of the Holy Spirit and preach the gospel, we have nevertheless made great sacrifices that every person who wished an education might obtain it; and this we have done simply because a man should be trained because he is a man, and because also with a developed mind he could better serve his Lord, the Christ.

One of the great triumphs of Christianity in our century is the magnificent work in the line of education done by the Northern Christians of all names for their poor, dark-faced brethren of the South. In this work Baptists have taken an honorable part. What the colored people would have been to-day without such timely help no man knows. Although the American Baptist Home Mission Society had, before the war, withdrawn its work from the South, in consequence of the difficulties and divisions growing out of slavery, yet as soon as the barred doors were thrown open, they immediately again entered this field, this time especially for the colored people. To show the zeal and purpose of this Society in the work of educating the Negro, even at a time when the general sentiment of the North was rather against him, I quote from the records of the Society.

A member of the Executive Board having been sent to Fortress Monroe in January, 1862, to inquire into the condition of the colored people, and having reported, on his return, as to the great destitution, material and spiritual, of these people, the Society, at its anniversary in Providence, R. I., May 29, 1862, adopted the following:

' *Whereas*, We recognize in the recent abolition of slavery in the District of Columbia, and in the setting free of thousands of bondmen by the advancement of our national armies into the insurgent States, a most impressive indication that Divine Providence is about to break the chains of the enslaved millions in our land, and thus furnish an unobstructed entrance for the gospel among vast multitudes who have hitherto been shut out from its pure teachings : and

" *Whereas*, We see in the entire reorganization of the social and religious state of the South, which must inevitably follow the sucful overthrow of the rebellion, the Divine Hand most distinctly and most imperatively beckoning us on to the occupancy of a field broader, more important, more promising than has ever yet invited our toils : therefore

" *Resolved*, That we recommend the Society to take immediate steps to supply with Christian instruction, by means of missionaries and teachers, the emancipated slaves—whether in the District of Columbia or in other places held by our forces—and also to inaugurate a system of operations for carrying the gospel alike to free and bond throughout the whole Southern section of our country, so fast and so far as the progress of our arms, and the restoration of order and law shall open the way."

On the 25th of June, 1862, the Executive Board voted—

"That immediate measures be taken for the occupation by our missionaries of such Southern fields as in the providence of God may be opened to our operations."

But few localities were accessible to the Society's laborers. The first points occupied were Beaufort, and the island of St. Helena, S. C., in the fall of 1862. Embarrassing questions arose concerning the constitutional right of the Society to undertake the work of education for the colored people. At length the solution thereof was found, and in September, 1863, the Executive Board announced their definite purpose to send

"Assistants to our missionaries in the South, to engage in such instruction of the colored people as will enable them to read the Bible, and to become self-supporting and self-directing churches. The Board will gladly receive all moneys contributed and designated for this purpose, and appropriate the same agreeably to the wishes of the donors; the money thus designated to be termed the Freedmen's Fund."

Hence, though initial and tentative measures were taken early in 1862, it was not until September, 1863, twenty-seven years ago, that a positive, pronounced policy was adopted.

When the war closed, it was entered upon more fully. Schools were planted, to become permanent. Teachers were secured and sent South. Money in large amounts was raised. This was the beginning of one of the greatest and most influential movements of modern times. About the same time that the Home Mission Society was beginning its work, another effort in the same line was being made by other friends of the Negro, under the guidance of Rev. Justin D. Fulton, D. D. The National Theological Institute was organized for the work of conducting Christian education among the colored people. It existed but a few years, however, performing a splendid service while it lived, and finally transferred its work to the Home

Mission Society. Among those who deserve special mention in connection with this work, at this time, is Rev. J. B. Simmons, D. D. He was Southern Secretary for the Society; and by his great energy and will, as well as because of his love for his unfortunate " brother in black," he caused school after school to be founded. His name and work should forever be gratefully remembered by colored Baptists. More than twenty-five years have passed away, and two million dollars have been spent in this work. To-day we have the following institutions:

Wayland Seminary, Washington, D. C., founded 1865.

Richmond Theological Seminary, Richmond, Va., founded 1867; incorporated 1876.

Shaw University, Raleigh, N. C., founded 1865; incorparated 1875.

Atlanta Seminary, Atlanta, Ga., founded originally at Augusta, 1867; transferred to Atlanta, 1879.

Roger Williams University, Nashville, Tenn., founded 1864; incorporated 1883.

Leland University, New Orleans, La., founded 1870; incorporated 1870.

Benedict College, Columbia, S. C., founded 1870.

Jackson College, Jackson, Miss., founded at Natchez, 1887; transferred to Jackson, 1883.

Bishop College, Marshall, Tex., founded 1881; incorporated 1885.

Selma University, Selma, Ala., founded 1878; incorporated 1878.

State University, Louisville, Ky., founded 1873; incorporated 1873.

Hartshorn Memorial College, Richmond, Va. (for women only), founded 1884; incorporated 1884.

Florida Institute, Live Oak, Fla., incorporated 1873; school opened 1880.

Spellman Seminary, Atlanta, Ga. (for women only), founded 1881.

Arkansas Baptist College, Little Rock, Ark., founded 1887.

Creek Freedman School, Tullehasse, I. T., founded 1883.

Howe Institute, New Iberia, La. (day school), established 1888.

Mather School, Beaufort, S. C.

Choctaw School, I. T. (day school).

Bible and Normal Institute, Memphis, Tenn.

The great increase in the number of our schools during the past ten years, and the general progress they have made, are due very largely to the untiring zeal of the present Secretary of the Home Mission Society, Rev. H. L. Morehouse, D. D. He has a high ideal for the education of the Negro, and is doing all he can for the building up of a solid Christian manhood among our people. All this is concerning the efforts of others for us. Now, have we nothing to do for ourselves? Let us consider this matter.

I. Do we owe a duty to our schools?

No demonination of Christians has ever increased and maintained a respectable standing which did not encourage and promote education, both in its ministry and in the masses of its membership. That its doctrines are evangelical is not sufficient. Truth, advocated by ignorance, will fail to succeed, while error, sustained by learning and skill, will at least for a time prevail. And so the history of all denominations in our country shows that they early felt the necessity of planting colleges. Harvard, and Yale, and Brown, are living witnesses of this fact. The best colleges in the United States to-day are denominational, and they came into existence in this way. The same belief shapes the policy of present missionary operations. In the Western field the feeble churches scarcely become self-supporting, before they take measures to lay the foundations of denominational schools. And in the foreign field the same thing is true. This practice is not peculiar to us, but it is the common policy of all the denominations. One denomination in particular uses its schools expressly for the purpose of promoting its growth. We may then accept the fact that our stability, and growth, and the integrity of our doctrines, depend upon our institutions of learning, and hence we owe a duty to our schools; and this duty is paramount, and immediate, and personal. For important as is the acquisition of property, the training of our ministry, and the elevation of the masses are more important. And the duty that we owe cannot be delayed in its performance. It is owing now. Nor can we discharge our obligation by proxy. We must do it ourselves. Our hands, and heads, and hearts must be placed under contribution, and their best products must be laid as cheerful gifts upon the altars of our schools of learning.

II. And since we owe a duty, let us see what it is, so as the better to discharge it.

1. We ought to make ourselves familiar with these schools. Their names, location, general character, and history, and the names of their presidents, ought to be intimately known to us. Wayland, and Richmond, and Shaw, and Benedict, and the others, should be as familiar to us as the letters of the

alphabet. Knowledge always gives birth to interest, and interest in a good cause will produce zeal and enthusiasm. It is not to our credit that we know so little about our schools, and have done so little for them; and our failure in the past to do our full duty in this direction is owing almost solely to a lack of knowledge concerning them. Call up a picture of what these schools have done. Think of the vast number of young men and women from whom the weight of ignorance has been taken, and who have been lifted into a higher life. Recall the thousands who have been brought to Christ. Think of the homes that have been reconstructed and purified, and the communities that have been regenerated. Consider the number of churches that have been blessed with a cultured ministry. Conceive, if you can, the numberless impressions for good which have been made. Place all these things side by side with mistakes that may have been made, then let us ask ourselves if we can reasonably and justly keep ourselves aloof from our schools, and refuse to learn of them, and thus fail to give them our most hearty and vigorous support?

2. We owe it to our schools to advocate their claims upon our people, and thereby induce them to send their sons and daughters as students. Our schools, taking them all in all, considering their number, the courses of study, and the ability and character of the instructors, are as good as those of any other denomination. We might in truth make the statement stronger, but we prefer to let it stand as it is. What reason is there, then, for us to send our young people to any but our own institutions? In our pulpits, upon the platform, in the homes of our people, and everywhere else, we

should commend these schools of ours. We should distinctly make it understood, *that no schools are better than ours; and that for our children ours are the best.* For our churches need cultured members, trained under Baptist auspices. Not that we so specially desire to have them, while pursuing literary studies, study the doctrines of our denomination; but that they should be kept from places and influences which will impress them with the idea that Baptist doctrines are heartless, and uncharitable, and selfish, and fit only for the uneducated and unenlightened. Too many of our young people who have been trained in schools outside of those of our own denomination have come back to us so weakened in denominational principles as to be almost ashamed that they were Baptists! We have all doubtless heard many such young people *apologizing* for our practice of restricted communion. They had been misinformed as to the reasons of our practice, and positively wrongly informed about the qualifications for the ordinance; and so, at their graduation, being completely undermined in their denominational convictions, they return home Baptists in name, but Pedobaptists in fact. Many others, yielding to persuasion, and other influences, have left the denomination entirely. This is not conjecture, but sober reality. No; we cannot afford to have our young people educated in any place where truths that are dear to us are slightingly spoken of. More than this, we need to have them trained where our doctrines are believed and practiced. While nowhere do we seek to unsettle the faith of any who attend our institutions, and while we do not teach our distinctive doctrines in the literary departments of our schools, yet we everywhere and always so exalt divine truth—*all* divine truth—that the beauty, and harmony, and truth of our principles are always made apparent, and, as a consequence, our young people return home at graduation to their churches, not with faith weakened, but strong, aggressive, and vigorous—Baptists, ready and willing, and anxious to take part in every movement that is calculated to promote the best interests of our denomination. By carelessness in this direction we have lost many of our young people. We must lose no more. Great measures are now crowding upon the attention of our churches. The evangelization of Africa, as well as missions at home, claims our intelligent consideration. We need a membership prepared by grace and education that will be able to take hold and do their duty. The Congo must be provided with laborers, and they must be supported. Our schools are prepared to train those whom God may call to go to this gold mine to dig for the precious metal, and also to train others whom God intends to remain at home and hold the ropes. We seek not the training of the head only, but over and above that, we seek the culture of the soul. Our aim is to raise up solid Christian workers, Baptist in sentiment, and simply because we believe that in this we are right.

Let no man's voice, then, be silent about our schools. Thank God for them. Bless their founders and supporters, and see to it that every young man or woman of Baptist parentage who desires an education is sent to one of our schools, and kept there.

One word more. We must cease tearing down our schools, and exalting, at our expense, those of others. We have our faults; so have others. Then show the bright side. No man is respected who is untrue to his own. An enemy may cheer you because you desert your colors and fight under his banner, but in his heart he will despise you. Be loyal to your own. If there be faults, seek to correct them; but lend your heart and hand to the development and support of what is your own, designed for the highest good of you and your children.

3. And we owe our schools a strong financial support. For these schools have come to us as a generous gift from benevolent friends. Except Selma Univerisity, and State University, and Arkansas Baptist College, and Memphis Baptist Bible and Normal School, these institutions were planted, and they are solely sustained at the expense of the American Baptist Home Mission Society. Even Selma and State and Arkansas are in large part supported by this great organization of American Baptists, while Memphis is the creation of the benevolence of the Howe family. White Christians all over our land have had to erect and sustain their colleges at their own expense, but ours have been given to us without money and without price. That such benevolence should be possible is proof of the strong interest felt for us by our more favored brethren. They have given freely, not only out of their abundance, but also, in many instances, from their scanty stores, in the expectation that we, rising at last out of the unfortunate condition in which our past history left us, into the higher life of Christian freemen, should be able and willing fully to enjoy "the liberty wherewith Christ hath made us free," and do our part in the great work of winning a lost world to our Master. Sufficient time has passed and development enough has been attained for our friends to expect from us some practical, tangible evidence of our appreciation. If now we refuse to give such evidence, then will it appear that

we are sadly lacking in manly character, or deficient in those higher moral qualities upon which our friends fondly based their hopes that we would rise, in the exercise of those rights to which the laws of nature and nature's God entitle us, and in those duties which our Christian obligation imposes upon us.

Our gratitude is placed under contribution, and rightly so. Look at these figures. In the past twenty-five years the Home Missionary Society has spent upon us, mainly for education, two million dollars. We can form no just conception of this amount. But if this money were in silver dollars, and these dollars placed side by side, they would make a silver line nearly fifty miles long. Moreover, the scholarship of our people is respected by the authorities of these institutions; hence, another reason why we should vigorously sustain these schools with our contributions. In nearly all of them colored instructors are employed. One-third of all the presidents, professors, and teachers are of our own race. Of all the missionary schools in the South, those that are Baptists employ the greatest number of colored educators. The talent and piety of the race are recognized and respected. No denomination has in this respect done as well as ours. Hence, no schools deserve from us such hearty recognition and respect in return as ours. And, again, not only are our young men and women of culture employed as instructors; our older men, those who are able to advise and govern, are either put on boards of trustees or committees of oversight. Recognizing that these schools are designed for us, the Home Mission Society is anxious that we, through experience in teaching and in governing and in supporting, should participate in full measure in this control. But in this great matter the first and the necessary condition is that we must *prove* our willingness and ability to provide full financial support. The management of a college is a thing of business, not of sentiment. Money, not good wishes, is needed to pay teachers and meet current expenses. If, therefore, we would like greater influence, we must afford larger support.

And, now, in conclusion, let me say that we have an abundant opportunity to manifest our love and devotion to our institutions. For they are poor. Not one has an adequate endowment. Many are yet needing buildings. If we do not feel able to give very much in this direction, we can give in two other ways. We can support teachers, and poor but worthy students. It would be an excellent thing, although it would be simply duty, for every State to support at least one professor in each school, and more, if possible. Really, we cannot afford to do less. Beginning in this way, we would gradually increase our gifts, developing our resources and benevolence as the years pass by, until we would be able at last to support our schools without any help from New York. There is reason to be grateful, and there is an incentive to hearty effort when we remember that no young man or woman desiring an education has any necessity for going to any institution but one of our own. We can give a good college course in most of our schools. We can give theological instruction in all of them, and a full and complete course, embracing Hebrew and Greek exegesis, in the Richmond Theological Seminary. If any desire to become physicians, they have but to go to the Leonard Medical College, at Shaw University, and receive a thorough course.

If any wish to become lawyers, the Law School at Shaw will give them the necessary training.

We thank God for our schools. We praise him for their noble founders. In our hearts, laid away in tender remembrance, are their names. We ask now only for inspiration and guidance as we, the leaders of one and a quarter millions of colored baptized believers, consecrate anew our hearts and heads and hands, and lead on to their fullest development this numerous host of men, women, and children, whom these schools of ours were planted to uplift and bless.

XXV.

BAPTISTS AND HOME MISSIONS.

REV. M. VANN,
General Missionary for Tennessee.

"Preach the gospel to every creature."—MARK 16 : 15.

NEARLY sixty years ago the American Baptist Home Mission Society, the general organization of American Baptists for home missions and church edifice work, came into existence. Founded by heroic spirits who appreciated the spiritual needs of the growing country, this great organization from a small beginning has grown to immense proportions, and has done, is yet doing, and will still do a work of untold value for our denomination. Its inspiring motto is: "North America for Christ." And so from Maine to Oregon, and from the great lakes of the North to Mexico, every section of our country has been tilled by its laborers, and every nationality has been blessed.

According to the annual report of the Board presented in May, 1890, it is shown that during the preceding year the Society conducted its work in forty-seven States and Territories; also in Ontario, Manitoba, British Columbia, Alaska, and in six States of the Mexican Republic. The whole number of laborers is eight hundred and thirty-three, being forty-three more than the preceding year. These missionaries have worked among thirteen nationalities or peoples, namely: Americans, Germans, French, Swedes, Danes, Norwegians, Indians, Negroes, Chinese, Mexicans, Bohemians, Poles, and Portuguese. From its very beginning this Society has steadily pursued its great work of preaching the gospel to the destitute. Its main instrument of work is *preaching*, and its work during nearly sixty years entitles it to the gratitude and earnest support of every American Baptist. The Society's greatest work is being done in the West. In this part of our country, where States are the creation of only a few years of work, and where the nations of Europe are emptying themselves, great and rapid work needs to be done.

It is difficult for us to conceive of the immensity of the West, and of its growth and necessities. Where to-day is the wilderness, to-morrow will be the village, and soon the city. The people who are filling up this portion of our country go there mainly to better their material condition. Those going from the East leave home and church and the Sunday behind them. Those who come from Europe bring with them their Roman Catholicism, their infidelity, their Nihilism, and their Mormonism. They seek to perpetuate their institutions and their languages on American soil. They need the gospel, must have it; and this Society is giving it to them. And the gospel must be given to these people *at once*. It cannot be permitted to allow anything hostile to our Christian civilization to take root here. The preacher must follow the pioneer; and he does. The services performed by our home missionaries on the Western frontier are in self-denial and heroic endurance equal to those performed by any missionaries anywhere. But although a mighty work has been done,

BAPTISTS AND HOME MISSIONS. 253

a mightier work is yet to be done by American Baptists; and every one of us ought to take part in it.

In this discourse it is desired particularly to speak of home missions in relation to the colored people. In the article on "Baptists and General Education," the action taken by the Society in the early days of the Civil War with reference to work among the colored people is clearly shown. In the footsteps of the soldiers the missionaries walked. The Bible followed the bullet. From "Baptist Home Missions in America," I quote the following:

"At a meeting of the Board of the Society, held June 25, 1862, it was voted that immediate measures be taken for the occupation by our missionaries of such Southern fields as in the providence of God may be opened to our operation.. At the same meeting, Rev. Isaac W. Brinkerhoff and Rev. Jonathan W. Horton were commissioned to labor among the blacks of St. Helena, S. C., and September 16, Solomon Peck, D. D., for many years Corresponding Secretary of the Missionary Union, who volunteered his services, was commissioned to Beaufort, S. C. Under his ministrations the colored members of the Baptist Church were collected, and hundreds of converts added to their number. For several years, in this locality, through the labors of Dr. Peck and others, great progress was made in the redemption of the people. In 1864, Rev. Asa Prescott and Rev. Thomas Hensen with an assistant, were at Norfolk, Va. ; Rev. E. T. Hiscox, with two assistants, at Alexandria, Va. ; Rev. Carlos Swift, at Washington, N. C. ; Rev. J. M. Mace, at Washington, D. C. ; Rev. Solomon Peck, with an assistant, at Beaufort; Rev. Andrew Wilkins, at Port Royal; Rev. W. S. Phillips, with two assistants, at St. Helena, S. C. ; Rev. J. B. White, Mississippi ; Rev. Isaac J. Hoile and Rev. H. G. Dewitt, with four assistants, at Memphis, Tenn. ; Rev. J. T. Westover, at Nashville, Tenn. ; Miss J. P. Moore, at Island No. 10, Tenn.; Rev. J. W. Horton, at New Orleans. These all have to endure hardness as good soldiers, their work involving discomforts and privations of no ordinary kind. How their hearts became wedded to their high calling is shown by the fact that nearly twenty years later some of them are still in the service, veterans, victorious!"

When the war closed, these workers were increased. Some of the ablest men in the denomination entered the service. Among those who entered at this time were Rev. C. H. Corey and Rev. James Hamilton, who did such splendid service in organizing churches in South Carolina, and Rev. D. W. Phillips, whose twenty-five years service has just closed by death at Nashville. At the same time large numbers of colored ministers, who had recently been ordained, were supported by the Society as pastors of young and growing churches; and many of these churches are now strong, numbering their members by thousands. Thus through all these years this Society has steadily pursued this work, until about two years ago it determined to give a more definite character to it by appointing Rev. William J. Simmons, D. D., of Kentucky, as District Secretary for the South. Dr. Simmons began at once to enlist the sympathy and co-operation of the colored churches in his district. His plan of operation was to appoint one general missionary in every State, generally in connection with the State Convention. The work thus organized has taken on additional interest and power. These missionaries are doing a work of incalculable value in building up the waste places, unifying the denomination, and organizing our forces for effective work. Home missions appeal strongly to us all. It is the foundation of all other mission work. All true missionary effort will be strong abroad in proportion as the churches at home are strong.

Another feature of the Home Mission Society's work is the Church Edifice Fund. This fund enables weak churches, usually in new settlements, either by gift or loan, or both, to build neat and suitable houses of worship. Hundreds of homeless churches have been helped from this fund. No worthy church is ever refused assistance. Whenever loans are made, a small interest is charged; and thus any amount which this fund may receive, having been loaned and then paid back, multiplies itself in its benefactions indefinitely.

After twenty-five years of this earnest and continued work among us, the Society expects our people to take hold and assist it. Only once a year are we asked for a contribution, and that is on "Home Mission Day." Every State has appointed such a day, and it should be observed. But the proper way to get the people to contribute to this or any other cause is by giving them information. Now the Society publishes a magazine once a month, known as "The Baptist Home Mission Monthly." It gives full and accurate information concerning the work of this great Society, and any one who reads it will have his soul fired with the spirit of missions. As the price is only fifty cents a year, it ought to be in the hands of every intelligent Baptist. "North America for Christ." What an inspiring motto! Just think of it! From end to end the land shall be given to our Saviour; and until this is done, we should increase our efforts and multiply our contributions. May God bless us and save our land for him!

XXVI.

BAPTISTS AND FOREIGN MISSIONS.

REV. P. H. A. BRAXTON,
Pastor of the Calvary Baptist Church, Baltimore, Maryland.

"Go tell my brethren. . . . Go ye therefore and teach all nations, baptizing them in the name of the Father, and of the Son, and of the Holy Ghost; teaching them to observe all things whatsoever I have commanded you: and, lo, I am with you alway, even unto the end of the world. Amen."—MATTHEW 28 : 10, 19, 20.

WE have now this command given by our blessed Lord and Saviour eighteen hundred years ago. It has been and ever must be the incentive and basis of all true missionary work; it is as human as man, as divine as God, and reaches as far as sin. Now let us see how far it has been obeyed. It is evident that the work of preaching the gospel to the nations of the earth is God's own work, and men are his instruments; because the love of God "constraineth" them.

There is a great gap in the history of Protestant missions. From 1732 to 1792 no great efforts were made for the propagation of Christianity; the true missionary spirit, as held by Paul and the apostles, seemed to have been eclipsed by the influences of the dark ages, the massacre of Christians, and the atrocities of the inquisition, until toward the close of the eighteenth century. In 1792, the Baptists of England organized the first missionary society. Members of different Christian communions longed to find ways of working together for a common Christianity in spite of denominational differences. The effect of this first Baptist missionary society throughout Christendom was unparalleled. Other societies arose in England and America, until almost every religious denomination had its own. Money was freely given, missionaries were sent abroad, and converts from Paganism were multiplied. It is not, then, without foundation that we say that the present advance in modern missions owes its existence to the Baptists.

In God's providence, Andrew Fuller and the humble shoemaker, William Carey, met in Carey's shoeshop, in Moulton, England. Andrew Fuller stepped in, perhaps to ask William Carey to fasten a shoebuckle, when, to his astonishment, he saw Carey sitting on a bench at work, with a book placed before him, and hanging up against the wall a very extensive map, of primitive make, consisting of several sheets of paper, which he had pasted together, and on which he had traced with a pen the boundaries of all the nations of the known world, and had entered on the vacant spaces such items as he had found in his reading relative to their religion and population. Here is the beginning of modern missions. It only needs a live coal to set all the world ablaze with the spirit of missions, and Carey was that coal; and the great Andrew Fuller was the tongs to take it from God's altar. For even now the bashful little shoemaker was gathering material for a pamphlet entitled "An inquiry into the obligations of Christians to use means for the conversion of heathen." It was published by a good deacon, at a cost of fifty pounds, he not being able to do it himself.

William Carey, the father of modern missions, was born

in Paulerspury, August 17, 1761. His father being a parish schoolmaster, gave his eldest son a better training in the rudiments of knowledge than most other children of his age enjoyed. At the age of fourteen, he was bound as an apprentice to a shoemaker. The exact time of his conversion is not known; he was baptized by Dr. Ryland, in the river Nen, not far from Dr. Doddridge's meeting house, at Northampton, October 15, 1783, who little thought what the poor journeyman shoemaker was to be, to do, and to dare. When first asked to preach, he complied, "because," said he, "I had not a sufficient degree of confidence to refuse." August, 1787, he was ordained pastor of the Baptist church at Moulton.

At the Association at Nottingham, May, 1792, Mr. Carey preached a sermon from Isaiah 54 : 2, 3. He took up the spirit of the passage in two exhortations, viz.: "Expect great things from God," and "Attempt great things for God." Speaking of this sermon and of its effect, Dr. Ryland says, that "if all the world had lifted their voice and wept, as did the children of Israel at Bochim, (Judges 2), I would not have wondered at the effect; it would have seemed only proportionate to the cause, so clearly did he prove the criminality of our supineness in the cause of God." The result was that it was resolved to propose a plan, to be laid before the next meeting, for having a Baptist society for propagating the gospel among the heathen; and accordingly, at the ministers' meeting at Kettering, October 2, 1792, the society was organized, and subscriptions made amounting in all to £13 2s 6d, the most memorable sum of money ever collected; we shall never see or hear the last of its influence. January 10, 1793, at the meeting held in Dr. Andrew Fuller's study,

Rev. Dr. William Carey was invited to accompany Dr. Thomas to India; and he readily accepted, and promised to go. After overcoming many difficulties, the collecting of money, the refusal of Mrs. Carey to go with him, and the diabolism of the East India Company in absolutely refusing to let them go out in one of their ships to preach the gospel, his band of missionaries, with Mrs. Carey, put to sea by a Danish ship, June 13, 1793. After a voyage of about five months, they arrived at Calcutta the eleventh day of November of the same year. After five years spent in preaching and studying the Bengali and Sanskrit languages, he fixed the scene of his labors at Mudnabati, but was not permitted by the Indian government to make a permanent establishment there. He next removed to the Danish settlement of Serampore, where he established that large and successful missionary post. Carey became an unremitting student of the Oriental languages, and lived to see forty different Oriental dialects become the channels of transmission for Christianity to as many tribes.

American Baptists were early brought face to face with the Lord's command: "Go and teach all nations, baptizing them in the name of the Father, Son, and Holy Ghost; teaching them to observe all things whatsoever I have commanded you." (Matt. 28 : 19.) To no other denomination do these words come with such emphasis as they have for Baptists. Truly, the Bible is our book, and we pay especial fealty to it. We have been and are to be the pioneers of truth. As early as 1802, the Massachusetts Baptist Missionary Society organized. Its object, as set forth in its constitution, was "to furnish occasional preaching, and to promote the knowledge of evangelical truth in the new settlements within the United States, or further, as circumstances should render it proper." The preachers who went out on this mission did not a little in awakening a wider interest in the spread of the gospel. "The Massachusetts Baptist Missionary Magazine," which started in 1803, had an extensive circulation throughout the country, and contained letters from Carey, Fuller, and Ryland, as also reports from the Serampore mission, which so fired the hearts of the American people that Dr. Carey said: "The Lord has wonderfully stirred up the whole religious world, of every denomination, to favor the work in which we are engaged, and to contribute pecuniary assistance to a large amount. Our American friends have a special claim upon our gratitude in this respect." Robert Ralston, Esq., of Philadelphia, himself being a liberal donor, was made the almoner of most of the American contributions to the Serampore mission. During the years 1806 and 1807, Dr. Carey gratefully acknowledged that he received from him six thousand dollars, but as early as 1804, female mite societies and numerous other associations were organized among the churches, and their contributions devoted mainly to the Serampore mission. But as yet there was no great denominational society in which the faith, efforts, love, brains, men, and money of this great Baptist denomination could be concentrated; but the formation of such an organization was daily approaching. In 1810, all denominations of Christians were greatly encouraged by the organization of "The American Board of Commissioners for Foreign Missions," which was national, but not denominational.

This society sprang from the pious zeal of several young

men, at that time students of theology in Andover Theological Seminary, who had submitted their views to a meeting of the Congregational ministers of Massachusetts, and declared their determination to devote themselves to preaching the gospel among the heathen. One of them was Adoniram Judson. He had corresponded with the friends of missions in England, and wrote the communication addressed by himself and associates to the ministers of the Massachusetts Association. He was sent to England to ascertain what assistance would be furnished by the London Missionary Society. He was received with warmest cordiality by the London Missionary Society, but they failed to unite with the American Board in sending him out as a missionary. At the meeting of the American Board at Worcester, his eloquence, together with that of his associates, triumphed over the continual delay, and he, Luther Rice, and the others, were ordained at Salem, Mass., February 6, 1812, and on the nineteenth of the same month, with his wife (Ann Haseltine), and Samuel and Harriet Newell, he sailed for Calcutta.

It was during his long passage across the Atlantic and Indian Oceans, and while engaged in the critical study of the Greek Testament on the subject of baptism, that his views underwent the change which had so important a bearing on the course of his subsequent life, and on the history of American missions. While thus removed from the controversies of men, amid the solitudes of the ocean, especially occupied in earnest study of the word of God, he adopted the belief that none but professed believers in Jesus Christ are intended to be subjects of baptism, and that immersion alone is the primitive mode in which the rite was administered. To this same conclusion Mrs. Judson was brought, and a few months later, Mr. Rice professed his faith in the same general views. They were subsequently baptized at Serampore, by Rev. Mr. Ward, of the English Baptist Mission.

When the intelligence of their baptism reached Boston, February, 1813, it caused no small commotion among the Baptists of that city. Immediately on the reception of Mr. Judson's letter, addressed to Dr. Baldwin, he invited several leading Baptist ministers to meet and consider the propriety of forming "a Baptist Society for Propagating the Gospel in India, and other Foreign Parts." The secretary, Dr. Sharp, was authorized to write to Mr. Judson, that the American Baptist churches would support him as their missionary in India. In September of the same year, at a meeting of the board of the Boston Society, Mr. Rice, who had returned from India, for the purpose of appealing in behalf of foreign missions, was appointed to attend a meeting of the Philadelphia Association, to represent the cause there, and among the Southern churches. Quite an interest was awakened on behalf of Foreign Missions. Accordingly, a denominational society was organized in Philadelphia, May, 1814, with Rev. Dr. Furman, of South Carolina, as president, and Dr. Baldwin, of Massachusetts, as secretary. It served to unite the distant and diversified churches in one vast, fraternal, self-denying, and beneficent purpose. What was afterward known as the Baptist Triennial Convention was organized. This convention, composed of the Baptists of all sections of the United States, continued to do missionary and educational work until 1845, when the great question of American slavery was agitating the land. The white Baptists of the

South in 1845 renounced all their rights in the Triennial Convention, and organized what is now known as the Southern Baptist Convention, which is doing effective work both at home and abroad.

The most prominent in African missions was Lott Carey, a colored man of Richmond, Va. The American Baptist missions in West Africa had their origin in the exertions of the colored Baptists of Richmond. About the year 1815, Lott Carey organized among his brethren "The Richmond African Baptist Missionary Society." The constitution specified that the money should be used for African missions only, there being no society of Baptists working in Africa at that time. Lott Carey, the pioneer missionary to Africa, was born in Charles City County, Va. As he was born a slave, no record was kept of the time of his birth, although it appears to have been about the year 1780. His father, like most of the pious Negroes of Virginia, was a member of a Baptist church. Being an only child, and his mother not being a professor of religion, Lott grew up in the company of his class, and like too many other slaves, he became intemperate and profane. In 1804, he worked as a slave in a tobacco warehouse in Richmond. Here he grew morally worse, until about the year 1807, when he was converted, and united with the First Baptist Church, in Richmond. After learning to read he was soon licensed to preach. For more than ten years he held meetings in and around Richmond, and became popular with people of his own race. He improved every spare minute in reading, and by seizing every moment not required for work in the warehouse, he picked up much miscellaneous knowledge. Some of the books he found time to read were of no immediate use to him; but, in the course of providential events, as we now trace them, they must have proved of very considerable service. As Lott Carey not only improved his mind, but was very industrious, he at length grew to be a first-rate man of business. He was likewise economical, and by saving the money he obtained from the sale of parcels of waste tobacco which were given him, and by the generosity of some of the merchants he had served, he was enabled to purchase his freedom, and that of his children.

Being now extensively known as a capable and trusty man of business, he found constant employment and earned a large salary. His first announcement of his intention to go out to Africa was made at a night school. After the leader had done speaking on African explorations, Lott Carey said : "I have been determined for a long time to go to Africa and at least to see the country for myself."

He had many inducements to stay at home. His employers offered to raise his salary two hundred dollars; he owned a good farm and a pleasant dwelling, which cost him fifteen hundred dollars. In spite of these attractions he accepted the appointment of the Triennial Convention to go out to Africa as a missionary. He was accompanied by Colin Teague, another colored man. In person, he was African all over; about six feet in height, broad shouldered, of erect frame, and of great strength. No one could handle a hogshead of tobacco with more dexterity and vigor than he. His face was square, his eyes keen, and his countenance grave and sedate. He was naturally reserved, and appeared cautious to excess. His pace, his gestures, his words were deliberately measured.

Carey sailed for Africa January 23, 1821, reaching Sierra Leone after a passage of forty-four days. The agents of the colonization society had not yet purchased any land, and therefore could not receive him and his friend Teague as cultivators of the soil. Hence they were obliged for some months to work as mechanics. Meanwhile, Carey lost his second wife, and was left with a family of young children. In 1822, he removed to Cape Mesurado, the first settlement in Liberia, where he was appointed health officer and government inspector. Very soon it was found that the little colony was threatened with invasions by the savage tribes that surrounded it. Weary of continual fear of extermination, the greater part proposed to return to Sierra Leone. But Carey resolved to stay, and he persuaded others to remain and face the enemy. During a war with the native tribes which raged for two months, he co-operated most wisely and bravely with the governor, Mr. Ashmun, in defense of the colony. At a moment when fifteen hundred wild and exasperated natives were rushing on to annihilate the settlers, he rallied the broken forces of the colony, and led them out to confront the enemy, and to drive them out of the territory. Having suffered from the diseases of the coast, he made them a study, and adopting such remedies as had proved efficacious, or had been suggested by physicians, he became a skillful medical adviser. He devoted much of his time to the sick, and contributed generously of his own limited means for the relief of the poor. Carey ever had at heart the real welfare of the colony. "He gave ample proof," says Governor Ashmun, "that he cherished the most ardent devotion to the colony, and would sooner have sacrificed life itself than jeopardize its interests."

Meanwhile, he did not neglect his duties as missionary. He was very active and efficient as pastor of the church at Monrovia, and in preaching occasionally at other places. He was likewise very useful in establishing schools, and in every way aiding the cause for which he had come. He made himself indispensable, not only as a minister of the gospel, but as a physician, and a public-spirited citizen. In 1826, he was unanimously elected vice-agent of the colony; and in 1828, when Mr. Ashmun returned to the United States, the whole executive business passed into the hands of Carey. On his death bed, Mr. Ashmun urged that he should be permanently appointed to conduct the affairs of the colony, expressing perfect confidence in his integrity, and in his ability to discharge the duties of the office. Very naturally the faithful discharge of all his various duties left Governor Carey little time for missionary work. He did not neglect any of the civil interests of Liberia; and it was while preparing to assert the rights, and to defend the property of Liberia, that he accidentally ended his mortal career. For many years after his death, there remained no other memorial of the great African than a little village in Liberia, called by the name "Carey." But in 1850, the late Rev. Eli Ball, of Virginia, while visiting all the Liberian Baptist missionary stations, as agent of the Southern Baptist Convention, searched for the spot where he was buried, and after considerable difficulty found it. The next year a marble monument was sent out, and placed over the grave.

In connection with African missions, Baptists cherish the memory of other brave men. In the year 1856, the Missionary Union withdrew its missionaries from Liberia, and offered to sell the mission premises at Bassa to the Southern Board. Messrs. Day and Jones, as early as 1846, had been appointed to labor as missionaries at Grand Bassa and Cape Palmas. John Day, a man of color, who was educated for the ministry by taking private lessons, went out to Liberia sixteen years before. He rose rapidly in influence and usefulness.

Rev. Benjamin Skinner and Rev. Lewis K. Crocker were also prominent missionaries in Africa. During the abandonment of the mission, the work was carried on by Revs. A. W. Anderson, John Lewis, and Hilary Teague, son of Colin Teague, who took charge of the above-mentioned church at Carey's death. Rev. W. W. Colley was sent out to Africa by the Southern Baptist Convention, and labored successfully there from February 8, 1875, to November, 1879. After the Southern white Baptists seceded from the aforesaid Triennal Convention, in 1845, an extra session was called by the president. A constitution was adopted, expressing the wishes of the members, and in May, 1846, the organization went into operation, under the name of the American Baptist Missionary Union, with a debt of the aforesaid convention, forty thousand dollars, which was provided for by subscriptions; and all of the property, together with the engagements and liabilities, was transferred to the American Baptist Missionary Union. All the missionaries, except Rev. Mr. Shuck, of the China mission, continued with the Union, but he joined the Southern Baptist Convention. The American Baptist Missionary Union has continued to grow in numbers, wealth, and influence, until to-day it is one of the largest and most influential missionary organizations on earth. In 1856, this society withdrew its missionaries from

Africa, and did nothing until about 1885, when, providentially, the Congo mission came into its possession from the English Baptists. Mrs. C. W. Hill, who has two schools in the Bassa country, is sustained by the Woman's Baptist Missionary Society of the West. This society was organized May 9, 1871.

There were no need, if space permitted, to enter upon a discussion of the causes that operated to bring about the organization of the American Baptist Free Mission Society. Suffice it to say, that it grew out of the anti-slavery sentiment of the country, and lived and did its work for many years, until the cause itself of its existence was removed. It sustained missionaries in Hayti, Burmah, Africa, Japan; it also supported eighteen missionaries in the Western States and territories, and during and subsequent to the rebellion some thirty missionaries in the South.

The work of the colored Baptists of America proper, in "Foreign missions," began in the fall of 1878, when the colored Baptists of Virginia, who have ever been foremost in mission work, and have since raised the major part of the money for the work, sent Rev. Solomon Crosby to Africa, where he labored with Rev. Mr. Colley at Abrokuta in connection with the Southern Board. On the arrival of Mr. Colley, in the fall of 1879, he was employed by the colored Baptists of Virginia to canvass the United States to organize a general denominational convention among colored Baptists; and on November 24, 1880, at his call, a meeting, composed of delegates from several States, assembled in the First Baptist Church, Montgomery, Ala., and organized the Baptist Foreign Mission Convention of the United States of America, with Rev. W. H.

McAlpine, of Alabama, president, and Rev. W. W. Colley, corresponding secretary. Since that time the said convention has met annually, and thousands of dollars have been collected by the colored Baptists of the United States to sustain men in preaching the gospel in Africa. In December, 1883, the aforesaid convention sent Revs. W. W. Colley and wife, J. H. Presley and wife, J. J. Coles, and H. McKinney, as missionaries to Africa, they establishing the mission at Grand Cape Mount. The health of Rev. and Mrs. Presley soon failed, she and her child both died there, and in less than a year he returned a helpless invalid. Soon Rev. W. W. Colley's health failed also, and he returned helpless. Then the work was put in charge of Revs. Coles and McKinney, who were called from their studies in the Monrovian College to this end. The work to-day is in the hands of the natives. The Baptist African Missionary Convention of the Western States and Territories was organized January 15, 1873, and employed a number of missionaries in the home field and in Africa.

Among the earliest efforts put forth by colored Baptists for Africa was the movement in South Carolina. At the meeting of their State Convention, in May, 1878, it was voted to send a missionary to Africa. Rev. Harrison N. Bouey was chosen missionary. He accordingly went to Liberia early in 1879, and remained three years, during which time he did an excellent work. He organized two churches, two associations, and so aroused a missionary spirit as to lead to the organization of a National Baptist Convention. Of this he became corresponding secretary and financial agent. Although he returned to the United States after remaining three years in Africa, the work he inaugurated is still growing. But though much has been done by us, as this brief survey shows, very much remains for us to do. With our large membership we ought to support hundreds of missionaries, and we should not confine our offorts to Africa. We should just as well seek to evangelize other parts of the world. Our money and our talents should all be given to the Lord. The world is our field, and God has sent us into it without regard to color. A movement has been inaugurated to consolidate all the colored missionary societies with the Missionary Union. Whether this shall be or not, we must do our duty. The field is before us, the means to some extent is ours, and a command has been given which we must obey.

XXVII.

THE WORK FOR BAPTIST WOMEN.

MISS MARY V. COOK, A. M.
Professor of the Latin Language and Literature in State University, Louisville, Ky.

"And it came to pass afterward, that he went throughout every city and village, preaching and shewing the glad tidings of the kingdom of God, and the twelve were with him, and certain women, which had been healed of evil spirits and infirmities. Mary, called Magdalene, out of whom went seven devils, and Joanna, the wife of Chuza, Herod's steward, and Susanna and many others, which ministered unto him of their substance."—LUKE 8 : 1-3.

"There was at Joppa a certain disciple named Tabitha, which by interpretation is called Dorcas: this woman was full of good works and almsdeeds which she did."—ACTS 9 : 36.

WHEN Christ came into the world to redeem man from the curse of the law, he found among his followers faithful women ready to do him service. After he had preached that wonderful sermon on the mount; after he had advised, warned, and given his disciples instruction for work after he should leave them; after he had laid the foundation for his kingdom on the earth—not only were the twelve with him, but certain faithful women, who from grateful hearts, because of his goodness to them, ministered unto him of their substance. He did not spurn their devotion, as his disciples often suggested, but acknowledged their love and good deeds, and commanded that wherever the gospel should be preached throughout the world that mention should be made of the woman who anointed his head, as a memorial of her.

Redeemed by Jesus, they gratefully came forward into his blessed service to give the best fruit of their hearts and hands.

Dorcas, the good woman at Joppa, is held in high esteem for her charitable deeds. Her good works had so made her known that when she died all the widows to whom she had shown kindness stood weeping, and showed the coats and garments which Dorcas made while she was with them. These women did heart and hand work—just such work as the indwelling of the Holy Spirit prompts all to perform through divine love and consecration to the Master. The Scriptures are filled with examples of faithful women. Phebe was a missionary as well as a deaconess, and labored with Paul. How delighted she must have been when entrusted with that letter to Rome! How her heart must have swelled with gratitude as she listened to the words of commendation, urging the brethren to give attention to her in whatever she had need, for she had been a succorer of many. Also in the same letter mention is made of a large number who had been co-laborers with Paul.

The little seed sown by those few women has continued to grow, while the number of laborers has increased. God is practically settling the question of woman's work in uprooting ignorance and dispelling the light of religion and education. For many years have devout women, in America and other countries, enriched the church and blessed humanity by their praiseworthy deeds and by demonstrating the power of God to save. They have been ready to lend a helping hand, and when they were free to do all their hearts desired they formed societies and organizations, that they might be able to develop and enlighten those in utter darkness, and to assist the brethren in their well-begun work. The organizations formed by women for the extension of the kingdom of Christ are fast becoming the potent factors in taking this country for Jesus. Inspired with love for the work, they throw off the garb of selfishness, and are only anxious to be instruments in God's hands for the good of mankind and the advancement of his cause. To attain the idea of enlisting the interest of the women in this work was winning a great victory. The walls of separation which heretofore debarred them have been broken down, and the combined forces of the two sexes are a strong power against sin and ignorance.

To speak more specifically, I will give a synopsis of the work of the organizations among the white sisters; then I will show the vast good that is being done among our own women. As early as 1800 it is said that a few women in the East formed themselves into societies and did much in supplying the needs of the heathen, while some attention was given to home work. But this feeble effort vanished, to appear again on a firmer and a more enduring basis. The events of that short season and the sentiments then cherished by those women as they plied the needle to make some garment or solicited means for some needy soul, come to us to-day with a freshness and interest which the lapse of time cannot efface. Among the thoughts that daily impressed them, no one was so absorbing, or attended with such deep and anxious feeling, as that which respected the labors to which they should give their lives. Many years elapsed before another organization was attempted. Hearing of the benighted heathen who were struggling in utter darkness without the light of the gospel, the interest of the women was enlisted, their hearts were warmed, and they were anxious for the conversion of these souls. The idea took possession of them. They made it a subject of prayer and conversation, and the result was soon apparent in the organization of the Woman's Baptist Foreign Missionary Society, April 3, 1871.

This Society has its headquarters at Boston, Mass. Its report for 1888 shows the number of 29 missionaries, 4 having been sent out during the year, with 1 under appointment. Total receipts for the year were $64,668.58; total expenditures, $63,446.88. The number of circles, or contributing churches, reported in the ten States and the District of Columbia was 1,221; of contributors, 29,295; Mission Bands, 557, with 12,196 members. They have sustained 102 schools, with 3,428 pupils, and the number of baptisms reported is 146. There were 58 Bible women engaged.

This organization has done untold good. Its influence spread, the women of the West feeling that it was also their duty to assist in sending the light of salvation to those burdened with sin and idolatry. They said: "If we have the spirit of Christ, we shall do what we can to save them." With this compassion for the perishing, they organized the Woman's Baptist Foreign Missionary Society of the West, May 9, 1871. It has its headquarters at Chicago, Ill. For 1888 the receipts were: From contributors, $27,876.55; savings on exchange, $2,306.46; on foreign appropriations, $1,931.30, making a total of $32,114.31. The expenditures were: Foreign appropriations, $27,775.48, leaving a balance of $4,438.83. "The Temple Builders" had contributed $1,376.00. Two new fields had been entered. One missionary had been sent to Japan. Miss Louise C. Fleming, who is the first colored woman sent from this country to her race abroad, was sent to the Congo. The territory of this Society contains 6,988 churches, in which there are 1,035 circles and organizations of young people. The Society engaged in the support of 24 missionaries, in connection with the American Baptist Missionary Union. Nine missionaries to the Karens have schools and jungle work; one to the Burmese, Bible woman's work; two to the Telugus, mostly Bible work, and one school work; two to the Assamese, school and country work; five to the Chinese, Bible work, one medical; one to the Japanese, Bible work, and two to the Africans, schools and country work.

When quite young, Miss Joanna Moore became deeply interested in the work among the freedmen by hearing an address given in 1863 by an agent of the Freedmen's Aid Society, on the need of teachers among them, and she greatly desired to respond to the call that thus came to her. The District Secretary of the Home Mission Society secured her a commission which pledged her a small salary, and she commenced teaching on Island No. 10 till the following spring, when, the colored people being removed to Helena, Ark., she aided in the care of a colored orphan asylum. While engaged as a teacher in the South, her attention was constantly called to the humiliating degradation of her sex among the freed people, and the need of loving, earnest labors in their behalf. Her mind was impressed with what could be accomplished by women in Christian work in the homes of that people, and she determined to go to New Orleans as an evangelical missionary. At first she was supported by collections taken especially for that purpose in the churches and Sunday-schools of Northern Illinois. Her work and demands to carry it on prompted the organization of the Women's Baptist Home Mission Society, which was organized February 1, 1877, and has its headquarters at Chicago, Ill. It adopted her as its missionary, and has since carried on a most successful work among the ignorant and degraded. The good this Society has done through Miss Moore can never be estimated. She has visited thousands of homes and changed the course of as many lives. She edits a little paper called "Hope," which has been a messenger of peace and good will to many a weary and disturbed soul. If ever a servant of God was loved, Miss Moore realizes it most truly among the people for whom she has given her life, and among the ministers unto whom she ministered daily. Total receipts for 1888 were $35,691.71. Of this, $6,060.18 was designated for the Training School, and $5,812.46 were expended in the schools and the work of the American Baptist Home Mission Society, in accordance with the plans of co-operation in the frontier missions. The balance in the general fund was $3,853.51, and in the Training School Fund $1,753.12. This Society publishes a monthly paper, the "Tidings," which has a subscription of 7,200. The income from subscriptions was $1,303.93. The actual cost of publication was $1,045.24. Receipts from the sale of the "Home Mission Lessons" and other literature was $153.19, making a total on this account, $1,457.12. The number of missionaries, including Bible women and helpers, is 71. This Society is spreading a wholesome influence wherever it has workers. They go into the homes of the people and teach a higher mode of living, "believing that the moral elevation of the women and girls is the first end to be sought."

On November 15, 1887, at Tremont Temple, Boston, the Woman's American Baptist Home Mission Society was organized. This Society is composed of the women of the East. The leading object of the organization is the evangelization of the women among the freedpeople, the Indians, the heathen immigrants, and the new settlements of the West, and to support teachers wherever, on this continent, schools shall be established by the Home Mission Society. It was also felt that by organization and united effort far better work could be accomplished than was possible by separate churches; that the Home Mission Society was in need of the organized help of women on its fields for the education of the young; for visiting and teaching in houses and Sabbath-schools; and assisting poor students in the institutions established in the South. There was reason to believe that, as the Woman's Foreign Missionary Society had been for some years successfully working, auxiliary to the Missionary Union, so a woman's society for similar objects in this land might co-operate in the same way with the parent society in New York. It was not desired to have an independent body, but to be subject to the direction of the board of the American Baptist Home Mission Society. The Home Mission Society cordially welcomed this co-operation as an important auxiliary in its educational work in the West and South, where large numbers of colored people are in dense ignorance and superstition, and where the Society is unable to support all the teachers needed without additional help. The Society sent printed appeals to the women of New England, and also sent earnest sisters to visit the churches and put the claim before them. "The conviction began to grow that there was a personal duty devolving on every Christian to labor for home and native land as well as for the heathen abroad." They say: "Some one must always be tending the fires which supply the power for the distant work. These fires must always be kept burning, and the work of those who serve, constant and arduous."

This Society has thirty-eight teachers and workers under its supervision. Some whose salary they now pay as teachers were supported by them when students. Though last organized, this body has been active in its labors and persistent in its efforts. The children are also organized into "Bands," that they may be trained to the missionary work. Their little mites are used to pay teachers' salaries, and for other necessaries. The Society says: "The patter of restless young feet may seem weak and childish now, but soon they will become the measured tread of men and women, who will fill our places and carry on our work." A monthly paper, "The Echo," is published, setting forth the work of all who are interested in the work. It has six thousand and two hundred subscribers. Receipts from it in 1888, were one thousand one hundred and thirty-four dollars and thirty-seven cents.

"Self-denial Week" is practiced once a year; last year the sum of thirteen hundred dollars was realized from it. It sends barrels to schools and missionaries to be distributed among the poor. These have kept many a student in school, and have been the means of saving many a soul from sin and ignorance. Total receipts during the year, twenty-seven thousand one hundred and ninety-nine dollars and ninety-four cents, which added to a balance from the year before makes thirty thousand seven hundred and forty-eight dollars and eight cents. It has one thousand and ninety-three life members. Thus ends a brief outline of the work that is being done by the women of the West and East. The reward for their labors cannot be given on this earth; but God, who has kept the record, will abundantly pay his ministering servants when they shall be gathered together in that home prepared for them from the foundation of the world.

As a pebble dropped into the sea will send its influence to the far-off shore, so the good work started by our sisters continued to exert its power till the worthy women of our race were inspired with the same zeal; and being filled with love for God, and anxious to do something for the elevation of the race, they set about to effect a similar organization. The idea was first suggested by Rev. Wm. J. Simmons, D. D., president of the State University, Louisville, Ky. He having visited the anniversaries where the white sisters met, and hearing them tell of their success and the extent of their work, and being an organizer, determined to institute such a movement among the colored women of the State of Kentucky, believing that more good could be accomplished by putting the women to work to assist the brethren in the educational enterprises they had undertaken. He put the matter before the General Association, which heartily endorsed the idea. The women received the message with grateful hearts, and went right to work. When it was found that the sisters could not meet with the general body as was first decided, a meeting was called for them, September 18, 19, 1883, at Louisville, Ky., in Fifth Street Baptist Church. The meeting was to be called to order by Dr. Simmons, and a temporary organization was effected till after the adoption of the constitution.

That was the beginning of the Baptist Women's Educational Convention of the State of Kentucky. Its object is: 1. To encourage the attendance of the youth of our State at the State University, that they may secure a Christian education. 2. To contribute to the funds for the payment of the debt on the property of the State University. 3. To develop in its members a greater missionary spirit.

At the first session, sixteen societies were represented, with money to the amount of seven hundred and eleven dollars and fifteen cents. It was a glorious meeting. Enthusiasm ran high, and the interest for the work took deep root in the hearts of the women. It keeps a missionary in the field, whose business it is to visit and organize societies in all the churches, and to arouse the people to the necessity of sustaining the well-begun work as a denomination and a race. Much of the success of the Convention has been due to the able and wisely selected missionaries it has kept in the field. It has a society in nearly every colored church in the State, and each session has been well represented. The delegates pay their own expenses to and from the Convention, that all the money collected may go to help swell the general fund. No officer of the body is paid, except the missionary; the services of the others are given for the good of the cause. The Convention fosters "Children's Bands," for the purpose of gathering and imparting information concerning the religious and educational work in that State, and the training of the children for Christ, and the collection of funds to pay the property debt of the University. The present officers are: President, Mrs. Amanda V. Nelson, Lexington, Ky.; Secretary, Mrs. M. B. Wallace, Danville, Ky.; Corresponding Secretary, Miss Mary V. Cook, Louisville, Ky.; Secretary of Children's Bands, Miss Lucy W. Smith, Louisville, Ky.; State Missionary, Mrs. Daisy E. Harvey; General Agent, Rev. Wm. J. Simmons, D. D., Louisville, Ky. The Convention has an excellent board of managers, of which Miss Lizzie C. Crittenden is the able chairman. What might be said in praise of one of these women could be truthfully said of all. All are interested, and labor zealously for the cause. Among the brethren who have ably assisted these sisters may be mentioned Dr. Simmons, Mr. Wm. H. Steward, Rev. C. H. Parrish, and Dr. D. A. Gaddie. Total amount collected since the organization, five thousand eight hundred and eighty-nine dollars and forty-six cents. Last year the amount brought in was one thousand two hundred and one dollars and sixty-six cents, and the Convention had the pleasure and privilege of paying the last dollar due on the debt of the University property, after the gift of seven thousand eight hundred dollars was given by the Home Mission Society. It is now laboring to help cancel the remaining debt of four thousand dollars due for repairs, etc., after which the money of the Convention will go to build a girl's dormitory, and to do such other things as in its judgment the Convention shall deem best. This body will hereafter hold its regular meetings at Louisville.

Rev. E. M. Brawley, D. D., after having visited Kentucky, and noted the work of the women there, determined to form a similar organization in his State, and by his urgent appeals and energies in this direction, the women were called to meet in a convention at Selma, Ala., and there he instituted what is now known as the Baptist Women's State Convention, of Alabama. Women's Educational and Missionary Societies are organized in all churches possible. A new feature has been added to the work this year in the organization of Children's Bands. At the last convention about sixty societies represented about ten thousand members. They have as their object Selma University and Mission work; but the erection of a hall for young women on the university grounds is at present receiving all of their attention. The work already done amounts to four thousand dollars, all of which has been paid by the women. A brick yard is in successful operation, thus furnishing employment for worthy students. These women have an agent, who is employed by the year to conduct their work. This band of Christian women have as their officers, Mrs. Rebecca Pitts, Uniontown, Ala.; Mrs. Sadie H. Wright, Montgomery, Ala.; Miss Susie A. Stone, Selma, Ala. As president of this Convention, Mrs. Annie Brooks deserves especial mention; and closely allied to her is Mrs. Rebecca Pitts: the two are a power for good. Mrs. Sadie H. Wright, the secretary, is a faithful worker, never tiring; through her much good has been accomplished. Miss Susie A. Stone has served this body as financial agent for two years. Educated in Selma University, she knows its needs, and labors faithfully "for Jesus' sake," knowing that only through an educated Christian womanhood can Alabama be taken for Christ. Mrs. Emma Ware, Miss Celia J. Walker, and Mrs. Lucy Gairy, are all prominent and earnest workers. The women of Alabama are thoroughly organized, and ready and willing to make any sacrifice the work demands. The new building is to cost ten thousand dollars, and with the generous donation given by the Home Mission Society, they hope to be ready to enter the building October 1, 1890. This Convention has given much for the support of worthy objects in its State, and is designed to be the leading organization of its kind in the South. It is only four years old, and compares well with any other similar to it.

The annual session of the Women's Baptist Missionary Association was held with the First Baptist Church, Little Rock, Ark., May 18, 19, 1888. Their preamble says: "Believing that in the great work of religiously training the world, and giving the gospel to the many who are yet in darkness, the women are equally responsible, in proportion to their ability, as the other sex, and feeling that we can better accomplish these duties by being organized, we therefore banded ourselves together in an association, and adopted the following constitution for the government of the same." The design of this Association is to promote the cause of religion, education, and other important objects connected with the Redeemer's kingdom, and to develop the powers of the women of our churches, thus advancing the interest of the Baptist denomination in the State, and aiding in the general organization of Christian benevolence. The Association is subordinate to the regular Baptist State Convention. President, Mrs. R. B. White, Little Rock, Ark.; Corresponding Secretary, Mrs. Carrie Woods, Pine Bluff, Ark. Collections during the meeting amounted to one hundred and thirty-eight dollars and eighty-five cents.

The women of Texas have a movement on foot, known as the Women's Baptist Mission Society, of Texas. Its object is to cultivate a spirit of Christian benevolence in its members, by personal labor and donations to the cause of missions through the respective treasuries of the Texas Missionary Baptist State Convention, the Baptist Foreign Mission Convention, and the Women's Baptist Home Mission Society. It was organized in 1886, and has held its meetings with the State Convention. The women show earnestness and zeal for the work. They keep missionaries in the field who work among the women and children, and organize missionary societies and industrial schools. Sixty-three societies were represented in the last meeting, and their three years' work shows them to have collected three thousand five hundred and forty-six dollars and seventy cents; and eleven months' work of Sisters J. L. Peck and F. Dysart, shows eight hundred and sixteen meetings held, and eight hundred and thirty-eight garments given away. These sisters and Mrs. Maggie Thomas are among the most active and faithful. Revs. A. R. Griggs, L. M. Luke, and I. Toliver, have given this work their hearty support.

The women of Georgia have a work which is yet in its infancy. It was organized May 23, 1889, and is called Our Women's Convention. It originated with Rev. W. J. White, of Augusta, Ga., and is to assist in the work of the State. President, Mrs. Josephine Muns, Augusta, Ga.; Corresponding Secretary, Mrs. Nellie L. Cook, Augusta, Ga.; Treasurer, Mrs. Mary A. Rutherford, Rome, Ga. Receipts of the meeting, one hundred and fifty-seven dollars and ninety-two cents.

The women of South Carolina have also lately organized under the efficient leadership of Miss Maria Jones. They are attempting some local work, but are devoting their

THE WORK FOR BAPTIST WOMEN.

energies mainly to education and missions. Not many years hence there will be an organization among the women in every State in the Union. We rejoice that so much has been accomplished. These noble exemplars of enthusiastic zeal and consecrated piety have ever been found at their posts, and when orders have been given, they have responded as soldiers of Christ. Nothing, so far, has daunted them; hard places have inspired and criticisms have been the fuel that has lighted the flame of their intense activity. Every minister of the gospel should see that the sisters are at work in his church; for if their help was necessary to Christ and Paul in their labors, surely it must be doubly so to those he has left to occupy till he come. If the women of the churches are made to feel that they too are personally responsible for the salvation of the world, and are enlisted to labor by the side of the men, it will not be many years before a revolution will be felt all over this broad land, and the heathen will no longer walk in darkness, but will praise God, the light of their salvation.

Give the women the scope the Bible gives them, and let them throw the influence of their spiritual power into the churches and communities. Let them feel that they have a higher calling than the love of fashion and worldly pleasure, and that God has called them to minister unto him. Let the women in the work sound the trumpet loudly to those women who are careless and at ease in Zion. Let them put forth every effort to arouse them and lead them from their path of indifference and idleness, that they may see Christ in his glory, and spend their lives in exhibiting his attractions to others. Oh, that God would give us grace to act worthy of our trust, to do what we can for dying men, to the intent that they might have an abundant entrance into a world where death never comes.

> " Do thou thy work : it shall succeed,
>   In thine or in another's day ;
> And if denied the victor's meed,
>   Thou shalt not miss the toiler's pay."

XXVIII.

THE DUTY OF COLORED BAPTISTS IN VIEW OF THE PAST, THE PRESENT, AND THE FUTURE.

BY THE EDITOR.

"Out of weakness were made strong."—HEBREWS 11 : 34.
"What hath God wrought!"—NUMBERS 23 : 23.
"Weighed in the balances."—DANIEL 5 : 27.
"Quit you like men, be strong."—1 CORINTHIANS 16 : 13.

THESE texts, taken entirely out of the connection in which they stand in the Scriptures, and viewed in the light of the theme for discussion, set forth four important facts concerning us.

I. That our past was that of weakness, but our present is that of strength.

II. That God has marvelously blessed us.

III. That the colored Baptists are being watched by the eyes of American Christians because of the opportunities which have been generously given them : they are being "weighed in the balances."

IV. That in view of our past, and the circumstances of our present, we should act the part of men, and exhibit a vigorous Christian manhood.

I. Our past was that of weakness, but our present is that of strength.

Twenty-five years ago we had, except in a few instances, no churches in the South. Now (1890) we have nearly twelve thousand church organizations, and connected with nearly every one of them is a Sunday-school. Then we had practically no ordained ministers; now we have fully eight thousand. Then there were but two or three colored associations; now there are nearly four hundred. Then we numbered a few hundred thousands; now we are more than a million and a quarter. Then we had not even one institution of learning; now we have forty, ranging from high-grade normal schools to colleges and universities. Then it was not possible for our young people to get a liberal or professional education in the South; now any young man or woman can get it, whether in the arts or sciences, in theology, law, or medicine. And he can get his training under Baptist auspices; for we now have schools of theology, law, and medicine, in addition to those which are purely literary. Then there was no education among our ministry, but few being able to read, and the masses were in the same condition; now we have hundreds of educated ministers, many of them having received their training in the best institutions of the North. Some of these men have taken high rank as scholars and orators. Then we had no educators; now we have college presidents and professors, and many thousand school teachers. One-third of all the professors employed in the educational work of the American Baptist Home Mission Society are colored. Then such a thing as a colored trustee of a college was unheard of; now all our colleges and seminaries have colored members on their boards. Then there was no general officer of a national organization; now we have one district secretary. Then we did practically no literary work, and could produce but few books; now we have a number of authors among us, and their books are read. Then we did not have any newspapers; now there are forty, edited by colored Baptists. Then we had no professional and but few business men; now we have a large number of lawyers, physicians, and merchants. Then our forces were not organized; now they are organized, and have reached a reasonable degree of efficiency. Then we did no mission work; now we are doing mission work in every State, and even in Africa. Then we had comparatively no church property; now we have considerable, some buildings costing between fifty thousand and one hundred thousand dollars, and the total valuation being millions. Then we had no personal property, scarcely so much as "a vine and fig tree" under which to worship God; now our total wealth is estimated to be many millions. Then we were regarded as being in character and in intellect children; now we are recognized as men. Such growth is without precedent in the history of mankind. Truly we were once weak; but out of weakness we are made strong.

But we have by no means attained the strength which we will have and must have. What we have attained is but the earnest of what we should seek after in the next quarter of a century. Our large numbers will even prove to be a source of weakness to us, unless we elevate them in point of efficiency and in moral and mental character. A tremendous work is yet on our hands. May God help us to realize it!

II. God has marvelously blessed us.

It is *God* who has blessed us. Let this fact not be forgotten. Much as we may praise the men who pitied us in the days of our misfortune, and they deserve all the gratitude which we may give to them, it must nevertheless be remembered that to God belongs the glory; for it was he who directed these his people to do the work that they have done, and they were the instruments—willing instruments, however, in his hands, to do his will. And so as our minds sweep over the past twenty-five years, being scarcely able to grasp the facts of our own growth, we are led to exclaim: "What hath God wrought!" God has indeed marvelously blessed us. He did not only give us release from physical bondage, but he also gave us the means whereby our mental and moral emancipation might be accomplished. And how quickly God sent his people to our aid! The Civil War had scarcely been begun before these people sent missionaries and teachers among us. We were not left to the fate predicted for us by some of our country's statesmen, nor were we carried through the experience of the Israelites who spent forty years in wandering until the whole land from the Red Sea to the Jordan became one vast graveyard. We were brought almost immediately into our promised land. Rapid, indeed, were the changes of our condition, and though we have not yet reached the great heights which we hope to reach, we must nevertheless not be discouraged; for we should measure ourselves from the depths from which we have come.

And we should be careful never to forget to give God the glory for all his wondrous kindness. There is a temptation which comes to people of education and wealth, of which the uneducated and poor are ignorant. It is the twofold temptation of pride of knowledge, and pride of money. Such people are in danger of exalting the mental at the expense of the spiritual; of praising reason at the expense of faith. The loving, child-like trust is made to give way to skepticism and unbelief. If there is one special thing for which we should always be grateful, it is that the higher education of our people from the very beginning was committed to Christian men and women who educated their pupils from a Christian standpoint and upon a Bible basis; and the result is that we have not raised up skeptics, and our cultured men and women are loyal to God's word. God has not only led us, but he has led us along safe paths; he has not only given to us development of mind and character, but he has conferred these blessings under the most favored conditions. How different, how vastly different would have been our condition, if God had not so graciously blessed us! To him, then, be all the glory, both now and forever.

III. The colored Baptists are being watched by the eyes of American Christians because of the opportunities which have been generously given them; they are being weighed in the balances.

1. Help was given to us for Christ's sake. He died for us and we needed the gospel. This was the great impelling motive that raised up both men and means all along the past twenty-five years. This is the reason why our national societies supported the work. In the face of opposition, much of it as severe and terrible in some respects as that endured by the early Christians, their laborers toiled. Although the surroundings were often dark, still they labored. "For Christ's sake" was their inspiration and mainstay. And now, after many years, when the earliest of these workers are nearly ready to retire from the work, having spent all they had of mind and body in it, they and the American people are weighing us to see if we weigh according to the weight of men.

2. Help was given to us also because we were believed

to be inherently worthy of it. Our friends took us on faith, and at full value. Many a good man believed that the Negro was incapable of a high degree of mental and moral training, and the opinion was often expressed that it was not worth while to attempt to give him any more than the rudiments of education. Happily for us, such a belief was not shared by those who controlled the work of our national organizations. Men like Nathan Bishop and John P. Crozer, who gave their thousands for our uplifting, did not believe that the Negro was only half a man but a whole man, with the same capacities of mind and heart as those of other men, but whose misfortune was the terrible legacy which ignorance bequeathed to him from an ancestry of two hundred and fifty years.

3. Help was also extended to us in order that we might be developed into American Christians. An *American* Christianity, not a race or sectional one, was the aim. Broad and generous as is our land—yea, as broad as the world is,—it was intended that the Negro's conception of duty and sympathy should be as broad. He must be made a citizen, an American citizen, a Christian American citizen —nothing less. That the objects aimed at should be fully realized, men and means were found and consecrated. These Christian missionary and educational sculptors went to work on the massive granite of untrained manhood and womanhood, cutting away and polishing that the hidden thing of beauty might be found. They did not find an angel, but they did find a man. But is he a broad man?

The results thus far secured in the line of mental and religious education are measurably a vindication of the wisdom of those who planned and executed all that has been done for us. But we have yet some things to prove. Will we come up to the ideal of our friends? Will we now begin to take our proper places in the general work of the denomination? Will we join hands and hearts with the denomination's recognized agencies, or will we keep aloof from them and form separate organizations on the race line? Will we seek to evangelize Africa alone, or will we interpret the Saviour's command as binding on us also to evangelize China and Burmah and Mexico as well? Will we give our hearty support to our institutions of learning by trying to endow them? *What will we do? We are now being weighed in the balances. How much are we going to weigh?* Will it be said of us in the coming years that we failed in completely vindicating the wisdom and judgment and philanthropy of our brethren? This is a serious matter. The eyes of all the Christian world are upon us. Many centuries will look down upon us. The angels are watching us. God himself is beholding us. Seeing we are compassed about with such a cloud of witnesses, let us take care that we do not in any degree fall short of what can properly and reasonably be expected of us; and, in determining upon any given course of public policy, let us never forget that we are in the balances.

IV. In view of our past and the circumstances of our present, we should act the part of men, and exhibit a vigorous Christian manhood.

1. We should show a thorough appreciation of what has been done for us; also, of the men and women who went down into the mines and toiled, and of those who remained above and held the ropes. Privileges bestowed create corresponding obligations. From him unto whom much is given, much is required. The first thing to be done is

to place its full value on the work done for us. Estimate its cost in money, brains, and heart, and be grateful for it. It has made us what we are. A generous benevolence has been lavished upon us. There are names of noble men and women which should never fade from our memory. Nathan Bishop, John P. Crozer, Mrs. B. A. Benedict, William Bucknell, Holbrook Chamberlain, J. D. Rockefeller, Mrs. Bishop, Judson W. Leonard, and many others. What names! What an influence they have had in the world! Some of those named are dead, and they have already received their reward from him whom they clothed and sheltered and lifted up in the persons of his poor and untutored brethren; but they nevertheless live in the manhood and Christian character of those whom they benefited. "I expect to stand side by side with these men on the day of judgment; I am determined to be prepared for that meeting," is what Nathan Bishop said when some people remonstrated with him for giving so much for the education of colored Baptists. What a Christ-like utterance! Grand, noble man, a fitting representative of those who shared his spirit, and gave as he gave, for our good! These men and women did not go down into the mines themselves, but they remained above and made it possible for others to go down and toil. And it should be remembered that all who gave were not wealthy. Many were poor in this world's goods, although rich in the spirit of Christ. They denied themselves in order that they might be able to give. And many who were rich, and could give their thousands, nevertheless denied themselves also in order to have still more to give. Nathan Bishop would not keep a carriage, because if he did he would not have so much to give away. Think of that. He denied himself. He need not have done it. He voluntarily chose to do it. What an example for us! Such people are indeed the grand army of the Lord. They have indeed built their monuments, not out of perishable marble or bronze, but out of mind and heart; and the Christian men and women whom they raised up, exerting, as they will, an endless influence in all the coming years, will make these monuments imperishable. And of the men and women who went down into the mines and toiled, what shall we say? Things are very different now from what they were; just as they are in foreign lands. It requires no especially heroic spirit to lead a man now to become a missionary to Burmah; but how was it in Judson's day? Neither does it require much of a self-sacrificing spirit to induce any one at the present time to teach or preach to us in the South; but how was it in 1865, and the years following? This fact is not mentioned for any other reason than to show the heroism and devotion of our early workers—men like Phillips and Tupper and Carey. The truth of history must be shown, and honor awarded to those who deserve it.

It is eminently proper that these first workers be honored. Earth has no grander men; for they toiled not for themselves, but only to make Christian character. They strove not to make fortunes, but men. They as well as the givers should always be remembered; and while some of them are yet living, it is but right to give to them the heartfelt tributes of appreciation they so eminently deserve. When they are dead they will not need it; they may not need it now; but it will be a source of satisfaction to them, and probably a means of comfort and cheer, as they still toil on in the work of educating the children of their earliest students. The human heart needs sympathy and appreciation to do its best work; and when physical vigor is fast declining, and the strong man is beginning to bow himself, the expression of appreciation is comforting and assuring. Let us not defer the proper meed of praise until these first workers are all gone, and are beyond the reach of our words. Let them have it now.

> "If I should die to-night,
> My friends would look upon my quiet face,
> Before they laid it in its resting place,
> And deem that death had left it almost fair.
> And, laying snow-white flowers against my hair,
> Would smooth it down with tearful tenderness;
> And fold my hands with lingering caress,
> Poor hands, so empty and so cold to-night.
>
> "Oh, friends, I pray to-night,
> Keep not your kisses for my dead, cold brow;
> The way is lonely; let me feel them now.
> Think gently of me; I am travel-worn;
> My faltering feet are pierced with many a thorn.
> . . . .
> When dreamless rest is mine, I shall not need
> The tenderness for which I long to-night."

Some years ago, when an eminent pastor in a Northern city was about to leave his pastorate to accept another in a different city, a banquet was given in his honor. One speaker alluded, in tender and generous terms, to the work of the departing pastor. Supposing that some would regard his remarks as too flattering to be made in the presence of him who was the honored guest of the evening, the speaker said: "If our brother were dead, I would say these words over his coffin; and why should I not say them in his presence to-night?" Even so, while our honored brethren are living, let us tell them how much we owe to their fidelity and earnestness and sacrifice. Why should we not do it everywhere, in home, and church, and business life? We are too chary of our praise. We blame for ill. Why not show appreciation for what is good? If an act be courteous, kind, right, why not tell the doer? If a sermon help us, why not speak of it to the preacher? If a life be inspiring, why not applaud? Let us not keep all our flowers for the dead; let us give at least a blossom now and then to the living.

2. We should give a hearty and undivided support to the agencies that have lifted us up, and to all others that are promoting the welfare of our denomination.

I plead for this not because of gratitude, which would not be an unworthy reason, but because it is right and best. The concentration, the union of our forces, not disintegration and division, is the proper thing to aim at. Our national organizations impose no race or color test. They cordially invite *all* Baptists to join them. We need only one American Baptist Home Mission Society for general missionary work, church edifice work, and Southern educational work. We need only one American Baptist Publication Society for Bible work, for colportage and Sunday-school missionary work, and the work of making Baptist books and periodicals. To attempt to found others, especially in our present condition, is but to rush poverty-stricken, comparatively, into the face of wisdom, experience, and might. We want no organizations on the color line. The kingdom of our Lord Jesus Christ knows no race or color.

But these organizations, that helped us when we could not well help ourselves, may with very good reason ask us to assist in helping others less favored than ourselves. The great West sadly needs more help. Why should we not aid in evangelizing the French, the Germans, the Chinese, and the Scandinavians? Why should white men love black men, and black men not love white men in return? Is there any gospel command for that? We should esteem it both a privilege and a duty to aid any man of any race or color who needs our assistance; and the proper thing for us to do is to give our undivided support to our national societies, and thus help to enlarge their work.

3. We should cease to be beneficiaries as fast as we can, then, provide the expenses of our own support, and, going beyond that, assist in helping others.

These three things we are to aim at. We are yet being aided. Not less than one hundred thousand dollars is annually spent by brethren North, for current work among us. This does not include amounts appropriated for new buildings at our schools. Just as soon as we can we should raise every dollar required for the prosecution of our Bible, missionary, and educational work; and we should not be very long in reaching the point where this can be done. Then we should heartily support all our denominational agencies. The Baptist family of our country is one, and

"Our aims and hopes and fears are one";

and there is no good reason whatever why there should not be the closest union and most fraternal feeling between all the members of this family, and union or co-operation in all their work.

4. We should merge race feeling in the broader spirit of an American Christianity.

This is the proper aim; for it is Christlike. And this

is expected of us. To show that the denomination is expecting this, let me quote from an address delivered by Rev. H. L. Morehouse, D. D., at Nashville, Tenn., Sept. 26, 1888:

"And this leads me to say: The ideal result of all this vast expenditure of energy is that the black man in America may arise to the full stature of American and Christian manhood. From necessity, he has hitherto been compelled to think of himself, his needs, the means by which he could attain to a better condition. But after these twenty-five years, has not the time arrived when he should be a man with sympathies as broad as those of any other human being, and with efforts directed to the betterment of all men irrespective of race, color, or condition? We hear much about the Negro in America. I want to hear more about America in the Negro—the American spirit of lively interest in all mankind. Let the American spirit be dominant over the race spirit. Let the feeling be: "I am first an American, after that a race man." I believe in the race feeling, I believe in efforts for the race—not, however, for a fragment or section, but for the whole human race. For we are all kin. No man can be a true, broad, Christly man, who lives merely for his own class of people with whom by birth or color or nationality he is identified—no man, whether Jew or Gentile, Anglo-Saxon, German, Irishman, African, Indian, or any other. As the white man is expected to have sympathies that embrace the black man, why not now proclaim that the black man is expected to pray for and help the white man; and wherever there is need of work to be done for God on this continent, or throughout the world, that he should have part therein? This is the ideal result for which all this expenditure has been made—and just in proportion as the black man of America broadens out in this manner, just in that proportion will he rise in his self-respect and in the estimation of all men. And toward this end, I am sure, from utterances at these meetings, are things tending. God hasten the day when narrow race feelings shall become less and less, being finally lost in the grander and all-controlling sentiment of Christian brotherhood."

And now my task as editor is done. It has been a pleasant one, this gathering of the productions of my brethren, the fruitage crowning the history of twenty-five years. We cannot be otherwise than grateful as we look back over it. It has been full of gracious providences on the part of God; full of consecrated purpose on the part of many of his people.

When Samuel overcame the Philistines, he erected a memorial stone, and called it "Ebenezer"—stone of help—saying, "Hitherto hath the Lord helped us." And so we sing:

> "Here I raise mine Ebenezer,
> Hither by thine help I'm come."

The future is in large measure in our own hands. What will the fruitage be when twenty-five years more shall have passed away? What will be the opinions expressed concerning us by those who will then occupy many of our places? What will God himself say to us when we shall have gone up before him to give an account of our stewardship? Will it be: "Well done, good and faithful servants"? May God grant unto us all that welcome plaudit!

THE END.

RENEWALS 691-4

DATE DUE